75199

THE SAVAGE IDEAL

THE JOHNS HOPKINS UNIVERSITY STUDIES IN
HISTORICAL AND POLITICAL SCIENCE

NINETIETH SERIES (1972)

1. The Savage Ideal: Intolerance and Intellectual
Leadership in the South, 1890–1914
BY BRUCE CLAYTON

2. Ultraroyalism in Toulouse: From Its Origins to the
Revolution of 1830
BY DAVID HIGGS

BRUCE CLAYTON

THE SAVAGE IDEAL

INTOLERANCE AND INTELLECTUAL
LEADERSHIP IN THE SOUTH,
1890-1914

THE JOHNS HOPKINS UNIVERSITY PRESS
BALTIMORE AND LONDON

The Johns Hopkins University Press, Baltimore, Maryland 21218
The Johns Hopkins University Press Ltd., London

Library of Congress Catalog Card Number 70-184955
International Standard Book Number 0-8018-1375-1

Library of Congress Cataloging in Publication data will be found
on the last printed page of this book.

FOR MY MOTHER AND FATHER

CONTENTS

CONTENTS

ACKNOWLEDGMENTS

Many people and institutions have helped in the making of this book. It is pleasant, at last, to acknowledge my gratitude to Professors Robert F. Durden and Richard L. Watson, Jr., of Duke University, who first aroused my curiosity about American history and the South and who gave friendly advice and warm friendship. I wish to thank my friends and colleagues who read the manuscript, either in whole or in part, and volunteered valuable criticism: Dr. M. E. R. Bassett, University of Auckland, New Zealand; Dr. John D. Kirkland, Bucknell University; Dr. Jay Luvaas, Allegheny College; Dr. James McDowell, Wake Forest University; Dr. Harold T. Parker, Duke University; and Dr. John Salmond, LaTrobe University, Australia. A. T. Brown, Kevin Cadigan, Forest Clonts, John G. Dowgray, Jr., Douglas W. Hix, James Held, Robert Hohner, Thomas Jacklin, William E. King, Edward Krekel, Kenneth LaBudde, Russell Moore, William E. Nelson, Thomas Piraino, Percival Perry, David Roller, and Paul G. Zolbrod also contributed to my understanding. I wish to thank the librarians of Allegheny College and Dr. Mattie E. Russell of the Duke University Library.

For scholarly encouragement and financial assistance I wish to record special gratitude to the Woodrow Wilson National Fellowship Foundation, the Cooperative Program in the Humanities (administered by Duke University and the University of North Carolina), the National Endowment for the Humanities, and the Humanities Faculty Enrichment Program for Allegheny College, and to Professor Paul B. Cares, Chairman of the History Department and Lawrence L. Pelletier, President of Allegheny College.

I reserve these remaining lines to thank Alfred Kern, my friend, neighbor, and colleague, and Horace E. Stoessel, my close friend and distant neighbor of Charlotte, North Carolina. They know how much I owe them. I alone, however, stand responsible for the argument made in this book. Finally, one other person's patient, gentle, and reassuring understanding must be recorded. My wife, Carrah, has been a constant companion all along the way.

THE SAVAGE IDEAL

INTRODUCTION

The Southern mind—how to know it, how to talk about it? In the brocaded sentiment of Margaret Mitchell or the defiant defensiveness of Donald Davidson? Does it demand an angrier man than Mark Twain, who scornfully described the "United States of Lyncherdom" and then—with an eye toward Southern sensibilities and sales—quietly put his manuscript away unpublished?[1] For many, the South (meaning the white South) has no "mind," no sensibilities save the crudest and most violent—Dixie is the Sahara of the Bozart. If H. L. Mencken's metaphor is too offensive, we can call upon Henry Adams to testify more calmly: "Strictly, the Southerner had no mind; he had temperament."[2] History has been made in the South, but does it offer a warning, a sign, or even a word of encouragement to those who come after?

Of all the attempts to capture the Southern mind, none was so grandly conceived and so successfully executed as Wilbur J. Cash's *The Mind of the South*, published in 1941. It was a masterpiece of impressionistic writing that began with the emergence of the "great South" (which started around 1820, he decided) and ended with a look into the future. Though short on historical "facts,"

---

[1]Justin Kaplan, *Mr. Clemens and Mark Twain* (New York: Simon and Schuster, 1966), pp. 364–65.

[2]*The Education of Henry Adams* (Boston: Houghton Mifflin Co., 1918), p. 57.

the book was long on insights. Cash's contention was that the white South, from top to bottom, from so-called aristocrats to so-called poor whites, had been paralyzed by a set of legends (the modern reader might prefer "myths"). He specifically indicted the white Southerner's intense individualism, his romanticism, and his hedonism, the last combined, paradoxically, with a self-denying puritanism.

The Southern mind was "of the frontier made" and was refined on the plantation, only to come under Yankee assault, first with words and then with rifles. This mind, an assortment of half-digested "truths," responded by turning back upon itself and inflating its values, particularly concerning the Negro, into absolute virtue, in the form of the Southern Way of Life. The white South, at best never more than a step away from its frontier origins, became solidly committed to maintaining itself intact, at whatever cost. Totems and taboos were constructed, first about slavery; "from the taboo on criticism of slavery, it was but an easy step to interpreting every criticism of the South on whatever score as disloyalty—to making such criticism so dangerous that none but a madman would risk it." In this way the Savage Ideal was created— "whereunder dissent and variety are completely suppressed and men become in all their attitudes, professions, and actions, virtual replicas of one another."[3] As it was, so will it ever be among men—that was Cash's message to his countrymen in 1941. The year was an ominous one, and as Cash looked out at the world from his desk at the Charlotte *News* he could find no reason for hope or optimism, either in the South or in the world. Fascism in Europe confirmed his fears that the Savage Ideal might be mankind's malignancy.

But has the Southern mind been so uniform? There is, of course, another way of thinking, pioneered more recently by C. Vann Woodward, a Southerner, whose *The Strange Career of Jim Crow* and *The Burden of Southern History*[4] announce the pres-

---

[3] *The Mind of the South* (New York: Alfred A. Knopf, 1941), pp. 93–94.

[4] *The Strange Career of Jim Crow*, 2d rev. ed. (New York: Oxford University Press, 1966); *The Burden of Southern History* (Baton Rouge: Louisiana State University Press, 1960).

ence of liberal men and movements in the Southern past. Their presence, says Woodward, indicates that Southerners have not been "virtual replicas of one another." And though, as he admits, a torrent of abuse silenced racial liberals like George Washington Cable in the 1880s and a similarly savage attack smashed the racially liberal Populists in the next decade, still Cable and the Populists did exist and represent, as do many other less well-known men and movements, genuine "alternatives" to the Southern way of life. Woodward's argument, detailed and documented, is that the mind of the South has never been so closed that it has not contained its antithesis. The disagreement between Cash and Woodward seems as total and unyielding as the Savage Ideal itself.

* * *

If one looks back to the generation of Southerners which preceded Cash's, one discovers an intelligentsia of native sons who criticized the entire life of the South—from lynchings to hookworm—searchingly, sometimes scathingly. The South had never before been faced with such concentrated criticism from its own. For the first time in its history it had a full-fledged intellectual community. Professors extolled intelligence and "candor" and worked for public education and other social reforms that would, they thought, convert Southerners to rationality and nationalism, rather than sentiment and sectionalism. Writers joined with the academicians to denounce illiteracy, demagoguery, and racism and their reflection, the Solid South and the Democratic Party—the self-proclaimed "white man's party." There were also several educated ex-preachers (the majority of preachers in the South were barely literate) who sought to combine their pastorates with social reform despite Protestantism's deep-seated allegiance to individual salvation. The combination turned out to be impossible for most clergymen, although several ex-clerics were in the vanguard of the educational crusade which swept the South in the 1900s and two led the fight to abolish child labor. By 1914 death, infirmity, or changing interests put an end to the generation's sense of common cause and destiny.

The generation was sustained by the conviction that man is, at bottom, rational and good—or would be if reason and intellect performed their ordained duties. Thus they "knew" that evil in men or in society resulted from causes external to man, whether it be ignorance, prejudice, corrupt institutions, or an unfortunate history. Partly as a result of such beliefs, or, one might say, assumptions, the intellectuals were forever looking to the past to find that time when the South had taken a wrong (by which they meant irrational) turn that had corrupted its people. Like Cash, who borrowed freely from their ideas, they urged Southerners to get free of history and become "men." Even Southerners could be changed, improved, made over.

Such assumptions about man, however, were not new to the South. It might be said that at the cornerstone of the Old South with all of its posturings and dependence upon mythology lay not only romanticism (and the other myths Cash censored) but rationalism. Antebellum apologists had defended slavery as the ultimate in rational social organization, the historical fulfillment of the Platonic and biblical blueprint for the republic of man. What was new was the intellectual's rather whole-hearted acceptance of their own century's faith in progress. The uniqueness of their conscious thought, then, lay in its unconscious blending of the eighteenth-century trust in man's rationality and innate goodness and the nineteenth-century conception of man. That blending, molded and modified ever so slightly by the experience of being both Southern and American, distinguished them from their antebellum relatives, who yearned for a static, uniform, monolithic society.

There was, as one might expect, an ancillary belief about the meaning and relevance of "work." To the hard-working intellectuals, work was a moral absolute, an outer sign of inner worth. Simply put, they had internalized the Puritan Ethic, an ethic which had ruled their fathers' lives. The sons, mostly secular men, unconsciously secularized their religious heritage. That heritage blended nicely into their middle-class values, giving their praise for work a grounding in faith. So, too, the ethic of work dovetailed with progress, supplying it with a directive for man and society.

4

In all this welter of words, however, one finds no genuinely emancipated mind or real understanding of racism's hold on the Southern mind. Several men spoke with understanding of the depths of racism among the white masses—the unlettered and unwashed—but no one grasped the singular fact that it had become firmly entrenched in the thinking of the intellectuals as well. One senses racism among even the most critical Southerners, in their identification of the white South with "the South" and in their determination to create a climate of "understanding" for the South's violence and brutality toward the Negro. One senses it too in their ignorance of Negro life, their obsessive concern for what the "Negro problem" meant for whites, and their acceptance of White Supremacy and its corollary, "Negro inferiority." There were several critics of the use politicians made of racial myths, yet even those with uneasy consciences finally—if grudgingly— accepted the racial segregation and disfranchisement that was legislated in the South all in a rush in their day. They were emotionally and intellectually unprepared for the new turn in Southern racism; most accepted the politicians' word that the new laws were "reforms." Sincere, trusting, benign men, the function of the intellectuals was to remind white Southerners of their traditional obligations to the blacks. In short, the intellectuals preached paternalism, but it was the paternalism of the plantation. They looked back to that mythical Garden of Eden, perfection frozen in time, when blacks and whites loved each other and treated each other decently, when, as the myth had it, master and slave "cooperated." How ironic that it was the New South's intellectuals— sons of the yeoman class, striving to break free of the plantation mold and restless to build a better world—who yearned for the spiritual regeneration of that very plantation to resolve the burden of Southern history in the twentieth century.

What accounts for the subtle—and, in some cases, not so subtle—racism in the best minds of the white South during a time of intellectual ferment? The question should be of compelling interest to those present-day Southerners, white or black, who yearn to obey their best humanitarian impulses and yet remain "Southern." The intellectuals of the New South were enthusias-

5

tically "American." When they returned to the South after their education in the North or abroad, they had added national values and ideals to their existing stock of racial myths, myths which had been refurbished during their absence. Racism characterized the national identity. It was present in the United States from the days of the founding fathers: one might say that the South's white intellectuals held racist assumptions and views not because they were Southern but because they were American. White America has always been able to accommodate itself to racism, as witness the constitutional provision that a slave is to be considered as three-fifths of a person or, more than a hundred years later, the Supreme Court decision in *Plessy* v. *Ferguson*, which sanctioned both the spirit and the fact of racial segregation. That historic decision, which was not reversed until 1954, came in 1896, two years before American troops rescued Cuba and the Philippines from Spain and began shouldering the white man's burden. Thus a tide of racism was sweeping over America in the 1890s, just when the South's first intellectual community was forming.

One last piece of evidence is entered, not to indict the past but to put the Southern mind in perspective. In 1912, with the overwhelming support of the South, Woodrow Wilson was elected to the presidency. A distinguished educator and man of letters—his writings included the celebrated book *Congressional Government*—and reform governor of New Jersey, Wilson was also a Southerner and a partisan Democrat. He had moved north and given his attention almost exclusively to national issues, but he was on record in such places as the *Atlantic Monthly* and in several books as favoring the political and racial "reforms" in the South. Thus he was a "Southern" candidate in 1912 and shared, in generous measure, the racist assumptions of his fellow intellectuals who had remained in the South.

One would not, of course, attribute Wilson's victory to his or the nation's racism—in no way could race be called an "issue," in the usual sense of the word, in 1912. Yet, as all successful politicians must, he mirrored the virtues and values that white Americans imagine in themselves and reward in a political leader. American politics was for white people; politicians were white. One remembers the overt racial consciousness of white America in 1912 and Wilson's own proclaimed sense of race. Had a black man seriously sought the presidency he would have been laughed or scorned out of such a notion. White Supremacy—the Southern slogan for the assumption that whites are the norm and blacks inferior—had become (or had remained) an unstated conviction of white America. So race, in this somewhat indefinable sense, was indeed an issue, just as it continues to be in American politics.

* * *

This book examines a dozen or so men and their relationship to the Savage Ideal. Three of the more prominent made their way as writers: Walter Hines Page, William Garrott Brown, and Thomas Nelson Page. The majority were academicians, either college professors or presidents: William P. Trent, John Spencer Bassett, Edwin Mims, William E. Dodd, John C. Kilgo (who was also a Methodist minister), Edwin A. Alderman, Samuel Chiles Mitchell, and James H. Kirkland. The intellectual community included Edgar Gardner Murphy and A. J. McKelway, both former clergymen. Woodrow Wilson was the twenty-eighth President of the United States.

After Wilson, Walter Hines Page was the most widely known Southern "spokeman" of the day. He seems to have been everywhere, known everyone of importance, and said just about everything on every conceivable subject related to the South. He started his professional life in the 1880s as a newspaper editor in his home state of North Carolina and culminated his career as American Ambassador to England, an appointment made in 1913 by a grateful President Wilson. In the years between he edited the *Forum* magazine and the *Atlantic Monthly*, spoke and worked tirelessly for reforms in the South, and founded the *World's Work* magazine in 1900. An eloquent, outspoken man, known to all as a crusader for change in the South, yet tactful and cooperative in his personal relations, Page worked as harmoniously with wealthy men who sought outlets for their charity as he did with aspiring Southern writers and scholars, white or black. Part intellectual, part bourgeois capitalist, Page had a knack for reducing complex ideas to practical expressions and selling them to those who shared his Jeffersonian bias for industrial capitalism. Page became so completely identified with the New South mind that the Fugitive-Agrarian poets and writers centered around Vanderbilt University in the 1920s slandered him for selling "the South's" birthright of true religion and tradition for the pottage of factories and modern ideas.

Temperamentally, William Garrott Brown could not have differed more from Page. A scholarly, shy, introspective man, he bore the stamp of the Alabama plantation country and had inherited a patrician view of leadership, a view that contrasted rather sharply with Page's rambunctious equalitarian rhetoric. He understood, as his famous book *The Lower South in American History* demonstrates,[5] that the day of patrician leadership had gone with the political democracy that swept the white South after the war. He knew intellectually that gentility had little to do with the modern world, yet he remained a gentleman, at ease with men of wealth and culture. As a newcomer to Harvard in the 1880s, he admired the genteel tradition of New England and continued to believe that gentlemen should rule, as they had ruled in Jefferson's day. Brown was no reactionary: he was, rather, a conservative man, in both his ideas and his habits. He loved reason, intellectual detachment, and enlightened leadership. Thus he felt estranged from his Southern home and, like Page and Wilson, lived and worked in the North. The Harvard Library and the editorial offices of *Harper's Weekly* served as his base as he sought to convince Northern and Southern leaders that the South needed to break free from the Democratic Party and become a two-party region like the rest of the nation. Aside from scholarship, which Brown secretly feared was irrelevant, political reform was his consuming interest.

Thomas Nelson Page, a Virginian of the planter class (he was only distantly related to Walter Page), had the social sympathies of a reactionary. He shared none of Brown's passion for "good government" or Walter Page's admiration for the common man lifted up by education. He gave himself to no causes, save the glorifica-

[5]New York: Macmillan Co., 1902.

8

tion of the "lost cause"—the Old South. In a series of popular romantic novels and short stories Page portrayed the vanished golden age of happy darkies and gay heroines lolling on magnolia-draped, mint-juleped plantations. He had no new ideas, nor did he want any, and he was not particularly "artistic." He was an apologist for racism, and to make sure that his reactionary ideas about race were clearly understood by Northern readers—he had a wide following in the North—Page turned to writing essays and historical pieces to make the case for keeping Negroes subservient, as they had been in slavery days. A loyal Democrat, a successful lawyer and benefactor of the University of Virginia, Page was chosen by Wilson to be his Ambassador to Italy.

Of the academicians, William P. Trent of the University of the South at Sewanee, Tennessee, was one of the first Southern professors to combine teaching with scholarship, and scholarship with critical social thought. He arrived at Sewanee in 1888 fresh from the invigorating intellectual atmosphere of the new Johns Hopkins University, where he had studied history with Herbert Baxter Adams. From the first, he dominated the staid Episcopal school: he was a brilliant teacher, an animated conversationalist, and a polemical and productive writer. In 1892 he established the *Sewanee Review* and made it a learned and sophisticated quarterly. That same year, he unleashed a full-scale, bellicose attack on the Old South that would reverberate through the Southern mind for decades. By nature a combative questioner, a skeptic, a polemicist who could dismiss John C. Calhoun and other saints of the past as easily as he could quote Matthew Arnold on society's need for criticism, Trent nevertheless felt strongly drawn toward the genteel tradition in American thought.

John Spencer Bassett, who preached history and the new learning at Trinity College from 1894 to 1906, might well be considered Trent's counterpart. A graduate of Johns Hopkins and Adams' seminar, Bassett's intellectual vigor and amazing literary productivity overshadowed everyone else at Trinity. Bassett's work invigorated the school; from the president on down to the faculty and students, everyone wondered where the young professor found the time and energy to write several histories, scores of articles, speeches and letters, along with stimulating lectures. In

1900 he founded the *South Atlantic Quarterly* and used it over the next few years as a battering ram against the wall of ignorance and prejudice he found around him. Sharply polemical in his writings—he curtly dismissed Thomas Nelson Page's romanticism—he was nevertheless a warm friend and sympathetic counselor to his students and colleagues. He was to need all his friends in the fall of 1903, when his words about the "Negro Problem" provoked the Savage Ideal.

Less outspoken and more temperate than Bassett was his colleague Edwin Mims, a professor of English. Mims joined the faculty in 1894 and committed himself to making Trinity a center of scholarship and what the faculty called "independent" thought about politics and other objects of Southern sentiment. His friends Bassett and Walter Page invited him to write for their magazines, and the graceful essays which resulted he transformed into a book, *The Advancing South*, in 1926.[6] By that time he had returned to his alma mater, Vanderbilt University, where he headed the English Department—the very department that later spawned the Fugitive-Agrarians. They respected Mims (while castigating his old friend Walter Page), and in return Mims's good will extended to the younger men even when they angrily aired their anti-New South biases in their manifesto of 1929, *I'll Take My Stand*, while he himself continued to put forth his old dream for the South.

William E. Dodd concludes the list of professors who played major roles in forming the Southern mind. Today he is remembered as President Roosevelt's Ambassador to Germany in the 1930s and, among fellow historians, as the author of *The Cotton Kingdom*.[7] Admirers of Woodrow Wilson remember him for his laudatory biography of their hero and for his collaboration with Ray Stannard Baker on an early, six-volume edition of Wilson's public papers. From Dodd's earliest days as a professor of history at Virginia's Randolph-Macon College, through his years at the University of Chicago after 1908, his writing reflects an abiding faith in man and an admiration for Jefferson, whom Dodd thought represented the "true" South before it was corrupted by feudal

[6]New York: Doubleday, Page and Co., 1926.
[7]New Haven: Yale University Press, 1918.

slavery. While in the South Dodd's words verged on political and economic radicalism of the Populist persuasion, but his enthusiasm cooled, and he became an advocate of Wilson's New Freedom.

President John C. Kilgo of Trinity College typifies the new sort of ambitious, energetic college leader who came on the scene in the 1890s to guide the schools into academic excellence and social relevance. Like the new professors whom he welcomed to Trinity, Kilgo came to his post as a young man—he was thirty-three years old when he was made president in 1894—with a robust enthusiasm for education. He arrived as a flamboyant, fire-and-brimstone Methodist preacher from rural South Carolina, but at Trinity he was transformed into an incorruptible champion of higher education, though he reasoned, in a way unique to his generation, that Christian education must remain superior to the secular education offered at the state universities. The presidency seemed to tap in him some deep, unexplored idealism, yet he lost none of his camp-meeting zeal. He resigned from Trinity in 1910, convinced that he had succeeded in his work, became a bishop, and settled into a quiet ecclesiastical routine.

By 1910 Edwin A. Alderman was in his sixth year as president of the University of Virginia. Before coming to the Charlottesville campus, he had served briefly and successfully as president of the University of North Carolina and of Tulane University. He brought to "Mr. Jefferson's University," as his friend Walter Page liked to call it, an intense enthusiasm for "service," an enthusiasm he had demonstrated as a leader in the Southern Education Board (the nonprofit independent administrative arm of the school movement). During a long and happy life at Virginia, Alderman built it into a major university. True to his generation's concern for the "word," Alderman helped establish the *Virginia Quarterly Review* in 1925. Throughout his career he remained a high-collared, high-minded, public-spirited administrator who walked circumspectly around the issue of the Savage Ideal. Circumspection came easier to him than it did to Bassett or Walter Page, however, because he shared abundantly, if in a benign way, in the racism of his era.

Joining the group of far-sighted administrators were James H. Kirkland, chancellor of Vanderbilt University from 1893 to 1939, and the historian Samuel Chiles Mitchell, who left the classroom of Richmond College in 1908 to head the University of South Carolina. Neither was a major figure in the intellectual community, but their willingness to speak out on social issues and their public commitments to reform gave Southern intellectuals added prestige. For almost fifty years (he was eighty when he retired) Kirkland worked to build Vanderbilt into a national university. He loosened its ecclesiastical ties with the Methodist Church, South; recruited dedicated professionals like Edwin Mims, Walter Fleming, Frederick Moore, and William Baskerville; and cooperated actively with other local educational leaders to build a federated university center in Nashville. Mitchell's years of service to the South were fewer and less distinguished, and he is included here because he was filled with enthusiasm for public education and helped bring the outside world to the South. Like so many other intellectuals of his day, he left the South in middle age and became president of Delaware University in 1914.

In that year, Edgar Gardner Murphy died. His rich, variegated life included, in the short span of forty-five years, a dozen years in the Episcopal ministry (including several parishes in the North) and a decade of involvement in reform movements in the South. When he discovered in 1901 that his parish responsibilities in Montgomery, Alabama, restricted his secular activities in the city, he stepped down from the pulpit, became secretary of the Southern Education Board, and proved to be an articulate, resolute, indefatigable leader. He brought the same qualities to the child labor movement, which he transformed (almost singlehandedly at first) into a national crusade for reform. But it was the larger issue of race that absorbed his thoughts, and here the historian can see the ultimately tragic failure of his mind and the mind of the New South.

A. J. McKelway succeeded his friend Murphy as head of the child labor movement in the South and promptly identified its goals with those of the National Child Labor Committee. A battler for reform on many fronts, McKelway came to his social activism—partly as a result of Murphy's example—from the Presbyterian ministry of North Carolina. He was born in Pennsylvania in 1866 but was raised in Charlotte, North Carolina. He attended a

Presbyterian college in Virginia and returned to Fayetteville as a pastor in 1892. Before the decade was out, he had seen enough sins more serious than dancing, card-playing, or whittling on Sunday to decide to leave the church and speak as a secular man. Pugnacious and polemical (he shared few of Murphy's mild manners), he could still see that most social ills, especially child labor, were intricately linked to national conditions. He was a scrappy fighter, rather different from the more sophisticated intellectuals who liked to believe that good manners and moral suasion would influence their opponents, particularly if they were business or professional men, to take a more humane view. McKelway's stumbling block was the race issue. He was, inexplicably, an insensitive racist.

In the course of writing this book I have often felt suspended between two perceptions of McKelway and his generation—the one shaped by Cash, the other by Woodward. Many were the days on which I felt deep admiration for the South's intellectuals for their good works and could understand Catherine Drinker Bowen's admonition that biographers should pick people whom they can admire, revere as giants in the earth. Yet I have also felt anger, hostility, and deep resentment over their shortcomings. Their major defect—their racism—threatens to overshadow everything else. There is much in these pages about this racism, and many times not the words themselves but the tone, the mood behind them, may be more subjective than a historian likes to admit. But there is, I hope, another bias in these pages, as well as the one that prompts praise and blame. That bias is toward understanding men and history. Perhaps the story of these men may illuminate history's hold on man and man's struggle to break free, to transcend his historical situation; perhaps it may help us to take a Nietzschean leap beyond what history presents as good and evil.

Part I

THE MIND OF THE NEW SOUTH

INTRODUCTION

Over the course of some twenty-five years the South's new intellectuals created a mind that was both a continuation of Southern traditions and a break with the past. There had been scattered writers and learned men in the South since Thomas Jefferson, but it was the generation of the 1890s who secured themselves in schools, organizations, and editorial offices and established scholarship and critical thinking as legitimate, worthwhile social goals. As Southerners, they drew heavily upon Jefferson's equalitarianism and the myths and illusions embodied in the optimistic call for a "New South" that went out from Dixie in the two decades following the Civil War. Led by the exuberant Henry W. Grady, editor of the Atlanta *Constitution*, the New South apostles of materialism extolled the benefits of industrialism, diversified agriculture, and a national outlook and fashioned a "creed," says Paul M. Gaston, that urged Southerners to become active (and uncritical) partners in Yankee capitalism. Prosperity was the creed's hope and promise, but as the 1880s wore on, the New South slogan became a "description not of what ought to be or would be but of what already was."[1]

There was a generous portion of this myopic optimism in the next generation, as the intellectuals added their immediate herit-

[1] Paul M. Gaston, *The New South Creed* (New York: Alfred A. Knopf, 1970), p. 7.

17

age to the ingredients in their prescriptions for social change, but the creed's booster spirit was tempered by a commitment to intellect and social reform and by a disturbing awareness of the depths of racism in the white Southern masses. One might say that the mind of the New South had matured and found its fullest expression by the turn of the century. If this mind was a little less sanguine and a good bit more self-conscious than it had been in the 1880s, still it could meld easily into the national mood of Progress and continue to hope that the white South would solve its many problems.

That hope was particularly strong in the early years of the decade, as the intellectuals finished school, became men, and settled down in the South to do their work. From the beginning, they were sustained by a youthful impatience to get on with the business of remaking the world, a pragmatic turn of mind, and a reassuring set of assumptions about man's malleable nature. Quite without realizing it, they had found a way to live with the evil which they and, later, Wilbur J. Cash condemned. But whereas Cash feared that evil, his predecessors possessed both a means of rationalizing it and a sense of their role in redeeming the South from it. However, exaltation of the social role of the critic was one thing; experiencing its effects in action was quite another. When these new critics took to task the history of the white South or its way of "handling" the Negro—when theory led to pronouncements and acts that infuriated their more conservative countrymen—they experienced a sobering confrontation with the Savage Ideal.

1

THE MIND IN THE MAKING

TO UNDERSTAND THE MIND of the New South in its maturity, we must know something of how these Southern boys became learned men. A glance at the biographies of the intellectuals reveals, with few exceptions, a common pattern: country-born, of farmer-merchant fathers and Protestant parents; graduates of the South's finest schools, first the private preparatory academies, then the colleges, usually denominational schools; then a trip north or abroad, always to Germany, never to England or France, for advanced training. Born in the decades from 1855 to 1875, a large group of them in the 1860s, they came of age too late to have experienced the traumatic upheavals of the nineteenth-century South: slavery, secession, war, defeat, and Reconstruction. The few born in the 1850s had shadowy memories of the Civil War and firmer images of its aftermath, but even they gathered their impressions and views from older folks, for whom the events of 1865–1877 took on more and more drama as the years passed.

The culture let no one forget the recent history. Teenagers in the 1870s heard of the past from relatives or from the seemingly endless parade of ex-Confederates who, to hear them tell it, almost won the war at this or that battle. Through it all, of course, ran the familiar litany that behind everything, in war or peace, stood the Negro, the "African," whose mere presence cast a black shadow across the land. The white South was saturated in racial consciousness, particularly strong in those areas which feared a repetition of the political "domination" of the blacks alleged to have taken place during Reconstruction. The myths of Reconstruction inculcated racial notions and feelings in the young that helped them in no small way to accept the claims of the latter-day disfranchisers that they were forestalling a new Negro domination, and the generation of the 1890s gave such myths intellectual and scholarly respectability and articulated the ethic of White Supremacy.

This generation also grew to maturity in a land that was experiencing industrialization for the first time. The economic changes that followed the Civil War exhilarated the Southerner, whose frame of reference was one of plantations and poverty. The promises of industrialism were heady—the North seemed to be reaping prosperity from the machine. The symbols of the brighter day were fledgling factories, the railroad locomotive, innumerable "land improvement companies," and industrial expositions.[1] Atlanta's International Cotton Exposition of 1881, impressive though it was, faded from the limelight two years later when Louisville put fifteen acres under one roof, and in 1885 the New Orleans Cotton Centennial Exposition dwarfed them all with thirty-three acres of covered exhibits.[2] The expositions got larger and larger in the following years, seemingly fulfilling one prophetic remark of the time made in the North, "Go South, Young Man."[3]

William Garrott Brown recalled in 1904 that in Marion, Alabama, the coal, iron, and steel boom in nearby Birmingham sent reverberations throughout the state: "I happened to see much and hear more of the industrial revival which in the late seventies and early eighties set everybody in the South talking and planning booms. It was mine not merely to observe but to share, with an

---

[1] C. Vann Woodward, *Origins of the New South, 1877–1913* (Baton Rouge: Louisiana State University Press, 1951), pp. 107–41.

[2] *Ibid.*, p. 124.

[3] *Ibid.*, p. 115.

accessory fever of growth, the curiously confident expectation of an immediate transformation which one Southern community entertained. I saw old fields staked out in broad avenues, the lots sold at prices which would not have been low in a city of several hundred thousand inhabitants, and big brick office buildings erected close alongside Negro cabins. I witnessed the collapse of more than one of these magic growths." Yet neither Brown nor his contemporaries permitted the several false starts of the 1890s to dampen their enthusiasm for industrialism. "For the present," Brown continued, "the true 'Southern Question' is how to make money out of the South's resources."[4]

One more incident will symbolize the sense of drama brought about by economic change. Edwin Alderman (whose leadership in the 1900s as president of the University of Virginia helped raise the level of Southern higher education) was graduated from the University of North Carolina in 1882, the year the Richmond and Danville Railroad completed a branch line to Chapel Hill, giving that university village a new outlet to the outside world. To celebrate the event, students and faculty sang a song which they had composed specifically for the occasion:

> Farewell, old wagon,
> Jolting hack and phaeton,
> Farewell forever,
> We're going to take the train.
>
> Farewell forever,
> Old road to Durham,
> Farewell forever;
> We'll travel now by train.[5]

Young Southerners like those who lustily sang out their final farewells to the old road to Durham had spent their boyhood in a region that everywhere seemed to be changing, or taking the first

---

[4] Stanton [William Garrott Brown], "The South at Work," Boston *Evening Transcript*, February 25, 1904. Why Brown chose to write under the name Stanton is unknown.

[5] Dumas Malone, *Edwin A. Alderman: A Biography* (New York: Doubleday, Doran and Co., 1940), p. 14.

steps toward those changes that the North had already experienced. They came from out-of-the-way places like Sandy Flat, Coffeeville, Laurens, Tarboro, Cary, Poplar Creek, Weatherford—some are just crossroads memories now. They knew the "country" of the South, the farms, streams, woods, and fields where one could spend a lifetime without meeting more than a minute proportion of the state's population. In the country Sunday services brought people together for social life as well as religious nourishment and a trip to the state capital or a nearby city was an adventure for country people, who had more time than money to spend around the courthouse square. When Walter Page and his father made the twelve-mile trip from Cary, North Carolina, to Raleigh, they marveled at life in the capital, a city of twelve and a half thousand. Though some were born in the "cities" of the South—Richmond, Wilmington, Charlotte—the typical homestead of the Southern intellectual was Cary or Marion, neither of which was large enough to figure in the census of 1890. Sometimes as young adults surveying the recent changes, they extravagantly assessed the inherent possibilities of the New South. John Spencer Bassett, a native of Tarboro, North Carolina, put it this way in 1896: "Our South is new—very new in some respects. The increase in factories, the growth of towns, the disappearance of the planter type, the cutting up of farms, and the citizenship of the negroes; all these witness a new order of living."[6] Inherent in Bassett's words was rejection of the old ways—the ways of the small town—and joyous acceptance of the "new way of living."

That same note of rejection came through clearly in much of the writings of other young Southerners, but few could match Walter Hines Page's disdain for the old ways. In one of his first writings, a "local color" piece for the *Atlantic Monthly* in 1881 called the "Study of an Old Southern Borough," Page summarized his views.[7] He probably had in mind Hillsboro, North Carolina, a hamlet that seems to have been bypassed by every wind of change that had blown since 1776; doubtless he also remembered Cary.

[6]"The Culture Problem in Southern Towns," *Methodist Quarterly Review*, 43 (1896):373.
[7]*Atlantic Monthly* 47 (1881):648–58.

Life there was "still" and "slow," Page began: "mental stagna-
tion" and "inertness" prevailed alongside the relics and remnants
of the past—planters, ex-Confederates, preachers, and women
whose entire education consisted of instruction in being ladies.
Though they were the backbone of the community, these women
were mired in religious fundamentalism and the ideas of the past.
From the "gentlemen of the old school," as Page characterized the
planters, came ceaseless chatter about politics—with never the
danger of a new idea about the past or the present. For the rest,
"it is not dullness, but immobility, that is their death." The dead
air of the community affected everyone but a few. "Sometimes,"
Page wrote somberly, "a lad from an old borough in the first
dawning of his thought, discovers for himself the mental stagna-
tion of his surroundings . . . and rebels against it. The only successful rebellion, however, is an immediate departure. For, if he begins
to deliberate, he is apt to be caught in the spell of inertness, and
live out his life and die before he decides whether to go away or
not." "Thus it has happened that the over-conservative spirit of
these old towns has driven many of the best men away." Only the
eager and ambitious merchant, the son of an overseer usually, Page
observed, had a fresh "tone of voice" and "energetic step."[8]
Page's words bring to mind Mark Twain's later description of the
"new men" of the South: "Brisk men, energetic of movement and
speech; the dollar their god, how to get it their religion."[9]

Deeper South, on the farms and in the towns of Mississippi and
Alabama, one could spend many a day without hearing even the
fresh voice or clicking heels of that upward-bound merchant. Page
remembered that the whir of his father's sawmill was one of the
few sounds to break the long silences of the woods.[10] William
Garrott Brown passed his youth in quiet Marion chopping down
trees and throwing pebbles at the occasional stranger who appeared on the streets. Without telephone, electricity, or factory,
the only accouterment of the modern age was the little branch

[8] *Ibid.*, pp. 654–56.

[9] *Life on the Mississippi* (Boston: J. R. Osgood and Co., 1883), p. 412.

[10] Burton J. Hendrick, *The Training of an American: The Earlier Life and Letters of Walter H. Page, 1855–1913* (Boston: Houghton Mifflin Co., 1928), pp. 13–20.

railroad line that ran east to Selma and west to Greensboro once a day. Coming back to visit years later, Brown complained that "they have changed nearly all the signs on the business street, there are new names and new faces everywhere. There are even some new houses and new fences and on one . . . of the houses there is a new front-porch and a fresh coat of paint. It is all very well to talk about progress, but isn't this taking the thing a little too seriously?"[11]

The social and economic status of the young intellectuals considerably eased the strain of growing up with the New South—perhaps one should say rather that their fathers' status and outlook did so. The fathers were, for want of a better label, "middle class," midway, that is, between the planters and the dispossessed poor whites and blacks. Thus their sons were admirably placed to find niches in a postwar South that offered its rewards (at least more so than in the past) on the basis of talent and not solely birth. They were far enough above the poor whites to sense the possibilities of personal advancement through work and to have the opportunities for taking advantage of those possibilities.

There are a few exceptions to this generalization. William E. Dodd's parents, for instance, lived so close to poverty that they might be more properly placed in the proletariat of white "farmers" who barely scratched a living from the soil.[12] Others, like novelist Thomas Nelson Page and historian and part-time lawyer Philip A. Bruce, were sons of Virginia planters, but only Bruce's father, with a five-thousand-acre plantation and five hundred slaves, would qualify as a genuine "aristocrat."[13] Oakland, the Page plantation, had fifty slaves, but the family lived just one step above the level of genteel poverty.[14] As far as I can determine, not one Southerner of intellectual prominence in the 1900s came from a background of academics, though several fathers held

---

[11]Stanton [Brown], "The South at Work," Boston *Evening Transcript*, March 26, 1904.

[12]Robert Dallek, *Democrat and Diplomat: The Life of William E. Dodd* (New York: Oxford University Press, 1968), pp. 3–7.

[13]L. Moody Simms, "Philip Alexander Bruce and the New South," *Mississippi Quarterly* 19 (1966):171–73.

[14]Harriet Holman, "The Literary Career of Thomas Nelson Page, 1884–1910" (Ph.D. diss., Duke University, 1947), p. 3.

degrees from well-known Northern schools and Woodrow Wilson's father combined parish preaching with some teaching at Columbia Theological Seminary near his home in Augusta, Georgia.

These fathers appear to have exemplified that overworked abstraction "yeoman." Almost to a man they were hard-working, upright men, devoted to their jobs and families, "clean, substantial, and vigorous," as one historian puts it.[15] In the history books they have taken a back seat to the planters and poor whites, but they made up the backbone of the Old South.[16] They appear to have been independent-minded and forward-looking men, capable of leadership—"solid," in the best sense of the word. They lived the work ethic and personified manly ideals, and their more urbane and literary sons drew strength from their fathers' example.

Frank Page and Richard Bassett (fathers of Walter Page and John Spencer Bassett) are prototypes of the yeoman of middling economic status. Page, an enterprising sawmill operator, cleared forests, founded towns in North Carolina, built hotels and railroads, and helped develop Pinehurst as a resort area. Richard Bassett was a carpenter and small-scale contractor; like Page he was a Piedmont Unionist and a critic of secession. Both men had criticized slavery, yet they served the Confederacy loyally. William P. Trent's father, who in 1861 was a prominent physician in Richmond, also had strong and openly expressed reservations about the wisdom of secession. But when the inevitable came he served loyally as a doctor, invested heavily in the Confederacy, and eventually lost the family's small financial holdings. Following the defeat, the Trent family struggled back to a measure of financial security.[17] War also dealt harshly with the fortunes of William Garrott Brown's family, but his father was able to recover and to re-establish himself in business.[18]

[15] Burton J. Hendrick, *The Life and Letters of Walter H. Page*, 3 vols. (New York: Doubleday, Page and Co., 1922–25), 1:5.

[16] Frank L. Owsley, *Plain Folk of the Old South* (Baton Rouge: Louisiana State University Press, 1949).

[17] Franklin T. Walker, "William P. Trent—A Critical Biography" (Ph.D. diss., George Peabody College for Teachers, 1943), pp. 18–27.

[18] Bruce Clayton, "William Garrott Brown: A Spokesman for the New South" (M.A. thesis, Duke University, 1963), p. 1.

Preachers Joseph Ruggles Wilson, Woodrow Wilson's father, and William Clark Kirkland, father of Chancellor James H. Kirkland of Vanderbilt University (1893-1929), further illustrate the force of personality and commitment to work characteristic of these yeoman fathers. When Dr. Wilson came south from Ohio in 1855, he brought his Scotch-Irish Presbyterianism along with him. From the first he and his family "fitted" into their new surroundings. They stopped first in Staunton, Virginia, where Woodrow Wilson was born in 1856, moving on the following year to a larger church in Augusta, Georgia. Dr. Wilson impressed his congregation and the citizens of Augusta as a "public-spirited and impressive man," to quote a recent historian, and "a preacher of remarkable power."[19] When the secession crisis drove a wedge in national church organizations, the Southern Presbyterians seceded into a separate body in Dr. Wilson's church. When the war came, he volunteered and served as a chaplain to the Confederate Christians.[20] Years later, in an admiring portrait of Woodrow Wilson, William E. Dodd used such words as "stern," "sober," and "earnest" to describe Wilson's parents.[21]

The portrait of sober sturdiness faithfully captures the Reverend Mr. Kirkland as well. When ill health forced him to retire from the Methodist ministry in the 1850s, he worked a small farm in South Carolina, saved his money, and accumulated a little property. By 1863 his health had improved enough for him to return to the ministry. Too old to ride the circuit, he nevertheless did so twice before his health broke for good. He died early in 1864, on a Wednesday: the preceding Sunday he had preached two sermons.[22]

In thinking about these fathers the image of the working builder comes to mind. Benjamin Few, father of educator William P. Few,

[19] Henry Wilson Bragdon, *Woodrow Wilson: The Academic Years* (Cambridge, Mass.: Harvard University Press, 1967), p. 5.

[20] Ray Stannard Baker, *Woodrow Wilson: Life and Letters*, 8 vols. (Garden City: Doubleday, Page and Co., 1927-39), 1:52-53.

[21] William E. Dodd, *Woodrow Wilson and His Work* (New York: Peter Smith, 1932), pp. 6-11.

[22] Edwin Mims, *Chancellor Kirkland of Vanderbilt* (Nashville: Vanderbilt University Press, 1940), pp. 15-16.

helped build the first church in Greer, South Carolina.[23] After building the town of Cary with logs from his own sawmill, Frank Page built its first schoolhouse. Whether as farmers, sawmill operators, or merchants, they tore down their barns and built bigger ones: they built, or helped to build, farms, towns, schools, businesses. The image of growth and the symbol of the working builder pervades the writing of Southerners in the 1890s and 1900s. Walter Page reprinted two of his most outspoken speeches calling for building schools in a book he called *The Rebuilding of Old Commonwealths*. He dedicated the work to his father, "whose work was work that built up the Commonwealth."[24] Page extended the imagery by naming the magazine which he founded in 1900 the *World's Work*. During his years as editor hardly an issue appeared without a full-page picture of some "captain of industry" and an accompanying feature article lauding the good works of such barons of commerce. Metaphors of manhood pervaded the chapel talks of the president of Trinity College, John C. Kilgo—a man who deeply revered his father, a Methodist minister, and equally admired the captains of industry for their labors.[25] "The Growing South" was one of Edwin Alderman's favorite speeches, which he eventually published in the *World's Work*.[26] William Garrott Brown did a lengthy series of travel articles for the Boston *Evening Transcript* in 1904 on "The South at Work."[27] Edwin Mims, a perceptive critic of the South for thirty years, a number of which he spent at Trinity during Kilgo's presidency, summed up in 1925 his three decades of reflection on Southern progress in *The Advancing South*, a book that heralded factories and mills and the good works of industrialists like Daniel A.

---

[23] Robert H. Woody, ed., *The Papers and Addresses of William Preston Few* (Durham: Duke University Press, 1951), pp. x-xi.

[24] New York: Doubleday, Page and Co., 1905.

[25] For a selection of Kilgo's chapel talks, see D. W. Newsom, ed., *The Chapel Talks of John Carlisle Kilgo* (Nashville: Publishing House of the Methodist Episcopal Church, South, 1922).

[26] "The Growing South," *World's Work* 16 (1908): 10373-83.

[27] February 25-May 28, 1904.

Tompkins of North Carolina and writers Walter Page and Edgar Gardner Murphy.[28]

Religion—the traditional American Protestantism of their fathers—played a part in shaping the Southern mind as well. Four of the men who gained national reputations as writers or critics during the 1890s and 1900s were sons of ministers[29] (Woodrow Wilson's biographers agree that his father's Presbyterianism was one of the "most pervasive influences in his inheritance"[30]). These fathers tended to be men of proper piety and conventional theology, blending a simple frontier fundamentalism with an equally simple life. Regular churchgoers of uncomplicated doctrine, they equated religion and moral life. The biographers of the sons speak constantly of the fathers' piety; in short, they appear to have been men who blended integrity, industry, hope, optimism, and a genuine belief in God's demands.

Yet at first glance it might appear that religion had little or no effect on Southern social thought of the period. Only one or two men made even halting attempts to fuse Christian principles with social analysis,[31] and not even preachers sought to make "religion" the foundation of their arguments about Southern society. Dr. Kilgo, a Methodist, preached often during his presidency of Trinity College, but he became a full-fledged minister only when he was elevated to a bishopric in 1910. After that, the secular South heard little from this formerly outspoken social commentator. In his weekly, and sometimes daily, chapel talks he often spoke out on social issues, but he never sought to identify "religion" with social life.

Kilgo's age, even in a religious sense, was the age of the Victorian ethic: salvation, whether religious or secular, was a personal matter. The intellectuals were unified in the belief that society's salvation ultimately and logically depended upon individual re-

[28] *The Advancing South* (Garden City, N.Y.: Doubleday, Page and Co., 1926), pp. viii–ix.

[29] John C. Kilgo, James H. Kirkland, Andrew Sledd, and Woodrow Wilson.

[30] Bragdon, *Wilson: The Academic Years*, p. 8.

[31] See, for example, John C. Kilgo, "Our Duty to the Negro," *South Atlantic Quarterly* 2 (1903):367–85; Edgar Gardner Murphy, "The Pulpit and the War," *North American Review* 166 (1898):751–52.

generation. Despite Southern Protestantism's lack of commitment to Christianize the social order, it did bolster the fundamental assumptions Southern intellectuals came to hold about man. One might have expected—given the Calvinistic basis of much of nineteenth-century Protestantism—that Christian indoctrination, Southern style, would have included a view of man as sinful, base, lifted up out of his natural depravity only by the outstretched hand of God. But such was not the case. Their religion gave them a concern for moral values and a regard for life which was manifested in their own seriousness and their demand that others live seriously as well. (Wilson's idealism and moral conception of life stemmed from his early Presbyterian Calvinism, which he never, apparently, questioned or doubted.) The notion had been instilled in them that life is serious because it is a constant confrontation with ultimate, unconditional values and truths. By insisting that men take, as they put it, the "manly" and "candid" view, they elevated rationality and goodness to the level of moral absolutes, and by insisting that the South would pay for its actions they betrayed a lingering belief in divine judgment. They had a marked tendency to invest secular goals with religious significance, portraying, for instance, education and industrialism as redemptive forces and suggesting to their listeners that men could be lifted up from their sad state of existence—ignorance, poverty, illiteracy—and saved by an act of individual will. This belief in personal salvation bolstered their later atomistic conception of human society. For them the world was essentially moral or immoral, the battle lines were drawn between good and evil, and the task of the "leader," as of the priest, was to laud the good and excoriate the bad.

In addition to providing their sons with a model of conduct, these parents introduced them to learning. Their mothers began by reading to them from the Bible and the classics. Later they went to school, usually a nearby preparatory academy headed by a classics "scholar." Some attended the new free public schools, but the majority went to the older private schools. Not many of the parents could afford the luxury, but they found a way. William Garrott Brown's father, whose attitude in this regard may not have been typical, ignored the public school in Marion and chose for his son the Marion Military Academy.[32] Dodd's parents, though poor and of the "undistinguished masses," made a similar decision and, though they needed help from a more affluent relative to do so, sent William to the Oak Ridge Institute to supplement his high school education.[33] Kilgo's father, whose salary as a parson provided only the barest living for his family, once exclaimed, "I will live on bread and water and wear patched clothes before I will throw my children on society uneducated."[34]

The young intellectuals of this generation attended the best academies the South afforded: Bethel Military, the Webb School, Jefferson Davis Military, Brundige Military, French Creek, Professor Norwood's Classical Academy, and the Classical Academy of Professor William R. Gath. In these enclaves from the past, dressed in Confederate gray, they studied classics with the "Professor," absorbed history, and prepared for college and the future.

Of those who played an important part in the development of the Southern mind after 1890, only one, Clarence Poe, editor of the *Progressive Farmer*, did not attend a college or university. Poe spent those years as a publisher's apprentice in Raleigh.[35] All of the others attended some college or university, with the majority taking degrees. More than half, perhaps two-thirds, attended the denominational colleges, with the Methodist schools of Wofford, Trinity, Randolph-Macon, and Vanderbilt the most popular. Of the state schools, the University of Virginia attracted more of them than any other. In the church colleges Bible courses (usually taught by some retired minister whose "teachings" were predictably "safe," as William Garrott Brown once observed[36]) and daily chapel services were mandatory, as was attendance at a local church on Sunday. Though the emphasis on religion was probably

[32] Clayton, "William Garrott Brown," p. 1.

[33] Wendell H. Stephenson, *The South Lives in History* (Baton Rouge: Louisiana State University Press, 1955), p. 29; Dallek, *Democrat and Diplomat*, p. 7.

[34] Paul Neff Garber, *John C. Kilgo* (Durham: Duke University Press, 1937), p. 5.

[35] Clarence H. Poe, *My First Eighty Years* (Chapel Hill: University of North Carolina Press, 1963), p. 13.

[36] Stanton [Brown], "The South at Work," Boston *Evening Transcript*, March 12, 1904.

qualitatively different at Episcopal Sewanee and at Baptist Wake Forest, throughout the South students were confronted with the perennial questions raised by the classics or the ethical and moral precepts of the Bible. There was a persistent emphasis—sometimes explicit, more often implicit—on personal responsibility and man's relationship to the truth, whether expressed in Plato or St. Paul. Southern education rested on the comforting belief that such training in such an environment taught people to think clearly.

Aside from the religious dimension of their education, the young scholars' experiences varied little from campus to campus, whether secular or parochial. Classical languages and literature made up the core of the curriculum, of course, with social science, history, and a smattering of science thrown in. Political economy—usually in the form of a thinly disguised apologia for capitalism and, following John Stuart Mill, the study of man the acquisitive animal—was also a favorite. Constitutional history, a staple, was based on Blackstone and on an unquestioned faith that the transcendent authority of the law constituted its majesty. Science education limped along with inadequate facilities, though William E. Dodd and Walter Fleming, both future historians, concentrated on mathematics and engineering.[37]

In college the South's ablest young men lived in an environment which nurtured and rewarded their special talents and told them in a thousand different ways that they were the leaders of tomorrow. They excelled in such an atmosphere, both in the classroom and outside. They worked hard, a trait which characterized their lives as it had their fathers'—Dodd's work habits earned him the nickname of "Monk"; Trent came close to suffering a nervous breakdown from overwork in his senior year;[38] and, whether from exhaustion or some other cause, Woodrow Wilson had to leave Davidson College during his freshman year and go home to recuperate. The others were more temperate.

All of these young men exhibited special talents as debaters and editors of yearbooks, newspapers, and literary magazines. Fre-

[37]Dallek, *Democrat and Diplomat*, p. 6.
[38]Walker, "Trent," pp. 52–53.

31

quently they attached themselves to a favorite teacher whose enthusiasm or candor touched a responsive chord in them. Such teachers returned the compliment with friendship and words of praise and helped define manhood for them. They met other young men who would one day be politicians, churchmen, professors, editors, writers. It was at this point in their lives that they began to feel a collective identity, began to sense their distance from the ignorance, poverty, and backwardness that was "the South." Simply to be in college in the 1870s and 1880s separated them from the mass of Southerners, gave them a language and a learning that made them part of a small elite. And that elite *was* small: Chapel Hill, for instance, had only two hundred students in 1900, and Princeton, with five hundred, maintained the atmosphere of a small college. Classes were small, relationships with teachers and fellow students were close, and activities were many and varied. Within college halls, in a history class at Trinity, a chapel service at Sewanee, an argument under a tree at Charlottesville, students were admonished by teachers and their fellows to think of themselves as the South's future leaders. They were eager to hear that message. "To a remarkable degree," Alderman's biographer observes, "the members of his college generation were imbued with ambition to serve the commonwealth."[39]

A word ought to be said here about the "influence" of contemporary English politics and literature on the mind of the New South. It is, admittedly, always difficult to say whether a man is influenced by others whose ideas and phrasing he subsequently reiterates or whether he has simply found in them ideas and assumptions which he "accepts." That question aside, Southerners took readily to the prose and poetry of the Victorians, finding Matthew Arnold most to their liking, then Tennyson—the Tennyson of *In Memoriam*—then Wordsworth and Coleridge. In defense of their own critical stance, Southerners frequently insisted, following Arnold, that society needed "sweetness and light." They found in Arnold and Tennyson reinforcement for the belief in rationality, progress, and individualism. The English emphasis on individualism was particularly important: these Southern intellec-

[39]Malone, *Alderman*, p. 23.

tuals later demonstrated a great concern for individual rights and a firm belief that society was a collection of individuals. As for English politics, Southerners came to English letters just at the moment when Whiggery was dominant in English thought, and with Gladstone and John Stuart Mill they came to treasure constitutions, "good" government, civil service, free trade, and political parties, and to extol the necessity for intellectual leadership. Wilson, precociously absorbed in everything English, hung a picture of Gladstone above his desk the year he joined the Presbyterian Church and enrolled at Davidson College. These young Southerners were beginning to take on the manners, assumptions and ideas of educated men; they were taking their first steps toward cosmopolitanism.

For many the next step following college graduation—usually after a year or so of teaching or casting about for a niche—was across the Mason-Dixon line for further education. A small but important number went to German universities, where they earned doctorates or did sustained scholarly work. Most stayed in America to attend graduate school or to study law or theology. Living outside the South tended to broaden them intellectually, to make them more tolerant of new ideas, different customs and habits. Life in prosperous and cultured New York City, Berlin, Baltimore, or Leipzig put into sharp relief the vast differences between the South and the rest of the world. They became more humane, tolerant men committed to creating an environment where ideas could grow and prosper.

Whether abroad or in the North, they attended the best schools—Harvard, Johns Hopkins, Columbia, Chicago, Leipzig, and Berlin—and studied with some of the outstanding scholars of the day. Of the formal disciplines, history, philology, and English literature were most popular. Woodrow Wilson, John Spencer Bassett, William P. Trent, Burr J. Ramage, and numerous others came to Johns Hopkins to study under Herbert Baxter Adams in his famous seminar on historical investigation.[40] After Adams' un-

---

[40] For the development of Southern historiography during its formative years and the influence of Herbert Baxter Adams, see Stephenson, *The South Lives in History* and *Southern History in the Making* (Baton Rouge: Louisiana State University Press, 1964).

timely death in 1901, Southerners interested in history tended to go to Columbia to study with William A. Dunning. At Leipzig William E. Dodd studied with Karl Lamprecht, one of Germany's leading scientific historians.[41]

Southerners in all disciplines worked diligently and earned high marks and words of praise. At the University of Berlin James H. Kirkland so impressed Professor Richard Wülcker that he invited Kirkland to conduct one of his classes in Anglo-Saxon poetry. "Privately he told me," Kirkland confided to a friend, "he was very much pleased with it and that I had done my work real well."[42] Adams was convinced that Bassett, Trent, and Wilson were three of his best students.[43] Walter Fleming and James W. Garner of Mississippi enjoyed the same pleasant standing with Dunning. At Harvard William Garrott Brown, who wrote a prize-winning master's thesis under Edward Channing, declined a doctoral fellowship, even though both Channing and the historian Albert Bushnell Hart urged him to accept.[44] Years later, Hart wrote to Brown: "I wish you were with us and of us in the University. You are one of the few men in the country who has both got something to say and can say it. Your reputation as a writer is steadily rising, and in my judgment we cannot spare you from Harvard."[45]

Southerners like Brown succeeded so well in school partly because they quickly and enthusiastically took to the teachings of their professors. Their teachers, or at least the ones they admired, held that "true knowledge" should be arrived at "scientifically." Science—symbolized in the achievements of Darwin—seemed to have gotten at the truth of the natural world. A number of prestigious people—in addition to Adams, Dunning, and Lamprecht—

---

[41] William E. Dodd, "Karl Lamprecht and Kulturgeschichte," *Popular Science Monthly* 63 (1903):418–24.

[42] Mims, *Kirkland*, p. 48.

[43] Stephenson, *Southern History in the Making*, pp. 72–73, 96.

[44] John Spencer Bassett, "My Recollections of William Garrott Brown," *South Atlantic Quarterly* 16 (1917):98–99.

[45] Hart to Brown, September 28, 1903, Brown Papers, Duke University Library, Durham, N.C.

were giving the scientific method an intellectual and scholarly foundation. At Yale, where William Graham Sumner rigorously upheld the new empiricism, the scientific mystique was so persuasive that William James was moved to say in 1896: "In this very University . . . I have heard more than one teacher say that all the fundamental conceptions of truth have already been found by science, and that the future has only the details of the picture to fill in." While that position was extreme—and neither Adams, Dunning, nor Lamprecht wholly accepted the view—the men who trained the South's intellectuals accepted the assumptions of the scientific method.[46] Simply put, these were that true knowledge rests on an "objective" investigation of the "facts." Temperamentally indisposed to accept the romanticism and sentimentality native to most Southern youths (it took even Wilbur J. Cash years to throw off the last vestiges of Southern romanticism[47]), Southerners entering Harvard or Hopkins or Leipzig in the 1870s and 1880s needed a way of thinking that promised objective truth, and not the mythology or boastful assertions that had been the bane of the South. With the exception of Thomas Nelson Page and, to some extent Woodrow Wilson, they had had enough of romance; they wanted realism—"candor," as they put it.

The theme of rationality was the message of the scientific method. True, it was not the traditional philosophical view that equated rationality with deductive and abstract theorizing. Here was no searching after First Principles or the mind of the Absolute in the manner of St. Thomas. In fact, it was all rather anti-intellectual, in that it subtly urged men to abandon abstract theories and introspective metaphysics and commit themselves to the brute "facts." The scientific method bridges the gulf between the objects of knowledge (the "facts") and the mind of the observer. In holding that knowledge should be based on "facts" and that scholars should allow those facts to speak for themselves, Adams and

[46]W. Stull Holt, *Historical Scholarship in the United States and Other Essays* (Seattle: University of Washington Press, 1967), pp. 15-28; Stephenson, *Southern History in the Making*, pp. 52-70.

[47]Joseph L. Morrison, *W. J. Cash: Southern Prophet, a Biography and Reader* (New York: Alfred A. Knopf, 1967), p. 12.

his counterparts were also assuring their students that such a conscious, intelligent act is possible—and that they can achieve it if they set their minds to it. This conception of man's power ultimately makes man into the knower whose thought is rational, once he realizes the world has a rational course and destiny, not irrational or capricious; critical, not sentimental; objective, not subjective. The adherents of this view are tacitly assured that they can identify their own biases and assumptions rather easily. Having done so, the rational scholar can exclude "bias" from his thinking, and his account will then be true and accurate. Adams and Lamprecht, themselves steeped in the Hegelian idealism of Von Ranke, inculcated in their students the notion that institutions and nations have their own course and direction, their own life, which the historian can chart.[48] Such a view appealed to these Southerners, who were eager to understand their society as a "whole"; it assured them that they could understand the past and, therefore, the present.

The scientific ethos was particularly strong in history and philology; Adams, Dunning, Lamprecht, and Wülcker were leading spokesmen for the new learning. Their message had the additional authority of Leopold von Ranke's dictum, "Report the past as it actually happened." Lamprecht had a few minor quarrels with the main strand of Rankean sentiment, but he stoutly upheld the belief that history should be a scientific study.[49] Philology, too, sought to become critical, rigorous, "scientific." Both Kirkland and John Bell Henneman, a graduate of the University of Virginia and a prolific writer during the years he taught at Sewanee during the 1890s and early 1900s, studied language in Germany from that point of view.[50] William Few studied under Harvard's renowned scholars, including F. J. Child and G. L. Kittredge, and earned a doctorate in philology with a dissertation on "The -ing Suffix in Middle English with Special Reference to Participles and -ing Verbals."[51]

[48] Dodd, "Lamprecht," pp. 418–24.

[49] Ibid.

[50] Mims, Kirkland, pp. 43–68; John Bell Henneman, "The Late Professor Baskerville," Sewanee Review 8 (1900):26–44.

[51] Woody, William Preston Few, p. 15.

Southerners accepted this notion of objectivity because they were "ready" for such a view. From birth they had been taught to respect rational thought. Several had had college teachers who upheld the scientific method and exemplified a critical spirit. In his undergraduate days at Auburn, Fleming had come under the influence of historian George Petrie, one of Adams' first students.[52] At Randolph-Macon Professor Thomas Randolph Price's defense of critical thinking won Walter Page and fellow student William Baskerville.[53] Baskerville, after earning a doctorate in philology at Leipzig, took a position at Wofford College. There he joined fellow Southerner Charles Foster Smith, also a Leipzig man, in the English Department. Both Smith and Baskerville believed that both language and literature should be taught "scientifically." One of their first students was James H. Kirkland, whom they persuaded to follow in their steps to Leipzig.[54] Kirkland was fortunate to find these two dedicated teachers. In paying tribute to Baskerville in 1900, shortly after his early, untimely death, John Bell Henneman observed that Baskerville and Smith brought such a fresh attitude to Wofford that they could almost be said to have turned the place upside down. The two men, whose income as professors was at the subsistence level, jointly subscribed to Northern papers and journals and eagerly discussed "questions and men and movements, in letters, in scholarship, and even in politics." According to Henneman, "It was a rubbing together of minds and keeping alive the flame of thought that was to do both good for many years,"[55] to say nothing of what it did for students like Kirkland and Kilgo.

For some of these men, particularly Walter Page, William Garrott Brown, Edwin Mims, and William P. Trent, their education and experience away from home led them to compare the "rational" North favorably with the hapless, reactionary, "thinkless" South, as Brown put it. Others, like Edgar Gardner Murphy and William P. Few, were not quite so enamoured of the North (too

[52] Stephenson, *The South Lives in History*, p. 96.
[53] Hendrick, *Training of an American*, pp. 60-66.
[54] Mims, *Kirkland*, p. 32.
[55] Henneman, "Baskerville," p. 33.

much crass Yankee commercialism) but nevertheless tended to identify the North with "America" and the South with "sectionalism" and to exhort the South to become "national."[56] Though even Page cautioned the South to spurn "Yankee commercialism" (never defined), the undercurrent of criticism of the South was intense, and its thrust was always that the Southerner needed to mend his ways and copy his Northern brethren. The intellectuals fell into the trap of equating their particular, but hardly representative, patches of "the North"—the Hopkins seminar or Harvard Yard—with the North. They forgot that Hell's Kitchen and the sweat shop were also part of the North, with the result that they measured the worst of the South against the best of the North.

Writing to a friend in 1907, Brown recalled what it had meant to him to go from Marion, Alabama, to Cambridge, Massachusetts: "You know, ten or fifteen years ago, whenever I passed from North to South I went through violent changes and revulsions of attitudes and feelings."[57] Similarly Nicholas Worth, the protagonist of Page's semi-autobiographical novel *The Southerner*, remarked about returning from Harvard to North Carolina, his home state: "As soon as I crossed the Potomac on my journey homeward, I was sure that I was coming into another world."[58] Murphy, less caustic than Page, nevertheless admitted that no Southerner could quite understand just how racially repressive the South was unless he had spent some time outside of it.[59] Others, like Kilgo, Mims, Henneman, and Samuel Chiles Mitchell (Mitchell did his graduate work at the University of Chicago), were given to praising every sign of the "national spirit" that appeared in the South.[60]

[56] Edgar Gardner Murphy, *The Basis of Ascendancy* (New York: Longmans, Green, and Co., 1910); William P. Few, "Education and Citizenship in a Democracy," *South Atlantic Quarterly* 7 (1908):1–10; Few, "The Standardization of Southern Colleges," *ibid.*, pp. 299–307.

[57] Brown to Charles M. Thompson, June 21, 1907, Brown Papers.

[58] [Walter H. Page], *The Southerner; Being the Autobiography of Nicholas Worth* (New York: Doubleday, Page and Co., 1909), p. 108.

[59] *Ascendancy*, p. 39.

[60] See, for example, John Bell Henneman, "The National Element in Southern Literature," *Sewanee Review* 17 (1909):88–105; Edwin Mims, "The Independent Voter in the South," *South Atlantic Quarterly* 5 (1907):1–7; Samuel Chiles Mitchell, "The Nationalization of Southern Sentiment," *ibid.*, 7 (1908):107–113.

Page went to the greatest extreme in measuring the South against a "national" ideal. He had his Nicholas Worth marvel at the contrast between Harvard and his native Piedmont: "We thought in rotund, even grandiose phrases. Rousing speech came more naturally to us than accuracy of statement. A somewhat exaggerated manner and tendency to sweeping generalizations came easy to us." But in the Yard thinking was exact, stimulating, exciting: "what an emancipation I owed to that candid and straight habit of life and thought which had no social or intellectual punishment for those who differed from it, at least on the subjects about which I was then especially concerned." Worth confesses to a certain social schizophrenia typical of many of Page's generation: "The earth itself seemed to revolve slowly" in the South, he says. "It *was* another country from the country whence I came. It must be accepted as it is, I reflected, and judged by its own standards."[61] But judging the South against its own standards—whatever that might mean—proved difficult, if not impossible. The temptation was to judge the South against another, more rigorous standard that few societies could have met.

As one charts the course of this generation, one becomes aware that conflict was an ever-present part of the lives of its members. Their education had made them "sensible" and "candid" (two of their favorite words), and, as such, set them apart rather sharply from the Chamber of Commerce booster and the hell-and-brimstone minister. Their commitment to Progress and its agents, the machine and the entrepreneur, separated them from the agrarian mystique. But their education and new-found vision were not solely responsible for their conflicts. Southerners were poor in a rich country (they had, as C. Vann Woodward puts it, "a long and quite un-American experience with poverty"[62]); they had failed to maintain their society and had lost a war, in a country that worshiped success; they had been "guilty" of human bondage and of "traitorous" secession, in a country that luxuriated in its assumed innocence of evil; they walked a tightrope between romance and realism, between romantic individualism and strict insistence on

[61]Pp. 89, 93, 96, 110.
[62]*Burden of Southern History*, pp. 17–18.

intellectual uniformity. All these conflicts were aggravated by the ever-present issue of race—whites and blacks living next door to each other, observing the etiquette of the color line. Walter Page was perhaps more perceptive than he realized when he wrote that three ghosts haunted the South, "the Ghost of the Confederate dead, the Ghost of religious orthodoxy, the Ghost of Negro domination."[63] In short, Southerners were tied to history: they were not, as Americans wanted to believe about themselves, "born free."[64]

The intellectuals of the New South worked out their own resolutions of these conflicts, reflecting, as one might expect, their basic assumptions: the South needed to work, to be rational about itself, to commit itself to progress. Then, and only then, would the Southerner become an American. Only on the racial issue did they falter. Some talked darkly of the African shadow and confessed that the problem was insoluble—at least, "in this generation." Most fell back rather lamely on theories about man's nature, arguing that rational criticism and constructive advice would produce a solution. There was nothing in their background which challenged existing racial beliefs. Some of their fathers may have held unpopular ideas about slavery, but there is nothing to suggest that they had emancipated racial views of the slave or the freedman. Nothing in Adams' seminar or Lamprecht's lectures, for all their attention to clear, unbiased thinking, put into question the view that Negroes were unable to think clearly—Dunning in fact argued that Negroes were inferior.[65] The sermons they heard as young men gave pious recognition to the fatherhood of God but little more than passing attention to the brotherhood of man.

That the South's new intellectuals resolved their conflicts is suggested by the fact that they appear to have reflected very little on what it meant to be a "Southerner." In their early adulthood, as noted earlier, they at times wondered how they, as educated

---

[63] Hendrick, *Life and Letters of Walter H. Page*, 1:91.

[64] Woodward, *Burden of Southern History*, p. 22.

[65] Alan D. Harper, "William A. Dunning: The Historian as Teacher," *Civil War History* 10 (1964):54–66.

men, would fit in, but they felt no necessity to define themselves as Southerners; their self-image was secure. Despite their fascination with history they felt that they had made a break with the past, but it was the plantation past, not the past represented by Jefferson and Lee, not their own past. There was no "generation gap" here, no rebellion against their fathers: sons and fathers shared a common view of the world.

In trying to resolve their tensions and conflicts, the new intellectuals turned to the examples of Thomas Jefferson and Robert E. Lee, two Southerners whose lives suggested ways in which a Southerner might live with prejudice and racial tension and yet make a noble and grand contribution to mankind. No one stood higher in the intellectuals' pantheon than these two Virginians. Lee's devotion to duty, first in 1861 and then in 1865, his calm, controlled passion for the South, in war and peace, exemplified the qualities the intellectuals would have liked to find in themselves and in the Southerner. He became their symbol of what a Southerner and an American might be—proud of the South, but devoted to America. Jefferson was the epitome of justice, guardian of the democratic tradition. He was learned, yet humane; he was devoted to the principles of the nation and of mankind. His high ideals, his love of free speech, his learning, and his unflagging faith in the people were cherished. Southern intellectuals were proud to acknowledge that the Jefferson of the Declaration of Independence was a Southerner. Lee and Jefferson, then, rather than Calhoun and Jefferson Davis, served as fitting symbols for a generation of Southerners who wanted to be Americans.

2

WALTER HINES PAGE: CATALYST
OF THE INTELLECTUAL CLASS

EVERAL DYNAMIC AND ARTICULATE MEN of the New South reiterated the beliefs and goals of their generation, and chief
among these was Walter Hines Page. He used the power of
his voice and his editorial office to draw public attention to the
South and its needs. In speeches, writings, and correspondence he
spread an infectious optimism and a sense of service to the South.
He defended education, spoke of the need to respect ideas and
men of ideas, and continually insisted that the South would realize
her "true" nature, given the proper leadership.

Page has been called by both friends and foes the archetype of
the New South intellectual.[1] He proclaimed ideals, and proclaimed
them boldly and enthusiastically. In so doing, he inspired in his
contemporaries a community of common concern. Part of Page's
persuasiveness was that he personified his message: he not only

---

[1] Page's friends and sympathetic critics include Edwin Mims, "Walter Hines Page:
Friend of the South," *South Atlantic Quarterly* 18 (1919):75-115: Robert D. W.
Conner, "Walter Hines Page: A Southern Nationalist," in Howard W. Odum, ed.,
Southern Pioneers in Social Interpretation (Chapel Hill: University of North Carolina
Press, 1925), pp. 53-67; Charles G. Sellers, "Walter Hines Page and the Spirit of the New
South," *North Carolina Historical Review* 29 (1952):281-99; and the ambitious,
uncritical account in Hendrick, *Training of an American* and *The Life and Letters of
Walter H. Page.* Page's unsympathetic critics include Donald Davidson, *The Attack on
Leviathan* (Chapel Hill: University of North Carolina Press, 1938), pp. 261-84; Frank
Owsley, "A Key to Southern Liberalism," *Southern Review* 3 (1937):28-38; Edd W.
Parks, *Segments of Southern Thought* (Athens: University of Georgia Press, 1938), pp.
273-92; and John Donald Wade, "What the South Figured, 1865-1914," *Southern
Review* 3 (1937):360-67.

talked about service and the necessity of working for the South—
he worked and served; he praised candor and independence
candidly and vigorously. As with Emerson, his message matched
his personality: when he spoke of optimism he was optimistic. He
was, as Paul Gaston has shown, an early and outspoken advocate
for "New South" values. Advocacy for the new and insensitivity
bordering on contempt for the old were his hallmarks. He wanted
change everywhere and in everyone in the South; he cared little
for "traditions"—and said so; he was convinced that the school
and the factory would root out the last vestiges of the past. More
exuberantly "Americanized" than most of his contemporaries, he
wanted the Southerner made over in the image of Yankee habits
and prosperity.

Greatly admired by the intellectuals of his own day—though
some found him a bit over-zealous—Page fired the imagination of
his generation and served as the model of liberalism in the Southern intellectual community. Yet here was a democratic idealism
that for all of its vitality and vision, for all of its robust Jeffersonian faith "in the people," stopped short at the color line. Like
Jefferson, when Page spoke of the common man, he meant the
white common man. And though he was concerned about the
black Southerner, and deeply alarmed about white racism, Page's
energies and vision were devoted to uplifting the whites, whom he
trusted to be ultimately rational and good.

Although in this respect Page was a typical Southern intellectual, few could match his energy, his idealism, or his commitment
to causes. He bore little resemblance to the out-and-out racists of
his generation and found some of his colleagues' ideas tired and
worn. He could only smile, for instance, at those who defended
the "Christian" basis for freedom or education. But in the eyes of
his fellows, Page rather completely typified what was known as
the New South mentality.

* * *

From his earliest years Page exhibited his father's industry and
individuality.[2] At the Bingham Preparatory School in Mebane,

[2] The following biographical information, except where noted, is taken from
Hendrick, *Training of an American.*

43

North Carolina, "Wat," as he was called, could not quite muster respect for the shallow artificiality of the school's traditions (the boys wore uniforms of Confederate gray) or the romanticism of Major Robert Bingham, headmaster. Not even the visits of old soldiers from the great war of 1861 or the students' ecstatic reception of them could prompt Page to mourn lost glories. When his classmates lamented their plain origins, Page found them silly and juvenile. When he once tried to console a distraught youth by admitting that his father held no colonel's rank either, his confession of humble origins only lowered his companion's respect for him. Later, at Trinity College, where his father hoped he would prepare for the Methodist ministry, Walter continued in his independent ways. The only teacher who inspired him was a man who advocated popular education and freedom of thought. The atmosphere was otherwise stultifying, and Page persuaded his parents to allow him to transfer to Randolph-Macon College. There he found people who shared his enthusiasm for talk about the South and her future. Speakers came to the campus, some to extol past glories, others to talk of learning and creative thought. A newspaper editor from Richmond whose credentials included service in the Confederate Army so electrified the students that for weeks they could talk of little else but his speech. Page also came under the influence of Thomas Randolph Price, a professor of Greek and English literature, who made his students feel his own deep love of knowledge. Wat spent many an afternoon talking with Price about the great literature of a past even more ancient than the Old South.

In 1876, following graduation, Page followed Price's advice and enrolled at Johns Hopkins to do graduate work in classics under Basil Gildersleeve. Gildersleeve, a Southern professor of the old school and a noted classicist, had just moved to the newly founded Hopkins. Page was impressed by his new mentor's profound feeling for the soul and the language of antiquity but found his unabashed glorification of the South wrong and irrelevant. He had moved too far from the old ways to accept Gildersleeve's equation of the Old South with the vibrant individualism of Athens. Wat Page's view of man and the universe had taken on a cosmopolitan coloring that made Gildersleeve's constant chatter about his days in the Confederate army seem woefully anachronistic. We glimpse Page's more emancipated outlook in a letter of 1876, outlining his mixed feelings about Hopkins' choice of the "modernist" Thomas Huxley to be a commencement speaker. Huxley's address and the university's decision to exclude prayers from the ceremony took him aback. The faculty, he wrote, was made up of "Jews, Catholics, and I suspect, atheists," as well as Christians. "But," he mused, "this must be so from the very nature of the institution."[3]

Page's two years at Hopkins proved to be troublesome ones. His parents' pious plans were constantly in his mind; so was his "ability" as a student. "Take for example my intellectual self," he confided to his mother. "Ever since I can remember, I have always been called smart, and many a foolish teacher and friend . . . has praised my *great abilities* to the skies."[4] Anxieties about his future plagued him also.

I wish, dear mama, that I could tell you my feelings tonight, my hopes, my fears. Life—what is it to be for me? Failure or success? Easy enough it is to talk about doing great things, but great talkers often times greatly fail. Have I the principles and the strength that make men? That's the question. Success at college—that is easy enough. I have learned its philosophy well. But how as nothing seems all my knowledge, all my experience, when I think of what I should like to be! Success at everything that I have ever tried is easy enough. But life—life, sure enough—how will that be?[5]

At such times Page felt that his education had not prepared him for "life." But he was wrong. His education had taken him beyond the borders of a narrow provincialism. He had learned from history how cultures and people vary. His view of man's aspirations and needs had been broadened: he had learned that the world had some "Jews, Catholics, and atheists" in it.

When he left the university in the spring of 1878 he was only partially clear about his goals. He did not want to pursue a schol-

[3] *Ibid.*, p. 71.
[4] Page to his mother (Catherine Francis), April 12, 1874, Page Papers, Houghton Library, Harvard University, Cambridge, Mass.
[5] Page to his mother, June 20, 1875, Page Papers.

arly career and considered teaching or journalism. As his friend William Garrott Brown said of his own life, he felt drawn away from history and the past toward the "living, real people of importance at one's elbow."[6] He spent the next few years casting about for direction. The summer of 1878 found him teaching at the University of North Carolina. His dress—a business suit rather than the traditional frock coat of the "professor"—symbolized both his own personality and the character of the intellectual class that was soon to emerge. In the fall, after a position offered him at the university failed to materialize, he did some freelance writing, and then taught for a year in Kentucky. Unsatisfied, he drifted west and joined the St. Joseph, Missouri, *Bee* as a cub reporter. Writing home in 1880 he sounded a note of confidence and self-assurance: "My place can be made one of influence. True, I am working hard and making little money; but isn't that always necessary? There *is* money in journalism in this country. And I expect to be comfortably situated one of these days."[7] In 1883 he took an important step toward that comfortable situation. He scraped together enough money to return to North Carolina to form a partnership with Josephus Daniels to buy the Raleigh *State Chronicle.*

From the beginning Page threw himself into causes. He joined a group of idealistic young men in a discussion club dedicated to exploring ways to improve the state and the South. Page was one of the prime movers in the Watauga Club (the name came from a stream in the western mountains and was meant to root the club in the land and the region's pioneer spirit), whose members included such public-spirited men as Charles B. McIver, Charles W. Dabney, and Josephus Daniels.[8] The weekly meetings provided an outlet for the energetic idealism of the young men. The talk was good and the friendships endured. A full fifty years later Dabney, who went on to be a forceful spokesman for public education as president of the University of Tennessee, vividly remembered its

[6] Brown to William R. Thayer, June 1, 1906, Brown Papers.

[7] Page to his mother, July 11, 1880, Page Papers.

[8] Charles W. Dabney, *Universal Education in the South*, 2 vols. (Chapel Hill: University of North Carolina Press, 1938), 1:180–85.

meetings: "The only entertainment was talk, and what 'talk-fests' these were."[9] The club was a microcosm of what the intellectual community would later become. Its faith lay in education and in an idealistic conception of a South redeemed through leadership.

One of the club's achievements was the founding of a state agricultural and mechanical college in Raleigh. The Watauga drew up a proposal for the state legislature outlining the need for such a school. When the legislature met to consider the proposal in 1885, Page and his friends called a mass meeting to demonstrate that the people wanted a new school. The legislators acquiesced and let the club leaders establish the guidelines for such a bill. Today North Carolina State is a tribute to the now-defunct Watauga Club.[10]

The *State Chronicle* also reflected Page's idealism. From the first, the paper was dedicated to uplift. It maintained proper respect for the "one true party" and championed the need for diversified agriculture and industrialism. In the fall of 1884 editor Page, in the spirit of the New South, helped persuade Raleigh businessmen to sponsor an exposition to advertise the state's "progress." A bulky "tobacco" issue of the *State Chronicle* heralded the marvelous attainments of Southern industry, with appropriate paeans to North Carolina's own home-grown capitalist, Washington Duke.[11]

But along with this orthodoxy Page held heretical and unpopular opinions which soon found their way into print. He revealed first dislike and then contempt for the Civil War, sectionalism, and the South's sentimental and romantic view of her past. To the Daughters of the Confederacy, just then embarking on a campaign to convince every Southern hamlet, no matter how small, to build statues to the "boys who wore the gray," Page suggested that they think more about building schools and less about erecting monuments to the dead past. The hope of the South, he announced, was its young men, not its doddering Confederate soldiers.[12] "What North Carolina needs," Page suggested, in an editorial that has

[9] *Ibid.*, p. 185.
[10] *Ibid.*
[11] Sellers, "Walter Hines Page," pp. 481–85.
[12] Hendrick, *Training of an American*, p. 168.

almost become synonymous with his name, "are a few first-class funerals."[13] Partly because of such intemperate remarks, the paper lost subscribers, and Page felt obligated to sell his share of the paper to Daniels.

The "people" had turned against Page. He had not been crucified or sacrificed to the Savage Ideal, but he felt betrayed. He decided to leave the state and move north, where his special talents would be appreciated. From New York came his bitter farewell, full of malice and vituperation. His acid-dipped "Mummy Letters" denounced the people of North Carolina as closed-minded and reactionary, dominated by "mummies" of the past—shibboleths that choked off any sign of modern thought.[14] The state had such a narrow and constricted mind that the better minds were forced out:

There is not a man whose residence is in the State who is recognized by the world as an authority on anything. Since time began, no man or no woman who lived there has ever written a book that has taken a place in the permanent literature of the country. Not a man has ever lived and worked there who fills twenty-five pages in any history of the United States. Not a scientific discovery has been made and worked out and kept its home in North Carolina that has ever become famous for the good it did the world. It is the laughing stock among the States.[15]

A close reading of the letters does reveal, however, that Page drew a distinction between "the people" and their "traditions" or leaders. Something prevented him from concluding that "the people" themselves were to be blamed for their actions. The state needed leadership: "I think the time has come for getting at the truth, for independent action, for a declaration of independence from the tyranny of hindering traditions."[16]

On that note a chapter in Page's life came to an end. Just thirty years old, too young to be considered a failure or to dwell overly long on his defeat, he turned his attention to a new job with the

[13]*Ibid.*

[14]The Mummy Letters are reprinted in part in Hendrick, *Training of an American,* pp. 176–91.

[15]*Ibid.,* p. 176.

[16]*Ibid.*

Forum magazine, and within a few years became its editor.[17] Then, in 1898, after an abortive effort to gain financial control of the *Forum*,[18] he left to edit the *Atlantic Monthly*. Two years later he found the financial support to start the *World's Work*.[19]

His criticisms of the South continued to follow, with slight modification, the pattern set by the Mummy Letters. The tone was less caustic, but the style was essentially the one he had developed earlier: a general criticism of an entire people coupled with an optimistic estimate of their potential. At times he struck out in anger, but the next sentence would offer a word of praise, a note of optimism, a resounding call for new leadership in the New South. Through his criticism and his active cooperation with other concerned Southerners, he hoped to create in the Southern conscience a will to attack the "causes" of evil.

* * *

Nowhere does Page's critical-optimistic voice ring more clearly than in his praise of Southern education and critical thought. Editorials on the subject dotted the *World's Work*. Through letters and speeches he popularized an emerging attitude toward intelligence and education. His passionate attack on the opponents of public education matched the fire and spirit of the words of Trent and Bassett during the 1890s. What was new in Page was an expanded, boldly articulated, democratic and idealistic concern for the white common man.

The most dramatic announcement of Page's views came in a historic speech he gave in Greensboro, North Carolina, in 1897. In "The Forgotten Man" Page reflected the best of his generation's

[17]Page's success in rebuilding the *Forum's* sagging sales and reputation prompted Woodrow Wilson to compliment Page for luring so many "important" people to its pages (Wilson to Page, December 5, 1894, Page Papers).

[18]For a full account of Page's feud with the stockholders and his abortive attempt to wrest control from them, see the Page-Charles F. Thwing correspondence of April–May, 1885, Page Papers.

[19]During Page's editorship, the *Forum* published thirteen articles on the South, including one by Page, "The Last Hold of the Southern Bully," 15 (1893):303–14. The *Atlantic Monthly* printed eight articles dealing with the South during Page's two-year stint as editor. In the 151 issues of the *World's Work* edited by Page the magazine carried some eighty-two articles on the South, or slightly more than one every other issue (Sellers, "Walter Hines Page," p. 492).

idealism and added a phrase to the language of the intellectuals.[20] He attacked the soothsayers and medicine men of special privilege, denounced ignorance and championed schools, lamented the lack of scholarship and libraries and the absence of a reading public to support an intellectual class and meet the needs of a civilized culture. The speech was publicized throughout the South, and from that moment on Page played the role of chief spokesman for Southern schools.

The burden of Page's remarks was that North Carolina—and, by extension, the South—had, under the dominance of the planters, politicians, and preachers, neglected the training of the common man. Everyone had been "corrupted," said Page, some by ignorance, others by false ideas. In the antebellum South the planter class had fostered the notion that education was for the few, the well-born. Such ideas were elitist, but not even war and its aftermath had been able to alter that mentality. In came the preachers after the Civil War, with only a slightly broader commitment to education. Page conceded that the churches built good colleges and took their stand for quality education, but he reminded his audience that only a few could afford to attend a Trinity, a Davidson, or a Wake Forest. Ignorance, superstition, and poverty denied the common (white) man a vision of a better life and made him an obstacle to Southern progress. The hapless "forgotten man" was duped by the rhetoric of the planter and by the insistence of the preacher that "the ills and misfortunes of this life were blessings in disguise, that God meant his poverty as a means of grace, and that if he accepted the right creed all would be well with him."[21] The educational schemes of the planters and preachers had, in fact, failed even in their self-appointed tasks, said Page. The whole South was impoverished intellectually. Was there really a first-rate college or university in the South? Did North Carolina's schools produce "a body of scholars that have been or are in any way famous"? To both questions the answer was no. "Make another test: there are no great libraries in the State, nor do the

[20] Page, *The Rebuilding of Old Commonwealths*, pp. 1-48.
[21] *Ibid.*, p. 23.

people yet read, nor have the publishing houses yet reckoned them as their patrons, except the publishers of school books."[22]

Page further extended his image to include the "forgotten woman." After applauding his old friends Edwin Alderman and Charles McIver for persuading the state to create the Woman's College in Greensboro, Page argued that the education of women was as imperative as the education of men:

Let any man whose mind is not hardened by some wornout theory of politics or of ecclesiasticism go to the country in almost any part of the State and make a study of life there, especially of the life of the women. He will see them thin and wrinkled in youth from ill prepared food, clad without warmth or grace, living in untidy houses, working from daylight till bedtime at the dull round of weary duties, the slaves of men of equal slovenliness, the mothers of joyless children—all uneducated if not illiterate.

She, too, Page warned, keeps the South poor. "She knows no better [life] and can never learn better, nor point her children to a higher life."[23]

Page went further than most Southern intellectuals in his liberalism. To his mind the logical conclusion to a free and public system of primary and secondary schools would be the establishment of equally free and public colleges and universities. A state with such a program would leave no Southerner forgotten. As he knew, Page was meddling in an issue that had touched off violent controversy in North Carolina a scant year earlier, in 1896. The proponents of the church colleges, ably and polemically led by John C. Kilgo (a man, incidentally, who also championed the higher education of women), maintained vehemently that tuition scholarships to the state universities meant "unfair competition" for the church colleges. Page, with a more secular turn of mind and an all-embracing faith in education, interpreted matters another way: the state needed educated citizens; citizens needed education; since the average citizen could not afford a church college, the state had a "duty" to provide free education—at all

---

[22] *Ibid.*, p. 20.
[23] *Ibid.*, pp. 22-25.

levels. There would be enough students to go around, Page maintained, and everyone would prosper from an educated citizenry, even the churches. To those who feared that state colleges would neglect the spiritual side of man, Page proposed that religious orders might send representatives to the state schools to minister to the spiritual needs of their students.

Page had to counter the familiar charge that the South was "too poor" to afford schools. He gave a typically Jeffersonian answer: "We pay for schools not so much out of our purses as out of our state of mind."[24] Besides, an educated citizenry creates wealth by providing a basis for an economy of supply and demand. "Too poor to maintain schools?" he asked. "The man who says it is the perpetuator of poverty. It is the doctrine that has kept us poor. It smells of the almshouse and the hovel. It has driven more men and more wealth from the State and kept more away than any political doctrine ever cost us—more even than the doctrine of Secession. Such a man is the victim of an ancient and harmful falsehood."[25]

This appraisal of Southern educational conditions naturally elicited a defensive reaction from Southerners. Newspaper editors and clerics who construed even the slightest questioning of the South's virtue and superiority as disloyalty struck back. Unperturbed by this teapot tempest, Page rather enjoyed the spectacle of one religious editor who gave him a proper dressing down. "I wrote him a gentle letter," Page said to a friend, "telling him that I hoped he'd have a long and happy life preaching a gospel of friendleness and neighborliness and good-will, and that I care nothing about 'excoriation.' " "Why should I or anybody read such stuff," he said. "I can't find time to do half the positive things that I should like to do for the broadening of my own character and for the encouragement of others." But he realized that "there is nevertheless a serious side to such folly. For it shows the need of education, education, education." Such critics "have such a starved view of life that they cannot themselves, perhaps, ever be educated into kindliness and dignity of thought. But their children must be—

[24] Ibid., p. 30.
[25] Ibid., p. 32.

must be. Think of beautiful children growing up in a home where 'excoriating' people who differ with you is regarded as a manly Christian exercise!"[26]

* * *

Page could view his detractors in this rather genial fashion partly because everywhere he turned he discovered men who applauded his work. He received numerous invitations to speak and letters of congratulations. In 1898, the year following his speech in Greensboro, he was invited to attend the North Carolina Teachers' Assembly. "I have many things to do in June, but I am going—going with great pleasure. I hope to see you there," he wrote to a friend. "I know of no other company of people that I should be so glad to meet. They are doing noble work—the most devoted and useful work in this whole world. They are the true leaders of the people. I often wish that I were one of them. They inspire me as nobody else does. They are the army of our salvation."[27] (Page attended the conference at his own expense, a thing he did many times throughout his life.)

On one such occasion in 1901 Page delivered a memorable address. He told his audience, the graduating class of the Georgia State Normal School at Athens, the story of Northwood, "The School That Built a Town."[28] Northwood was a small, nondescript Southern borough, undistinguished in either its citizens or its economic level. The only educational adornments were a ladies' seminary and an academy for boys. Nothing was happening to change the town, to open windows to the future. Then some civic leaders built a public school, and the result was astounding: "The school has made the town. It has given nearly every successful man in it his first impulse in his career and it has given the community great renown."[29] Industrious and dynamic men were attracted to Northwood: "The architects are high-school men; the

---

[26] Hendrick, *Life and Letters of Walter H. Page*, 1:81–82.
[27] *Ibid.*, p. 82.
[28] *The Rebuilding of Old Commonwealths*, pp. 49–104.
[29] *Ibid.*, p. 69.

engineers who graded the streets and made a model system of sewers are high-school men; the roads were laid out by high-school men. There is a whole county of model farms and dairies and good stock farms. High-school men have in this generation made the community a new community. They conduct all sorts of factories—they make furniture; they make things of leather, they make things of wrought iron; they have hundreds of small industries."[30]

But, Page reminded his audience, for such a town to exist in every county in every state, Southerners would have to discard the notion that education is for the few and that public education costs too much money. He charged that any man who might uphold such anachronisms was thinking "in terms of the Middle Ages, and the sooner you know it the better for the community, and I am glad of a chance to tell you." To any man who might oppose his proposal to build a schoolhouse in every school district in the state, Page said:

You are a dead weight on Georgia. You are one of the reasons why its property is not now worth five times what it is. You are one of the reasons why the products of its soil are not five times as great as they are, for such schools as I mean would make most farmers highly successful farmers. You are one of the reasons why the population of the State is not twice or thrice what it is, for such schools as I mean would attract good people from every part of the world, and cause more children to grow into healthful maturity. You are one of the reasons why Georgia is not one of the greatest manufacturing States in the Union, for such schools as I mean would turn thousands of the best-trained hands and minds to the making of beautiful and useful things.

Then he administered the *coup de grâce*: "Last of all you are not a democrat. You have never thoroughly read Thomas Jefferson." "Of course," Page went on to assure his listeners, "there is no such man in your community."[31] For Page "education" had a transcendent quality and a religious sanctity. The school, and not the church, would save men from the despair and hopelessness of ignorance. He concluded his speech with his "creed":

[30] *Ibid.*, pp. 70–71.
[31] *Ibid.*, pp. 75–77.

I believe in the free public training of both the hands and the mind of every child born of woman.

I believe that by the right training of men we add to the wealth of the world. All wealth is the creation of man, and he creates it only in proportion to the trained uses of a community; and, the more men we train, the more wealth everyone may create.

I believe in the perpetual regeneration of society, in the immortality of democracy, and in growth everlasting.[32]

The cadence, wording, rhythm, tone, mood is of the sermon. It is the voice of the believer; it is the glad tidings of salvation. It is the sermon of a lay preacher, the secular idealist: the Alpha, "I believe," stands appropriately juxtaposed with the Omega: "the regeneration of society, the immortality of democracy, and growth everlasting." Of course, Page knew his congregation. The imagery and tone would be immediately recognized and accepted as the language of truth in the Bible Belt, and no doubt Page chose his language carefully. Yet his creed says explicitly what he and his generation *believed* about education. He had enunciated the same creed years earlier in Raleigh during the 1880s and members of the Watauga Club had taken his words to their hearts. Notice the similarity between his creed and the aphorisms Charles McIver was fond of repeating:

"Education makes democracy possible."

"Education is not charity, but our chief duty as citizens."

"Education cannot be given to anyone. It is as personal as religion; each one must work out his own mental as well as his spiritual salvation."

"Education is simply our effort to live life more abundantly."[33]

Such was the faith of rational men.

* * *

By 1901, the year of his speech in Athens, Page had good reason for his optimism. The *World's Work* was selling: in fact, he was even making money. In the South an army of young, energetic academicians and writers followed in his footsteps. Through a voluminous correspondence with those who shared his values, he

[32] *Ibid.*, p. 102.

[33] Dabney, *Universal Education*, 1:201.

kept in touch with almost every liberal thinker. The men—and women—who benefited from Page's editorial enthusiasm and support represent a roll call of the South's new intelligentsia: fellow writers William Garrott Brown, Clarence Poe, and Joel Chandler Harris; educators William P. Trent, John C. Kilgo, Charles D. McIver, Edwin Alderman, James H. Kirkland, Samuel Chiles Mitchell, and David Houston. Southern Negroes, too, found him to be a friendly editor. He published Booker T. Washington, of course, but also Charles W. Chesnutt, Robert Russa Moton, and even W. E. B. Du Bois. Through his connection with the publishing house of Doubleday, Page and Company, he sought out and encouraged Ellen Glasgow, as well as a number of others like Grace King and Mary Johnston.

Page's relationship with Edwin Alderman illustrates the dynamic role he played. Their acquaintance went back to the summer in 1878 when Page taught at Chapel Hill. Alderman, a freshman at the time, was captivated by the new teacher's intensity, earnestness, and modern outlook. In the 1890s, when Alderman and McIver were serving as propagandists for better North Carolina schools, he listened to McIver's stories of the Watauga Club days and of what Walter Page thought about this and that, particularly education, and Page's Greensboro speech of 1897 served to bring the two men closer together. Alderman was by this time the president of the University of North Carolina, and he appreciated Page's words. In 1898 Page came to Chapel Hill to give the commencement address,[34] and from that time on the two men followed each other's careers with interest. Page had mixed feelings when Alderman left North Carolina to become president of Tulane University, a private school, but Alderman stood for quality education—that fact retained Page's admiration. Page went to the New Orleans campus in 1902 to accept an honorary degree which Alderman had secured for him.[35] Two years later, when Alderman

---

[34] Page came even though the university could not afford an honorarium; see Alderman to Page, November 14, 1898; Page to Alderman, November 29, 1898, Page Papers; Malone, *Alderman*, p. 93.

[35] Page to Alderman, n.d., 1902, Page Papers.

assumed the presidency of the University of Virgina, Page publicly lauded the new president in the *World's Work.*[36]

Privately, too, Page supported Alderman's decision and his dedication to public education. Remember Jefferson's boldness, Page admonished his friend: "It was the man, not the time. Virginia was a nest of old fogies in his day, too."[37] Alderman was encouraged: "Your letter . . . did me a great deal of good. Somehow you have the note of conviction in your talk. After being with you for an hour or two I feel that I could get anything and do anything!"[38]

Page continued to support his friend. In 1906 a feature article in the *World's Work* described the good work being done at Charlottesville under Alderman and placed him in the vanguard of a new breed of men who were leading the South to a better day. Page coupled Alderman with another friend, David Houston, president of the University of Texas, and full-size portraits of the two men were published in the magazine. That year, at Alderman's request, Page gave the commencement address at the University of Virginia.[39]

Others also found Page a welcome ally. Edgar Gardner Murphy, an outspoken critic of Alabama's educational system, welcomed Page's support. You are, Murphy wrote to Page, "helping wonderfully to make the whole country *conscious* of the South—of its needs—its interests—and its possibilities."[40] In 1904 Murphy invited Page to address a conference on education in Birmingham. Impressed by Murphy's success in persuading Alabama's governorelect, Braxton Bragg Comer, to speak out forcefully for public education, and aware of the need to support Murphy against those who were saying that the state could not afford education, Page went to Birmingham and spoke on "Education and Prosperity."[41]

[36] Page to Alderman, June 22, 1904, Page Papers; Page, "The University of Virginia and Its President," *World's Work* 8 (1904):5224–25.

[37] Page to Alderman, June 22, 1904, Page Papers.

[38] Malone, *Alderman*, p. 190.

[39] Walter H. Page, "Two Leaders in Educational Statesmanship," *World's Work* 12 (1906):7731–32; Alderman to Page, June 2, 1906, Page Papers.

[40] Murphy to Page, March 5, 1902, Page Papers.

[41] Murphy to Page, February 10, 1904, Page Papers.

That same year the *World's Work* gave Murphy's new book, *The Present South*, a favorable review.[42]

Sympathy and public support characterized Page's relationship with Kilgo of Trinity and Kirkland of Vanderbilt. At Kirkland's request Page gave the commencement address at Vanderbilt in 1908. Three years later, when the school administration clashed with the clergymen on its Board of Trustees, Kirkland received Page's moral support.[43] At Kilgo's invitation Page went to Trinity in 1903 to dedicate its new library; he took the occasion to call attention to the accomplishments of the school under Kilgo's administration. The *World's Work* publicized the school's achievements and congratulated Trinity for upholding academic integrity.[44]

Part of Page's high regard for Trinity stemmed from his friendly relations with the faculty, particularly with Professor Edwin Mims. Their friendship started in a way that reveals a great deal about each man. In the spring of 1902 Mims protested to Page that one of his recent editorials was unfair to the South.[45] Recognizing Mims's earnestness, Page conceded the point: "Now, never give the matter another thought, I pray you. Let's turn to bigger tasks and nobler aims. They can't get us into a silly personal controversy—not on your life! We've too much to do!"[46] The following year, when historian John Spencer Bassett's words touched off a violent controversy at Trinity College and plunged the school into a bitter struggle over academic freedom, Page stood by the college and turned to Mims for information about the controversy. In addition to supplying Page with the facts, Mims wrote several unsigned editorials about the matter for the *World's Work*. The Bassett incident cemented the relationship between the two men. Mims

[42] W. H. Heck, "The Educational Uplift in the South," *World's Work* 8 (1904):5027–29.

[43] Kirkland to Page, May 2, 1904, November 16, 1908; Page to Kirkland, November 19, 1908; Kirkland to Page, August 12, 1911, Page Papers.

[44] Earl W. Porter, *Trinity and Duke, 1892–1924: The Foundations of Duke University* (Durham: Duke University Press, 1964), pp. 97–98.

[45] Mims, *Advancing South*, p. 33.

[46] *Ibid.*

looked to Page for encouragement and leadership whenever ominous events took place in the South, and Page in turn aroused Mims's flagging will. In the spring of 1904, just after the Bassett controversy had been resolved in favor of academic freedom, he wrote Mims: "What the South's got a chance to do is *lead*. There's no use in stopping short of that. The effect of the croakers and the critics and all kinds of narrow men has been to make us forget the we once had leadership. They keep us forever in the lowlands of complaint. Let's keep sounding the note of leadership and the next generation will hear it and take it up and *do it*, praise God!"[47]

A few years later, shortly after Mims had moved to the University of North Carolina, he received an offer from Kirkland, his old friend and former teacher, to come to Vanderbilt as chairman of the English Department. He asked Page's advice, and Page responded:

I should make dead sure that this Vanderbilt situation is absolutely one, not simply a probable one [for service] before I play with that at all. If those Bishops should get the lead or even if their influence should continue to be great I should almost despair of the accomplishment of any broad thing at Nashville. They are a pestiferous lot, they are persistent and vindictive. Unless they are knocked out completely they will come again. Moreover the angry controversy that has arisen is itself a very serious handicap to that institution. Looked at in a long range way the state institutions are the big things. Of course I know their limitations and disadvantages also.[48]

Mims decided to go to Vanderbilt, but, like Alderman's decision to go to Tulane, the move failed to undermine the friendship. Page returned to Mims for material for the *World's Work*. In 1911 he proposed that Mims write a series of articles describing the progress of the South. Page outlined the theme, in his best rhetorical style: "With 15 to 18 cent cotton, with profitable manufacturers, with the broadening influence of trade, with the results of modern

[47] Page to Mims, May 15, 1904, Page Papers.
[48] Page to Mims, January 5, 1911, Page Papers.

education, the old land is really just coming into its own. The next ten years will see such a development as was never seen elsewhere in the world except when the West was settled." Mims's instructions were "don't once mention the War, nor the Old Nigger mammy, nor the old civilization, nor the poor white trash. Write in the terms and the vocabulary of the world today, not of the historical or legendary world."[49]

Mims's three articles followed Page's guidelines. The first celebrated the industrial changes taking place in Hartsville, South Carolina;[50] the second and third described the forward-looking men who were working out ways to tap the South's natural and human resources in order to bring wealth and happiness to the South.[51] Page was ecstatic. The articles, he said, were "first-rate in every respect." The third, "The South Realizing Itself: The Remakers of Industry," was "a howling success." When Mims grew slightly discouraged that the articles had aroused no reaction from the South save a few unkind remarks, Page consoled him. True, the magazine had not had one single new subscriber from Hartsville, but "that's all right. The people who speak to you (as a rule) have not read the article but only something in the newspapers about it. Try the next fellow and see! But that's all right. We'll get 'em in the 3rd or 4th generation. But *this* generation is an awful liar about subscribing to magazines and buying books—simply awful!"[52] Two days later Page wrote to Mims again in an encouraging vein: "I'm pleased—pleased to death." He, too, he said, had worked "hard for the old land," "But as for visible concrete appreciation or reward—Lord, no, no—no." "It's the same old thing," he went on, "100 years behind in intellectual curiosity and the oratorical habit of speech which means lying (almost comically) about Religion, Women, and Reading. . . . You don't have to pay for a magazine—to talk about Prof. Mims' article; you have read a

<hr/>

[49] Page to Mims, April 6, 1911, Page Papers.

[50] "The South Realizing Itself: Hartsville [South Carolina] and Its Lessons," *World's Work* 22 (1911):14972–87.

[51] "The South Realizing Itself: Redeemers of the Soil," *ibid.*, 23 (1911):41–54; "The South Realizing Itself: Remakers of Industry," *ibid.*, pp. 203–19.

[52] Page to Mims, October 23, 1911, Page Papers.

piece about it in the paper. Why read any more, then? Reading comes hard to many men that you know: don't you know it does? . . . But 50 years hence you fellows will have educated *all* the people: that's the trick. Only 1 in 100 is yet really educated to the point of really waking up or reading anything."[53]

Such talk, of course, was easy for Page in New York, but he also knew that it was what Mims needed. Page knew the South; he remembered how it felt to be immersed in teaching young Southerners and in writing for people who refused to read what you had written. Mims needed a boost, and Page therefore proposed, early in January, 1912, that he make no commitments for the coming summer but devote it and the next few summers exclusively to writing for the *World's Work*.[54] Two weeks later he returned to Mims with a request for more writing and a proposal sure to warm the heart of any optimistic Southerner. He was to write on "North Carolina and the Industrial Order," Page proposed, and to write as though he owned the state "and had power to develop the land and the people in all better ways—what would you do?"[55] Though Page found the piece unsuitable for his magazine, he sent Mims fifty dollars and a suggestion that the piece ought to be published in, say, the *South Atlantic Quarterly*. "Now," Page closed, "what is the next thing you ought to take up for us?"

Mims took heart, and his writings echoed the sound of Page's voice. Looking over his pieces in the *World's Work*, one finds Page's imprint on many passages, which in turn found their way into his later writings. Mims's major work, *The Advancing South*, followed, he said, "substantially the point of view" of Walter Page and Edgar Gardner Murphy.[56] The optimism, the commitment to serving the South, the idealism, and the conviction that the South's problems were ultimately amenable to enlightened leadership and education all point to Page. After Page's death in 1919 Mims summed up his feelings about his old friend: "He was in

[53] Page to Mims, October 25, 1911, Page Papers.
[54] Page to Mims, January 4, 1912, Page Papers.
[55] Page to Mims, January 22, 1912, Page Papers.
[56] *Advancing South*, p. ix.

many ways the best friend I ever had—the most stimulating and inspiring personality that ever touched my life. He was certainly one of the three or four best friends that this section has had in this generation."[57] In a public eulogy Mims praised Page as a prophet of a new day. His little book *The Rebuilding of Old Commonwealths*, Mims wrote, "ought to be read and reread by every Southern man who would understand the significant forces that are now making a new order of society."[58]

[57] Mims to Wallace K. Buttrick, December 27, 1918, Page Papers.
[58] Mims, "Walter Hines Page," p. 113.

3

WILLIAM P. TRENT: JEFFERSONIAN
IN THE NEW SOUTH

AFTER WALTER PAGE, no man did more to establish in the South a commitment to scholarship and rationality than William Peterfield Trent, an outspoken and vastly productive professor at Sewanee during the 1890s. Throughout the decade Trent's historical and literary works demonstrated what critical thinking promised and what it demanded. He was one of the first scholars to wrest Southern history from the hands of the ex-Confederates and "lady writers" and to plant firmly in the minds of Southern intellectuals the notion that, buried beneath the layers of mythology and romance in the history of the South lay the key to understanding the present. In 1892 he founded the *Sewanee Review* and also published a scathingly critical work on the Old South. On all issues he spoke boldly and fearlessly, not hesitating to go his own way or to champion an unpopular view. His Jeffersonian cast of mind was manifested in a practical, concrete approach to problems and an impatience to get on with the business of improving the South in a rational way.

* * *

In 1888 William Peterfield Trent, twenty-six years old, came to Sewanee College, officially the University of the South, to take up duties as Professor of History and Literature. A native Virginian of some social standing, graduate of Jefferson's university at Charlottesville, a favorite of Herbert B. Adams, Trent was a prize addition to the faculty of fifteen. He did not expect to stay there long, partly because Sewanee sat in effective isolation atop a mountain twenty miles from Chattanooga, the nearest outpost of civilization, and partly because he hoped to return to Hopkins soon to complete work for a doctorate in history.[1] But during the next few years, as his interests shifted to literary studies and his scholarly work in that field became substantial enough to attract the attention of the Ivy League colleges, he decided to forgo further formal education.

Trent wanted to do everything—teach, read, write, think, argue—and Sewanee, his "mountain fastness," as he called it,[2] allowed him time to pursue his interests. He soon earned a reputation as a stimulating teacher and personality, though some thought him a bit sarcastic and brash. Possessed of little humility and a sharp tongue, he liked to stand on the steps of the college chapel following Sunday services and, to the students' delight, acidly analyze the chaplain's sermon.[3] His seminar on John Milton prompted admiring students to paint, on a fence reserved for campus pranks, "For Sluggish Minds Take Trent's Miltonic."[4]

Trent's pace was indeed far from sluggish. In addition to teaching what seems to have been half the courses in the college catalogue—and in one class he had seventy-two students—he found time to write.[5] During his twelve years at Sewanee he published more than two dozen articles and reviews in national magazines, including two feature-length pieces at Walter Page's invitation in the *Atlantic Monthly* in 1897.[6] Also in that year his *Southern*

---

[1] Trent to Herbert B. Adams, June 9, 1890, Herbert B. Adams Papers, Johns Hopkins University Library, Baltimore, Md.

[2] Trent, "An Academic Sermon," *Sewanee Review* 14 (1906):274.

[3] Walker, "Trent," pp. 52–53, 192.

[4] William S. Knickerbocker, "Trent at Sewanee," *Sewanee Review* 48 (1940):152.

[5] Trent to Herbert B. Adams, September 30, 1890, Adams Papers.

[6] Page to Trent, August 22, 1896, Page Papers; Trent, "Dominant Forces in Southern Life," *Atlantic Monthly* 79 (1897):42–53, and "Tendencies of Higher Life in the South," *ibid.*, pp. 766–78.

Statesmen of the Old Régime, a series of impressionistic essays, and *The Authority of Criticism*, a collection of literary essays, were published. Two years later his *Robert E. Lee* (every Southern writer did something on Lee sooner or later) appeared. "I am living proof," he reminisced a few years later, "that it is entirely possible to teach eighteen hours a week in a bewildering range of subjects—I blush to say that at a pinch I have been known to teach French and Greek, mathematics and the history of English law of real property—I repeat that it is possible to teach a multitude of subjects and not completely lose one's health or one's self-respect. It is even possible at the same time to do some writing and editing."[7] His pace prompted Brander Matthews to write him, "I am moved to indignation to learn that you are working so hard and writing so much. Take care not to overdo it and fatigue your public!—to say nothing of yourself!"[8]

In 1892 when Trent somehow found time to establish the *Sewanee Review*, the South had no literary or historical publication of either critical or national scope, and this fact, he thought, was more than a little responsible for the lack of any sizable or significant body of writing in the South. Southerners had to take their wares to Northern periodicals and hence to Northern readers and critics. A Southern author might have his work reviewed by a fellow Southerner in a Yankee magazine, but he had little chance of being reviewed critically by a Southerner for other Southerners. But Trent had far more than the health of Southern letters in mind. The *Review* was to be a voice of reason in the republic, North and South. The intention, his colleague and coeditor John Bell Henneman recalled on the *Review's* tenth anniversary, was to publish a magazine on the best English model, one of high literary and critical standards based on reason and intellect.[9] It would say to a busy and bustling America that basic

[7] "Academic Sermon," p. 274.

[8] Quoted in Walker, "Trent," p. 214.

[9] John Bell Henneman, "Ten Years of the *Sewanee Review*: A Retrospect," *Sewanee Review* 10 (1902):489–90.

freedoms of thought and conscience must be preserved. In the manner of Matthew Arnold, whom Trent and Henneman admired, the magazine would array culture against anarchy.[10]

From the first, the *Review* fulfilled Trent's purpose. In addition to serving as a forum for Southerners whose names were rarely seen in print, it brought out the best in several Sewanee professors.[11] Henneman pointed to "The South's Opportunity in Education," lauded the emerging "National Element in Southern Literature," and praised the new critical, "scientific" spirit that pervaded "Historical Studies in the South since the War."[12] The historian Burr J. Ramage, another of Adams' protégés, contributed historical studies, political commentary, and observations on the international scene.[13] Though the *Sewanee Review* never attracted as many leading Southern writers as the *South Atlantic Quarterly* in the next decade, Trent was able to attract such a well-known Northerner as Theodore Roosevelt to contribute.[14] Trent himself was not very sympathetic to the theological trappings of Sewanee, but he nevertheless welcomed writings from the theology professors there and elsewhere. Most of the articles on secular issues were couched in the idealistic, optimistic language of the Age of Progress; in fact, there were few attacks on specific facets of Southern life, though Ramage did single out lynchings and the Solid South for criticism.[15] No muckraking organ, the journal

[10] Edgar Gardner Murphy, who graduated from Sewanee at the end of Trent's first year on the faculty, later caught the spirit of the quarterly in an article "The Task of the Leader" (*ibid.*, 15 [1907]:1–30).

[11] See, for example, Carl Holliday, "One Phase of Literary Conditions in the South," *ibid.*, 11 (1903):463–66; Colyer Meriweather, "Social Changes in the Black Belt," *ibid.*, 5 (1897):203–9; George F. Milton, "Industrial Crisis at the South," *ibid.*, 2 (1893):227–38; Milton, "Material Advancement of the Negro," *ibid.*, 3 (1894):37–47; and Milton, "Relations of Labor and Capital," *ibid.*, 4 (1895):67–72.

[12] John Bell Henneman, "Historical Studies in the South since the War," *ibid.*, 2 (1893):320–29; "National Element in Southern Literature," *ibid.*, 11 (1903):345–66; and "The South's Opportunity in Education," *ibid.*, 17 (1909):88–105.

[13] "Wade Hampton," *ibid.*, 10 (1902):368–73; "Dissolution of the Solid South," *ibid.*, 4 (1896):493–510; "The Railroad Question," *ibid.*, 3 (1895):189–208; "Homicide in the Southern States," *ibid.*, 4 (1896):212–32; and "Remedies for Lynch Law," *ibid.*, 7 (1900):1–11.

[14] Theodore Roosevelt, "National Life and Character," *ibid.*, 2 (1894):353–76.

[15] Ramage, "Dissolution of the Solid South," pp. 493–510; "Remedies for Lynch Law," pp. 1–11.

stood solidly in the genteel tradition of late nineteenth-century American letters. Lincoln Steffens and Ida Tarbell would have found it tame, fine for high-minded, sedate readers who believed that their ideals, if set before the public over and over again, would ultimately carry the day.

That the *Sewanee Review* was relatively tame (even when compared to the *South Atlantic Quarterly*) is somewhat surprising, in view of Trent's combative temperament. Perhaps the explanation lies in his conception of the magazine's purpose as a literary journal in which specific social criticism would always be subordinate to literary considerations. The book section, for instance, was given over almost exclusively to literature and theology, with some attention to history and only passing notice paid to books of social comment. Moreover, during Trent's eight years as editor, from 1892 to 1900, the journal became increasingly focused on history and literary criticism. Only one of the eight pieces he himself wrote, "A New South View of Reconstruction," dealt directly with Southern society, and that appeared in 1901, a year after he left the South.[16] The remainder were either literary criticism or essays on large themes such as "War and Civilization" and "Cosmopolitanism and Partisanship."[17]

The *Sewanee Review's* genteel ethos is certainly not attributable to any vacuity of mind on Trent's part. He was intensely critical of the South in such publications as the *Atlantic Monthly*, where he denounced intellectual intolerance, the political status quo, and the anti-intellectual apologists for Southern sentimental writing. Perhaps integrity kept him from using his own journal an an outlet for his personal views. The quarterly never reviewed or even noticed his own books, which received wide attention in the North. And when the Southern press vilified him for unkind remarks he made about the Old South, he made no attempt to defend himself or denounce his detractors in the pages of his magazine. The *Review* was consistently sedate and high-minded.

[16] *Sewanee Review* 9 (1901):13–29.
[17] "War and Civilization," *ibid.*, 8 (1900):385–98; "Cosmopolitanism and Partisanship," *ibid.*, 7 (1899):342–65.

Trent's standing in Southern letters rests only partially on his magazine articles and work with the *Sewanee Review.* He is better remembered as the biographer of William Gilmore Simms, the antebellum writer.[18] Trent used the book to lash into all the myths and legends surrounding the Old South. Published in 1892, it represented a major breakthrough in Southern writing. It served notice, boldly and brilliantly, that a new critical voice devoted to speaking the truth had been heard in the South—a voice, Trent knew, not universally appreciated in Dixie. Though "the South" responded with a chorus of condemnation that resulted in a minor controversy over academic freedom, the book established Trent's place in American scholarship and emboldened a generation of Southern writers. Had either his detractors or his admirers looked closely into the text, they would have discovered that his criticisms of the old ways were grounded in a Jeffersonian faith in learning and "the people."

William Gilmore Simms's historical romances of South Carolina were still read and remembered in 1892. He ranked with Edgar Allan Poe as one of the few antebellum Southerners of genuine artistry. Yet Simms was convinced that aristocratic Charlestonians snubbed him and dismissed his writings because of his humble origins. Eager for recognition, he became a States' rights apologist and a spokesman for South Carolina's sectionalism and secessionist course. He changed from artist to polemicist, from novelist to apologist. But all to no avail. Until his death he was convinced that he and his books had been shunned in Charleston because of class prejudice.

From the beginning, Trent accepted without question Simms's high estimate of his own work and his explanation for his low literary reputation. Trent's Jeffersonian equalitarianism made it easy for him to think that the planter class in Charleston must have treated Simms unfairly because it lacked the capacity to form a rational, critical estimate of talent. They had never worked themselves and, worse yet, lived off the work of others. Thus, in

[18] *William Gilmore Simms* (Boston: Houghton Mifflin Co., 1892).

Trent's view, they were utterly incapable of recognizing creativity and worth in others, except in the most superficial sense.[19] The planters of Charleston and the Old South were blind, self-indulgent snobs, said Trent, made soft by leisure and doomed to extinction in the emerging competitive society of the New South. Intellectually "decadent," their attitudes were "primitive," their judgments "emotional"; they called nondescript academies colleges and universities, foolish gallantry (usually their own) manhood, and the parroting of conventional wisdom free and candid thought. Theirs was "a life that choked all thought and investigation that did not tend to conserve existing institutions and opinions, a life that rendered originality scarcely possible except under the guise of eccentricity." The Old South was a "feudalistic," vicious class structure that oppressed everyone, whites and blacks alike, even corrupting the values and ideas of the privileged planters.[20]

In this backward state the South—for Charleston and its environs were the South in microcosm—lacked the spirit of the age, its *Zeitgeist*, Trent said, echoing Hegel and Von Ranke.[21] Locked in a social structure that exalted sectionalism, emotion, intolerance, rigidity, and backwardness, while the rest of the country and the western world followed the high road of nationalism, rationality, liberty, and freedom, the secessionists, though they saw themselves in the mainstream of life, were in reality fighting "for the perpetuation of a barbarous institution and of anarchy disguised." The secessionist South was a "world of nightmares"; Gettysburg was the triumph of civilization over barbarism.[22]

Although Trent's criticism of the secessionist leaders was scathing, he did not, in the final analysis, blame them: they had been "corrupted" by slavery and feudalism. As happened with his friend Walter Page, Trent's preconceptions about man's nature kept him from finding *in man* the roots of the evil in the world

[19] *Ibid.*, pp. 28–36.
[20] *Ibid.*, pp. 36–41.
[21] *Ibid.*, p. 270.
[22] *Ibid.*, p. 274.

which he so sensitively described. Evil, he believed, was not innate in man; it was fostered by his corrupt institutions. Moreover, Trent's denunciation of slavery and secession stemmed from a set of assumptions about the "direction" of history. Every page of *William Gilmore Simms* indicates that for Trent "true history" is rational, purposeful, directed toward Progress. In Trent's judgment, slavery and secession might have been orderly and purposeful developments in themselves, but not in the light of the *Zeitgeist* that had enveloped the North. The Old South's history was unreal; it was "irrational"; secession was a "nightmare." Years later Trent's view was echoed by Wilbur J. Cash: "In general, the intellectual and aesthetic culture of the Old South was a superficial and jejune thing, borrowed from without and worn as a political armor and a badge of rank; and hence (I call the authority of old Matthew Arnold to bear me witness) not a true culture at all."[23]

Trent did, at times, talk obliquely about Progress, but he never seemed aware that he had measured the South against a cosmic concern.[24] For all his struggle to find the Old South in history, he felt no corresponding necessity to place the New South in historical perspective. Perhaps that is too much to ask of any man. At any rate, his assumptions were real and vital; they give *Simms* its flavor, its distinctiveness, and its optimistic vision.

Trent's contemporaries North and South took the book at face value. Southern newspapers, pouncing on the attacks against Charleston "society" and its treatment of Simms, denounced the book and the author's "intentions."[25] Most of them characterized Trent as another Yankeefied Southerner only too eager to please Northern readers—and pocketbooks. One reviewer denounced Trent's "rage for realism" as a device to distort the facts in order to denigrate the South. Another, writing "A Defense of the South" for the Charleston *News and Courier*, anathematized Trent for his

[23] *Mind of the South*, p. 97.

[24] See, for example, his "War and Civilization" and "Cosmopolitanism and Partisanship."

[25] Stephenson, *Southern History in the Making*, pp. 80–82.

"calumnious misrepresentations" of the people of South Carolina.[26] Numerous commentators charged him with "disloyalty."
Only one Southern newspaper, the Louisville *Courier-Journal*, gave
the book a favorable notice.[27]

Northerners liked what they read, particularly the criticisms of
secession. Theodore Roosevelt, writing in the *Atlantic Monthly*,
represents the common mood: "the most valuable portion of the
book is that portraying Simms' relation to the political movements
which culminated in the civil war. Mr. Trent strikes his true theme
when he writes as a historian; and if he fulfills the promise of this
book he will eventually stand in the first rank of our politico-his-
torical writers."[28] A writer for the *Dial* found the book so objective that it was "hard to judge whether the author is a Southerner
or a Northerner."[29] Brander Matthews concluded that "it is not
only a good book; it is a good deed."[30]

The reviews touched Trent deeply. He confided to Brander Matthews: "Such a review from such a critic [as you] goes far to take
the sting out of the attack on the part of the Southern press to
which I have been subjected for the past few months. I was of
course prepared for a certain amount of adverse criticism, but I
was considerably surprised at the virulence and the *density* of
some of the gentlemen who honored me with a notice."[31] Trent
needed all the praise he could get. In his home town of Richmond
old family friends openly snubbed his mother, and one of his
former professors at the University of Virginia publicly called for
his dismissal and accused him of perverting the youth. His personal
friends wrote privately to applaud his courage and convictions, but
only one fellow professor openly came to his defense. For several
days the situation at Sewanee was confused: the students and
faculty stood by him, even in the face of rumors that a disgruntled

---

[26] *Ibid.*, pp. 81–82.

[27] Walker, "Trent," p. 126.

[28] *Atlantic Monthly* 69 (1892):838–40.

[29] *Dial* 13 (1892):109.

[30] "Two Studies of the South," *Cosmopolitan* 14 (1892):322–23.

[31] Trent to Matthews, October 25, 1892, Brander Matthews Papers, Columbia University Library, New York, N.Y.

board of trustees would deal severely with him. Trent had reason to worry: three trustees were Charlestonians, and all were Southerners.[32] The question was "settled" quickly and unofficially, but suspicion lingered on for years in the minds of some faculty and trustees that Trent was untrustworthy.[33]

In the years that followed, as the Southern intellectual community took shape, Trent's name became synonymous with courageous scholarship. The new intellectuals read *Simms* in graduate school or heard Trent's name mentioned by a professor. "The book was a brilliant affair," John Spencer Bassett wrote in the mid-1890s, adding that Trent represented the true South.[34] Both Walter Page and Samuel Chiles Mitchell concurred in that view. Edwin Mims, who graduated from Vanderbilt in 1892, knew *Simms* and the *Sewanee Review*. Trent's critical, unsentimental voice, he later recalled, was one of the major influences saving him from the common malady of romanticizing the South's past. Trent set the pace of Southern scholarship, said Mims. Years later, in his own book, *The Advancing South*, Mims congratulated Trent and his generation for rejecting the "sentimental tradition" and maintaining universal standards of judgment.[35]

Idealism and a commitment to critical standards characterized Trent's other writings in the 1890s. His historical writings and social commentary applauded good works, social responsibility, and the free expression of ideas. He roamed over a variety of subjects from politics to education, urging Southerners to be national-minded, to free themselves from corrupting institutions and progress in the "American" way.[36] These assumptions are explicit throughout his next book, *Southern Statesmen of the Old Regime* (1897).[37] Although Trent claimed no originality for his "portraits," the book nevertheless gave him the opportunity to express

---

[32] Walker, "Trent," pp. 151–52.

[33] Trent to Herbert B. Adams, January 8, 1898, Adams Papers.

[34] "History As It Relates to Life," *Methodist Quarterly Review* 45 (1897):355.

[35] Pp. 19–20.

[36] The best introduction to Trent's philosophical outlook would be the two pieces he did for the *Atlantic Monthly* in 1897: "Dominant Forces in Southern Life" and "Tendencies of Higher Life in the South."

[37] New York: Thomas Y. Crowell Co., 1897.

once again his opinion of the nature of the leadership in the Old South, from George Washington to Jefferson Davis, and to make further pleas for leadership in the New South. His temper had mellowed somewhat since *Simms*, but his words were still pungent. The first page of *Southern Statesmen* announced that he had not retreated one step from his previous attitude toward scholarship: he still "regarded his subjects from the point of view of an American who is at the same time a Southerner, proud enough of his section to admit its faults, and yet to proclaim its essential greatness." To "certain hypersensitive portions of the Southern people," he wrote, "my opinions are the results of my own studies . . . and I am willing to change all or any of them, when they are proved to be erroneous, but I am certainly not to be turned from them by unstinted personal abuse."[38] Not surprisingly, in following the path of the old regime's statemen, Trent described a downward course and concluded that the South had failed because "the people" had been unwisely led by those who mistook their reactionary ideas for the mainstream of history.

Yet the Old South began with brilliant leadership. Both Washington and Jefferson were true nationalists and cosmopolitans, and they placed their trust and faith in the people.[39] Jefferson may have been a bit of a "visionary," when compared to the more "practical" Washington, but, said Trent, he "never committed the absurd blunder of despising and underrating the people."[40] The great Virginians were succeeded, however, by men of narrow minds and lesser understanding who both despised and underrated the common man[41] and put their faith in caste and class: they were corrupted by feudalistic conceptions of man and privilege.

Trent was harshest on John C. Calhoun. He saw in Calhoun, the architect of the Old South's defense of an unchanging feudal order, not a brilliant mind—as some have been inclined to do—but a rigid and reactionary theoretician who had warped and twisted the

---

[38] *Ibid.*, pp. ix–x.

[39] *Ibid.*, p. 36.

[40] *Ibid.*, p. 68.

[41] Trent discussed John Randolph, John C. Calhoun, Jefferson Davis, Alexander H. Stephens, and Robert Toombs.

original Jeffersonian dream of a free society. Calhoun could not understand, said Trent, that he had corrupted the Constitution by turning it into a defense of inhumanity. Nor could he understand what Jefferson had so clearly perceived, that the Constitution and the Declaration of Independence were created to lead men toward greater freedom, not back into bondage. Therefore, Calhoun's theory of "Nullification" was "ludicrous"—as were most of his other ideas. "Calhoun lacked the power of creative and truthful imagination," said Trent. "His foresight was largely the result of deduction; and as his premises were always mixed with error, except in the matter of antagonism between slavery and modern civilization, his foresight was of little practical service to himself or others." The author of treatises on majorities and minorities "led thought rather than men, and lacking imagination, he led thought badly." Nevertheless, since Calhoun had been corrupted by slavery and feudalism, he himself was not entirely to blame.[42]

And if one could not expect a man of Calhoun's stature to grasp the ideals of Washington and Jefferson, then one could hardly demand that his successors do so. Jefferson Davis was a "sincere" man but not a great one; he lacked "originality" and could not "overleap the barriers of thought set by heredity and environment."[43] Comparing him with Jefferson, Trent could only conclude that Davis had his eye on the past instead of the future; thus the "idea for which he struggled was negative rather than positive, and so his place is with the failures of history."[44] To relegate Jefferson Davis to the "failures of history" and to dismiss Calhoun's theories as "ludicrous" required courage in 1897—the sort of courage that had characterized *Simms*. Trent had not changed his mind about the South's history. His reference to Calhoun's thinking as "nightmarish reasoning"[45] recalls the concluding words of a chapter in *Simms*, quoted earlier: "But perhaps we have tarried long enough in this world of nightmares."[46]

[42] *Ibid.*, pp. 155–69.
[43] *Ibid.*, p. 270.
[44] *Ibid.*, p. 291.
[45] *Ibid.*, p. 181.
[46] P. 190.

During the 1890s, however, Trent did not limit himself to exorcising the devils of history, nor was his vision limited to the South. He spoke out on national issues: he championed the mugwumps, lashed out at corruption in Washington, advocated the popular election of senators, and, adopting the orthodox Southern attitude, denounced the protective tariff. In language as caustic as any he had used to describe the Old South, Trent denounced American imperialism of 1898-1899.[47] He was also, as a subsequent chapter will show, one of the first Southerners of intellectual stature to criticize the South's emerging one-party politics and to outline his reasons for opposing its capitulation to the Democratic Party.[48]

* * *

In 1900 Columbia University lured Trent north. The Columbia offer attests to his reputation as a man of letters (his publications by this time included scores of literary essays) and to how far he had traveled since leaving Professor Norwood's Classical Academy. In addition to giving him the opportunity to work with distinguished colleagues, Columbia offered a better library and a reduced teaching schedule that would allow him to concentrate his research energies on Daniel Defoe, whom he had recently come to see as his main scholarly interest. Columbia also held out the possibility of academic advancement, which Trent had concluded was denied him at Sewanee because of his heresies, past and present: he confided to Herbert B. Adams in 1898 that he was "continually made the object of prayers and other pietistic propaganda for my spiritual regeneration. As a man gets older this sort of thing becomes more insulting and ridiculous." Besides, he said, "there is no Southern institution that would touch me—and I must look for advancement either to the North or the West."[49]

His critics maintained that he had been looking for "advancement" all along—that he had been writing for the Yankee eye, if not the Yankee purse, in order to land a job in a Yankee college.

[47] "The Opportunity of the Mugwump," *Sewanee Review* 3 (1894):1-9; "In Re Imperialism: Some Phases of the Situation," *ibid.*, 6 (1898):478-99.
[48] See his "Dominant Forces in Southern Life," pp. 42-53; "Cosmopolitanism and Partisanship," pp. 342-65.
[49] Trent to Herbert B. Adams, January 8, 1898, Adams Papers.

The implications are of "disloyalty" and "treason" to the South, charges that had been made even by Trent's "friends" at Sewanee. They were based on a parochial view of loyalty that elevated the South above the nation, and Trent and his generation, many of whom moved north, had become too fully "Americanized" to equate patriotism with the Southern way of life. In the 1870s Sidney Lanier, poet laureate of the New South and a man Trent greatly admired, summoned up a new Southern man "tall enough to see over the whole country." While Trent perhaps did not fulfill that vision in all respects, he had become a national-minded man, who chose to live and work in New York rather than in Tennessee.

Trent left the South at the age of thirty-eight, when most men begin to put away their hopes of remaking the world and take up more mundane tasks. He had given the South perhaps the twelve best and certainly the most energetic years of his life. At Columbia he climbed the academic ladder to become a full professor, and, although he never fulfilled his original promise as a literary historian, he devoted himself to Daniel Defoe. When his tenure at Columbia ended in 1928 he had in manuscript a ten-volume work on the author of *Robinson Crusoe*. Except for an occasional glance over his shoulder, he never looked back at the South.

4

CHALLENGING THE SAVAGE IDEAL

By 1900, THE YEAR Walter Page founded the *World's Work* and William P. Trent took up residence in New York City, the new intellectuals had come to have a shared set of ideals and goals; they had become an intellectual community. Page and Trent had shown the way. Their critical standards and social vision would dominate the mind of the Southern intellectual for the next twenty years. They had taken, as they liked to say, a "candid" look at just about every aspect of Southern life—except one. Neither they nor any other major figure had addressed themselves directly, in the new critical spirit, to the central issue of Southern life, the Negro Question.

In mid-1902, at Emory College in Georgia, Professor Andrew Sledd, one of the new school of Southern academicians, openly condemned Southern lynchings and white racism. He was publicly vilified and driven off the faculty for his trouble. Less than a year later, in July of 1903, Dr. John Spencer Bassett of Trinity College categorically condemned Southern racism. Though a distinguished historian and a man of letters, he too suffered public obloquy as part of an unsuccessful attempt to run him off, as Sledd had been. In each incident the Savage Ideal was invoked, and each incident sent tremors through the Southern academic community and tended to confirm what the intellectuals had been saying—that the white South was opposed to new ideas in general and was specifically and violently opposed to criticisms, even from professors, of any fundamental tenet of the Southern way of life.

* * *

In 1902 Andrew Sledd was a professor of Latin at Emory College.[1] He had ideal credentials for that small and struggling Methodist school: he was a Virginian of good stock, a graduate of Randolph-Macon, with an M.A. from Harvard. When he married Annie Florence Candler in 1899, one year after joining the faculty, most people thought that he had done well. She was the daughter of Bishop Warren A. Candler, past president of Emory and one of the most powerful churchmen of the denomination. An ordained minister, like his father, Sledd's sermons suggested that he was sound in the faith, though some thought him a little too intellectual. On neither religious nor social issues, however, had he given any indication that he harbored heretical views. Yet he had become appalled by the excesses of White Supremacy. In 1902, in an angry article for the *Atlantic Monthly*, "The Negro: Another View,"[2] Sledd denounced racial prejudice and mob violence and demolished, one by one, the popular shibboleths about race relations in the South. Seldom has a Southern white man of prominence spoken with such sorrow about the white man's treatment of the Negro.

The article began conventionally enough. Sledd reproached the North for talking about Southern race relations from "preformed theories, rather than actual facts." Then, after paying lip service to the dogma of Negro "inferiority," he acknowledged that most people were now well aware that talk about "social equality" was just "ill-advised cant." He agreed with "informed minds" that "racial amalgamation" was repugnant; the words were "sickening." Then came the heresy: despite all of its protestations and affirmations about its own virtue, the white South daily brutalized the Negro. He was told where he could work, worship, sit, stand;

---

[1] See Henry Y. Warnock, "Andrew Sledd, Southern Methodists, and the Negro: A Case Study," *Journal of Southern History* 31 (1965):251–52.

[2] *Atlantic Monthly* 90 (1902):65–73.

he was the object of vile slurs; worst of all, he was lynched. While the last shreds of the Negro's "inalienable rights" disappeared, the white man lauded his own inherent superiority and benevolence. The South, said Sledd, "has carried the idea of the negro's inferiority almost, if not quite, to the point of dehumanizing him."[3]

What prompted Sledd to call down such a judgment upon his people? The immediate cause was a recent lynching in Georgia, a "Sunday burning," rather—for a throng had taken Sam Hoss out on the Sabbath and burned him to death while a crowd of onlookers cheered. The spectators then proceeded to ransack the cooling embers for "souvenirs": kneecaps, finger bones, or an ear still intact. "It is the purest savagery," Sledd wrote.[4]

Such savagery, Sledd knew, was not new or infrequent. Since the end of Reconstruction, both the number and the manner of lynchings had become a disgrace to the region. From 1888 to 1906, 3,500 lynchings occurred in America, and 2,770 of these took place in the South. Over two thousand of the Southern victims were black—lynching in America, as everyone knew, was primarily inflicted by Southern whites on Southern blacks. In those years more Negroes were lynched in Mississippi (which led the nation with 334), Georgia (275), and Louisiana (224) than in all the northern and western states combined.[5] Had one grown up in Mississippi in those years he would have seen or heard about a lynching on an average of once every twenty-seven days. "Lynching" meant hangings, burnings, shotgun murders, and various forms of mutilation. Mass lynchings took place on occasion. A surviving photograph from a Texas lynching of 1893 shows a black man about to die, standing above the mob on a newly constructed wooden scaffold, 15 or 20 feet high. Someone has scrawled "Justice" on the scaffold beneath him. Below, the mob mills in anticipation.[6] Then, a scene frequent throughout the next two decades,

[3] *Ibid.*, pp. 65–67.

[4] *Ibid.*, p. 71.

[5] William H. Glasson, "The Statistics of Lynching," *South Atlantic Quarterly* 5 (1906): 342–48.

[6] Woodward, *Origins of the New South*, facing p. 352.

came the burning. Even the conservative Thomas Nelson Page admitted that the figures were "enough to stagger the mind."[7]

What explains such barbarity? Were lynchings, as whites traditionally thought, the result of the outrage of rape? Were lynchings merely a violent justice administered by a temporarily enraged mob? Both John C. Kilgo, a blunt critic of racism, and Thomas Nelson Page, an apologist for it, tended to think so—how else could they explain their countrymen's actions, particularly to themselves? Yet both men admitted that lynchings were usually brought on by some other offense.[8] "The world," wrote Sledd, "is familiar with the usual defense of lynching," but even white Southerners know that lynchings only rarely ("in some years one-tenth") result from rape.[9] The majority of victims were suspected of far less serious crimes, such as robbery, arson, or being "uppity." More damaging to the familiar argument was the known fact that many lynchings were planned and publicized executions. A lynching in Texas in 1917 prompted seventy-five parents to write to the school principal requesting that their children be excused to attend the affair.[10] In some instances whole families came, carrying blankets, picnic baskets, and loaded shotguns. Blacks, too, were welcomed: the whites hoped, said Thomas Nelson Page, that seeing a lynching would deter other potential criminals. Usually the blacks formed an outer ring of onlookers, some shouting final farewells or jibes or cheers for the departed, while others, probably friends, family, or older people, stood by somberly.[11]

The lynching of Sam Hoss, then, was neither an isolated nor unfamiliar affair, nor was it the work of a crazed mob—it was

[7]Page, "The Lynching of Negroes—Its Causes and Preventions," *North American Review* 178 (1904):36.

[8]John C. Kilgo, "An Inquiry Concerning Lynching," *South Atlantic Quarterly* 1 (1902):4–13; for the views of other apologists who admitted that lynchings resulted from a wide variety of causes, see Clarence H. Poe, "Lynching: A Southern View," *Atlantic Monthly* 93 (1904):155–65; James W. Garner, "Lynching and the Criminal Law," *South Atlantic Quarterly* 5 (1906):333–41; Ramage, "Homicide in the Southern States," pp. 212–32; "Remedies for Lynch Law," pp. 1–11.

[9]"The Negro," pp. 69–71.

[10]*Ibid.*, pp. 71–72; W. D. Weatherford, ed., *Lawlessness or Civilization: Which?* (Nashville: n.p., 1917), p. 10.

[11]Page, "Lynching of Negroes," p. 38.

planned well in advance. The crowd was particularly large that day partly because an enterprising local railroad official had arranged for two special trains to carry people to the site. Knowing that, Sledd dismissed as shallow and hypocritical any ideas that lynchings represented a "righteous public sentiment, aroused and administering rude justice." A mob of lynchers knows nothing of justice, and when the whites boast that lynchings teach "the niggers a lesson," he wrote, they betray their real motive, which is to "teach the negro the lesson of abject and eternal servility, [and] burn into his quivering flesh the consciousness that he has not, and cannot have, the rights of a free citizen or even of a fellow human creature." "The radical difficulty," he concluded, "is not with the negro, but with the white man."[12]

And it was to the white men that Sledd spoke: "We must, as a whole people, candidly and honestly, recognize a certain set of underlying facts, which may or may not differ from our theories, cross our sympathies, or contravene our wishes." He implored the South to become rational, to look at the facts—"a frank consideration of all the facts, with no other desire than to find the truth, the whole truth, and nothing but the truth, however contrary to our wishes and humiliating to our section the truth may be." The white South's racial record is "an unpalatable truth; but that it is the truth, few intelligent and candid white men, even of the South would care to deny."[13]

Racism sprang, Sledd believed, from the "lower classes," poor whites who had been "inflamed" by reactionary ideas. "Our lynchings are the work of our lower and lowest classes. What these classes are is hardly comprehensible to one who has not lived among them and dealt with them." The "cause" of the evil lay in this irrational South, not in the real South. "No candid man who has seen the average lynching mob, could think otherwise. Our lower classes must be made to realize, by whatever means, that the black man has rights which they are bound to respect."[14]

[12]"The Negro," pp. 69–71.
[13]Ibid., pp. 66, 69.
[14]Ibid., p. 72.

It is not clear whether Sledd thought he could challenge the myth of White Supremacy and remain unscathed, but the repercussions soon became apparent. For a full month after the *Atlantic Monthly* appeared in Atlanta in late June, nothing happened to indicate that Sledd would soon be the object of a fierce attack.[15] The Atlanta *Constitution* editorially rebuked him for his "northern foolosophy" but offered no hint that the Savage Ideal was about to be invoked. Mrs. W. H. Felton, wife of a prominent Georgia politician and an extreme racist, led the actual onslaught. This lady was a curious blend of provincialism and cosmopolitanism; she crusaded vigorously for governmental reform and women's rights and with equal vigor denounced blacks and advocated lynchings to stop "the crime." "Her busy pen and dreaded letters," writes one historian, "often threw erring public figures into sheer panic."[16] Mrs. Felton, whose racism bordered on the psychotic, may also have seen in Sledd an opportunity to injure Bishop Candler, who had opposed her crusade for woman suffrage. At any rate, for whatever reasons, she launched a vituperative barrage that quickly stimulated a general denunciation of Sledd which the intellectual community interpreted as a slanderous attack on one of their own.

Mrs. Felton's opening sally, a letter published in the *Constitution*, suggests how vulgarly the Savage Ideal could be applied. Sledd's words were "rot" which he had "vomited" onto the *Atlantic's* pages for "filthy lucre"; for him the time-honored treatment for traitors, tar and feathers and the train north: "Pass him on! Keep him moving! He does not belong in this part of the country. It is bad enough to be taxed to death to educate negroes and defend one's home from criminal assault, from arson and burglary, but it is simply atrocious to fatten or feed a creature who stoops to the defamation of the southern people only to find access to liberal checks in a partisan magazine."[17]

[15] Warnock, "Andrew Sledd," pp. 256-71.

[16] *Ibid.*, p. 257.

[17] Quoted in *ibid.*, p. 258.

The press and irate citizens fully supported Mrs. Felton's denunciation. The *Atlanta News*, though less hostile than the other papers in the city, called Sledd's article "treason." The *Journal* printed a number of slanderous letters about the matter and agreed that Emory should follow Mrs. Felton's advice and "pass him on" to the North. Candler tried to convince the president of Emory that Mrs. Felton was really trying to strike at him through his son-in-law, but his protestations were of no avail in the face of the press attack. The college administration accepted Sledd's resignation, and the faculty, which had taken no stand in support of Sledd or the principle of academic freedom, acquiesced. However, his colleagues persuaded the trustees to grant him one thousand dollars to allow him to start graduate work at Yale. Sledd departed angrily, but he did earn a doctorate the following year with the money given him.[18]

The Sledd affair was a major shock to the intellectual community. Some feared that the incident might touch off a general demand for intellectual conformity in Southern schools.[19] Walter Page watched the events anxiously from New York.[20] The reaction at Trinity College was one of nervousness and sympathy for Sledd. Kilgo and Candler were old friends, and the Bishop turned to him for aid in finding another position for his son-in-law.[21] Kilgo replied that he did not know the man, nor had he read his article, but that he stood firmly for academic freedom and understood the implications of the affair. "The only hope of freedom," he said, "is in the colleges of the church, and these have been marked for the slaughter. . . . Well, Trinity shall be free tho' all the Bishops, preachers, politicians, and wild women on earth decree otherwise, and I will get out only when shipped out, and then I will leave the church on record for a crime, the stench of which

---

[18] *Ibid.*, pp. 259–71.

[19] Charles F. Smith, "Professor Sledd and Emory College," *Nation* 125 (1902):245.

[20] See Walter Page to B. N. Duke, November 13, 1903, Trinity College Papers, Duke University Library, Durham, N.C.

[21] See Candler to Kilgo, August 13, 1902, Trinity College Papers.

will never cease to rise to heaven."[22] Within a year Kilgo faced the obligation to make good his promise.

* * *

The Bassett affair of 1903 dwarfed the fracas in Atlanta. The onslaught by the press, the dramatic stands taken by Kilgo and his faculty, the tense deliberations of the trustees, the dramatic victory celebrated by the students with bonfires, the tolling of the school bell, and the burning in effigy of Josephus Daniels (Walter Page's former friend), whose role in this incident was equivalent to Mrs. Felton's, all made it a *cause célèbre*.

At the center of the controversy was an unlikely candidate for notoriety. John Spencer Bassett was a hard-working scholar, author of numerous books and articles, many of which appeared in the *North Carolina Christian Advocate*, and was highly respected by the students and by Kilgo. He returned to Trinity, his alma mater, in 1894 from Johns Hopkins, where he, like Trent, had been one of Herbert B. Adams' outstanding students.[23] He plunged into the writing of history, pumped new life into the Trinity College Historical Society, preached the doctrine of "objective" history, and stimulated fresh interest in collecting materials for a research library at Trinity. In 1895, to promote publishing, he established the Trinity College Historical Papers, which he edited and aided with contributions. He had equal energy and enthusiasm in the classroom: he taught American history, ancient, medieval, and modern European history, and a "troublesome" French class, and also served as college librarian.[24] In 1902 he established the *South Atlantic Quarterly* and edited it until 1905. Scarcely an issue of the journal appeared without something from his hand, yet he found time to write for other magazines as well, including the *World's Work*. Other faculty members marveled at his pace. Mims wrote to Page, "His lamp, burning into the wee

[22] Kilgo to Candler, August 14, 1902, Trinity College Papers.

[23] For a detailed look at Bassett the historian, see Stephenson, *Southern History in the Making*, pp. 93–118.

[24] Bassett to Herbert B. Adams, January 24, 1898, Adams Papers.

small hours of the morning night after night, is the greatest inspiration to scholarly work that I have found on this campus."[25]

When he came to Trinity Bassett envisioned a quiet life of teaching and scholarship, but he became outraged by events in North Carolina. Everywhere in the South, and particularly in that state, the Democratic Party in the 1890s faced a major threat to its unquestioned rule when Republicans, Populists, and scattered dissidents of both races allied themselves and made a joint appeal to the Negro and the poor white voter. The Fusionists offered a platform of representation and social legislation that boldly challenged the Bourbon policies of the Democratic Party. Fusionists won control of the state legislature in 1894 and captured the governorship in 1896. In retaliation, in the elections of 1898 and 1900, the Democrats, past masters of political manipulation and infighting, raised the familiar cry of "White Supremacy" and exploited racist sentiments in the most blatant way. At dusk, night riders in red shirts harassed the blacks and gave them a foretaste of their place in the new order; a race riot at Wilmington in 1898 ended with twelve Negroes dead and hundreds injured; and by 1900 the black man had lost his vote and most of his civil rights, and had seen racism become the cornerstone of the Democratic Party's appeal and support.[26]

Bassett was filled with dismay at these events. Publicly he said little, but to Adams he wrote frankly: "As to the election, I might write you a whole book. We are crowing down here like children because we have settled the negro question. We don't see that we have not settled it by half. At best we have only postponed it. We have used a great deal of intimidation and a great deal of fraud, I fear; although it is hard to get information about the latter. I do not have the honor to agree with most of my fellow Anglo Saxons on the negro question." Everywhere the Negroes are "really cowed," and "it is now said that 21 will die" in Wilmington.

---

[25] November 24, 1903, Page Papers.

[26] For a detailed account of racism and disfranchisement in North Carolina, see Helen G. Edmonds, *The Negro and Fusion Politics in North Carolina* (Chapel Hill: University of North Carolina Press, 1951); Woodward, *Origins of the New South*, pp. 350–51.

"Considering the violence of [the] attack it seems to me the negro has acted admirably. Vilified, abused, denounced as the unclean thing, he has kept his peace; he has been patient. He has borne what no other people in history have borne." Bassett added, "the white man will continue to run over the negro until the negro learns how to defend himself. If about 25 white men were dead as the result of the Wilmington riots the whites would be a little more careful of how they go into a riot there again." He closed by saying that Adams "won't have a chance to hear this side of this miserable story from many North Carolinians."[27]

When the "white man's government" of North Carolina put into practice its campaign promises with new election laws supposedly based on a non-discriminatory "education clause," everyone knew that the disfranchisers would apply the new restrictions only to blacks or persons known to be recalcitrant Republicans who would not accept the new order. Bassett privately labeled the new law an "enamelled lie." "If it honestly provided for an intellectual standard for suffrage it would be a good thing," but such dishonest practices are "one more step in the educating of our people that it is right to lie, to steal, and to defy all honesty in order to keep a certain party in power."[28] Bassett was no Leveller (when he wrote earlier to Adams that the Negro might be given full citizenship, he added, "nauseating as the dose is"),[29] but he never wholly accepted the logic of the disfranchisers and Jim Crow. Privately he found it disgusting.[30]

By the turn of the century, with racism now legalized, Bassett became convinced that the South needed a critical awareness of both its past and its present. He had reiterated in the 1890s that the South was too emotional, too sensitive to criticism, and basically intolerant and suspicious of new ideas. "We have not cultivated the spiritual to excess," he wrote in 1896, "but we have in many respects failed to cultivate the intellectual enough. We are

[27] November 15, 1898, Adams Papers.
[28] Bassett to Adams, February 18, 1899, Adams Papers.
[29] Bassett to Adams, November 15, 1898, Adams Papers.
[30] Bassett to Adams, November 3, 1911, Adams Papers.

accordingly emotional, loyal, orthodox, religious—and that is a good thing; but we are not so thoughtful, rational, self-cultured as we might be."[31] And the following year, "We are as a people emotional, loyal, warm-hearted, but not very intellectual."[32] He admired Trent's work with the *Sewanee Review* but felt that a new magazine was needed that would devote more attention to history and social problems.[33] After persuading his colleagues at Trinity to help with the proposed venture, Bassett launched the *South Atlantic Quarterly*. He would, "in a business way," as he put it, speak to that small "audience of serious minded people of the South"[34] and try to make the South rational, even on the race issue.

Bassett's colleagues set the tone of the new journal. In the lead article of the first issue President Kilgo denounced Southern lynchings, and Edwin Mims and William P. Few upheld literary and educational values.[35] Articles were submitted from all parts of the South. The contributors during Bassett's editorship provide a guide to the important scholarly and literary voices of the New South: William E. Dodd, Burr J. Ramage, Walter L. Fleming, U. B. Phillips, Frederick W. Moore, Enoch Marvin Banks, Henry M. Snyder, Franklin G. Woodward, Samuel Chiles Mitchell. All agreed with Bassett that the South needed leadership based on the middle-class doctrines of work, optimism, and purpose.

No one rivaled Bassett himself in blunt speaking, however. In his first contribution, "The Bottom of the Matter," he lambasted the South for lacking "vital literary activity" or concern for ideas and literature.[36] He found the source of "The Problems of the Author in the South"—a concern close to the heart of his genera-

---

[31] "The Culture Problem in Southern Towns," *Methodist Quarterly Review* 43 (1896):371.

[32] "History As It Relates to Life," *ibid.*, 45 (1897):353.

[33] *Ibid.*, p. 355.

[34] Bassett to John M. Vincent, December 8, 1901, Adams Papers.

[35] Kilgo, "An Inquiry Concerning Lynching," *South Atlantic Quarterly* 1 (1902):4-13; Few, "Some Educational Needs of the South," *ibid.*, 3 (1904):201-11; Mims, "The Functions of Criticism in the South," *ibid.*, 2 (1903):334-45.

[36] *Ibid.*, 1 (1902):99-106.

tion—in the region's "provincialism."[37] Recalling the Trent incident, Bassett wrote: "To speak truly we write as a people who are
not yet out of the stage of uncultured animalism."[38] Readers got
more of the same in the next installment, "The Reign of Passion,"
which Bassett considered to be his most outspoken piece. It lo-
cated the source of the South's intolerance in the blatant racism of
its politicians.[39] Bassett carefully noted that the South's racism
sprang from "history," but he went on to say that the "reign of
passion" created by the politicians "has robbed politics of fair
judgment; it has accustomed the citizen to party hatred; it has
made well intentioned men tolerate, even justify, political fraud; it
has helped preserve the South's provincialism; it has produced a
one-sided press; it has made it possible for the South to be 'solid',
and this has pauperized the intellects of her statesmen—for it is
true that men who do not battle for their ideas against opponents
do not have the capacity for forming vigorous ideas."[40]

In Bassett's next article[41] he reiterated Trent's view that the
aristocrats of the slave South had become soft and weak because
of their luxurious and artificial social status and that, having never
"worked," they were incapable of making their way in the postwar economy of competitive capitalism, which bestows its rewards
upon labor and industrial genius. Bassett admitted that planters'
sons had occasionally succeeded in this new world but insisted
that the real leadership of the New South had come from "the
sons of the middle class." They had "shown the way"; they had
the proper attitudes toward work and social status; "they have
been, for these reasons, steady gainers in the struggle for existence. . . . The rise of the middle class has been the most notable
thing connected with the white population of the South since the
war."[42] To anyone who had been listening carefully to this new

[37] *Ibid.*, pp. 201–8.
[38] *Ibid.*, p. 202.
[39] *Ibid.*, pp. 301–9.
[40] *Ibid.*, p. 308.
[41] "The Industrial Decay of the Southern Planter," *ibid.*, 2 (1903): 107–13.
[42] *Ibid.*, p. 112.

breed of intellectuals, Bassett's words had a familiar, optimistic ring.

By 1903 Bassett had developed a habit of speaking his mind frankly, sometimes sarcastically. The *South Atlantic Quarterly* carried articles by him and others about everything conceivable in the South except the evils of the factory system and some of the questionable labor practices by which the captains of industry prevailed. On the sensitive issues of race and politics Bassett was about as critical as any Southerner had dared to be. With the exception of Sledd, not since George Washington Cable's essay of 1885, "The Freedman's Case in Equity," had any prominent white Southerner dared attack White Supremacy head on. In October, 1903, he published "Stirring Up the Fires of Race Antipathy," his "waker," as he called it,[43] and in one torrent, all his hatred of Southern racism burst out. Self-seeking politicians, he began, had fastened on the racial prejudice and fears of the white masses to the point of ruthless and shameless exploitation. That, united with the frustrations felt by whites in the face of the educational and economic progress of the blacks, poisoned the racial atmosphere. Bassett well knew that the Democratic Party's conversion to the politics of White Supremacy in the 1890s following decades of paternalism had been brought about by the Populist uprising that challenged the Democrats' hold on the Southern voter, white and black. He anticipated C. Vann Woodward's argument[44] that the Southern black man lost his vote and his civil liberties not because he was black, or a former slave, or a "menace to civilization," as one racist put it at the time, but because the Democratic Party saw in White Supremacy a method of regaining political supremacy.

Certain of Bassett's observations in the article aroused particular furor. His detractors seized upon one sentence: "Booker T. Wash-

---

[43] Bassett to Charles Francis Adams, November 3, 1911, John Spencer Bassett Papers, Duke University Library, Durham, N.C. The article appeared in *South Atlantic Quarterly* 2 (1903):297–305. Writing to Edwin Mims in 1909, Bassett recalled that he had said: "I guess that will wake them up" (Mims, "Early Years of the *South Atlantic Quarterly*," *South Atlantic Quarterly* 51 [1952]:38).

[44] *The Strange Career of Jim Crow*, 2d rev. ed. (New York: Oxford University Press, 1966), pp. 49–96.

ington is a great and good man, A Christian statesman, and take him all in all, the greatest man, save General Lee, born in the South in a hundred years."[45] But Bassett made other, more incisive, comments: "The race feeling is the contempt of the white man for the Negro"; the Negro now considers Jim Crow laws "a badge of inferiority, a mark of intolerance which he will some day seek to wipe out." "In spite of our race feeling," Bassett continued, "of which the writer has his share, they will win equality some time." Though the blacks "are now weak," he said, "some day they will be stronger" and will bring down the South's "solutions." "I do not know just what form the conflict will take. It may be merely a political conflict; it may be more than that," but "the conflict will be fiercer in the future than in the present."[46] "The 'place' of every man in our American life is such as his virtues and capacities may enable him to take," he concluded: "Not even a black skin and a flat nose can justify caste in this country."[47] Astonishing words for any white American in 1903, and almost beyond comprehension from the pen of a white Southerner.

Astonishment does not begin to describe the reaction of Josephus Daniels as he read the article. No doubt he felt personally vilified because he was one of the chief exploiters of racial prejudice in the state and an acknowledged spokesman for the White Man's Party. Apparently Daniels had forgotten that he and the disfranchisers had assured the white community the right to think freely about all social issues once the Negro was removed from politics. Daniels opened the attack on Bassett in his paper, the Raleigh *News and Observer*. Does Bassett "pray with his face turned toward Tuskegee?" one editorial asked, and he was frequently referred to in headlines as "bASSett."[48] The North Carolina

---

[45] "Stirring Up the Fires," p. 299.

[46] *Ibid.*, pp. 298, 301, 304.

[47] *Ibid.*, p. 301.

[48] See Daniels' rather candid autobiography, *Editor in Politics* (Chapel Hill: University of North Carolina Press, 1941), pp. 428–37. See also Porter, *Trinity and Duke*, pp. 110–24; Joseph L. Morrison, *Josephus Daniels Says... An Editor's Political Odyssey from Bryan to Wilson to F.D.R.* (Chapel Hill: University of North Carolina Press, 1962), pp. 121–49.

press—with only three exceptions[49]—followed the *News and Observer's* example, some referring to the blacks as "mASSes." Bassett was called "disloyal," unfit to teach Southern youth, and a "nigger lover" whose words would only give blacks an exalted opinion of their "rights."[50]

From the beginning of the controversy the faculty and administration at Trinity stood firmly behind Bassett and the principle of free speech. When the college trustees assembled in December to take official notice of the incident and to determine whether to accept Bassett's resignation, which he had offered, Kilgo stepped forward and, in an impassioned speech of over three hours he, who had himself spoken plainly against lynchings, argued that the issue was not one man or one man's pronouncements, but freedom. Was there not, he asked, one place in the South where a man could speak his mind honestly without abusive criticism? Kilgo's was no empty rhetoric: though he did not mention it at the time, he too carried in his pocket a letter of resignation, to be offered immediately should Bassett's be accepted.[51]

Dean William P. Few spoke for the faculty. He read a lengthy statement signed by twelve of the thirteen full professors (the thirteenth was away at the time).[52] The statement had actually been written by William Garrott Brown, Few's classmate at Harvard, who had just arrived on the campus to spend a month with Few when the uproar began. A close friend of Bassett's, Brown

---

[49] The Charlotte *Observer*, the *Progressive Farmer*, and the *Biblical Recorder* (John Cline, "Thirty Eight Years of the *South Atlantic Quarterly*" [M.A. thesis, Duke University, 1940], pp. 49-122).

[50] Daniels reprinted editorials from various other papers, including the following from the Charleston (South Carolina) *News and Courier*, which suggests that Southern intolerance had a long memory: "It ought not to be a very hard matter for Bassett to get a place in some Northern college. He has made good his claim to scholarship and teaching ability . . . and when he shall go to his new place in the North, Prof. Bassett will find that he has been preceded in that country of liberal endowments and fat places by such men as Prof. Trent, formerly of the University of the South, and George Washington Cable, and others of like attainments" (*ibid.*, p. 76).

[51] Porter, *Trinity and Duke*, p. 132.

[52] The statement, titled "Memorial From the Faculty to the Trustees," is reprinted in William B. Hamilton, ed., *Fifty Years of the South Atlantic Quarterly* (Durham: Duke University Press, 1952), pp. 64-67.

had watched the "screaming onslaught" with disgust and immediately came to the support of the faculty.[53]

The statement, which clearly showed the influence of John Stuart Mill's views on liberty, elevated the issue from the personal to the universal level of human freedom: "It is far better to tolerate opinions which seem to be wrong than to punish the expression of opinions because they are contrary to those generally accepted." It appealed to patriotism: "There is a question in the mind of the world whether there is a genuine freedom of speech throughout the South. This college has now the opportunity to show that her campus is undeniably one spot on Southern soil where men's minds are free, and to maintain that the social order of the South need not be shielded from criticism because it has no reason to fear it, because it is not too weak to hear it." Other colleges, the trustees were reminded, "have been called upon to face the same issue which you are to decide. Such as have failed have been disgraced in the eyes of the academic world." The point was clear: "It is the cause of academic freedom, and we, the professors of Trinity College, by reason of the very circumstances that we do not assent to the views of our colleague which are being criticized, feel that we are left exceptionally free to devote ourselves to the great and general principle involved. We should be recreant to the principle and false to our brothers in other colleges if we did not now urge upon your body the gravity of the crisis at hand."

To the rumor spread by Daniels in his newspaper that there would be a mass exodus of students if Bassett were retained, the faculty statement replied: "We realize with you that we may be in danger of losing some students, perhaps of losing friends, but we are willing to risk our future standing for the great principle of free speech and to accept all the consequences of this choice. For we believe that our chance to build up here eventually a great institution among the colleges of the world will be far better if we stand for truth and freedom, than if we silently consent to yield

[53] See Bassett to Frederick Bancroft, December 8, 1903, Frederick Bancroft Papers, Columbia University Library, New York, N.Y.

our minds to any sort of intellectual bondage." To lose our freedom, Dean Few read on, "would be a calamity, to throw it away would be unpardonable folly. Money, students, friends, are not for one moment to be weighed in the balance with tolerance, with fairness, and with freedom."[54] The faculty was serious: twelve signers had already written letters of resignation, which were to be submitted immediately upon word that Bassett's had been accepted.[55]

One of the trustees was Benjamin Duke, one of the founders of the Duke dynasty that built the American Tobacco Company into a multi-million-dollar trust and, like his father Washington Duke, a generous benefactor of the college. Once he learned that Bassett's position was in jeopardy, Walter Page attempted to persuade Duke to use his extensive influence in Bassett's behalf.

Page was genuinely fond of Bassett and admired his scholarship, and he also considered Trinity an intellectual oasis in the South. Three times in November Page wrote to Duke that the battle lines had been drawn and that he had an unparalleled opportunity to stand for freedom and put Trinity College permanently on the map. It was of no importance, Page wrote Duke, whether Bassett was right or wrong, but it was "of the highest importance that a professor from Trinity College should be allowed to hold and express any rational opinion he may have."[56] Then Page appealed to Duke's competitive spirit: "The fight is squarely drawn. It is a fight for free speech—for the freedom of Trinity College." "I wish I had a hand in it myself," he exclaimed. "I'd give a year's growth for a chance to stand up and say what I think and how I feel."[57] Page's words may have influenced Duke's decision to reject Bassett's resignation.[58]

---

[54] "Memorial From the Faculty to the Trustees," pp. 65–67.

[55] Porter, *Trinity and Duke*, p. 131.

[56] November 13, 1903, Trinity College Papers.

[57] November 25, 1903, Trinity College Papers.

[58] He was, in any case, reminded of Page's admonition by Few, who pointed out in his address that "a Southerner of national and international reputation" had written to a member of his audience to say that the issue was freedom and the future of Trinity ("Memorial From the Faculty to the Trustees," p. 66).

Support for Bassett came from other quarters also. James H. Southgate, chairman of the board of trustees, received numerous letters from alumni and friends of the college urging Trinity to stand by Bassett. A recent graduate wrote from Harvard: "I earnestly beg that you will not permit the resignation of our very highly esteemed History Professor. As a student under Dr. Bassett for three years I realize what a great loss the college would suffer should he give up his chair."[59] Three other alumni wrote to Southgate from Yale: "Dr. Bassett's statement was unfortunate, perhaps unwise, but we cannot hear of the acceptance of his resignation by the Board without a feeling of deepest regret for we consider him to be one of [the] men that has done much to raise the name of our Alma Mater to such glory throughout the educational institutions of our country."[60] Several businessmen in the state supported Bassett. One wrote Southgate an eight-page typed open letter in defense of Bassett, which he said he was also sending to the Charlotte *Observer*.[61] Another, Jacob Long, acknowledged proudly that he had fought with Lee at Appomattox and had since voted the straight Democratic ticket. "I am a full-blooded-southern-confederate-democrat," he declared, adding that he wanted to say a few words about academic freedom and freedom of speech in North Carolina:

This tempest will soon blow over. I can remember when a man could not say publicly that he favored the emancipation of the slaves. Who now would have the hardihood to say that he favored putting them back into slavery—just as they were in 1860? This change has come within the last thirty years—inside of the next twenty years—we will see, those who live that long, as great changes as what we have seen in the last twenty. No sane man will contend that the negro will ever be equal of the white man—but the negro is now entitled to equality in treatment before the law—forty years ago he had only the right to live.[62]

[59] Ralph O'Dell to James H. Southgate, November 28, 1903, Trinity College Papers.

[60] Stewart L. Mims, S. G. Winstead, and W. A. Lambeth to Southgate, November 19, 1903, Trinity College Papers.

[61] G. S. Bradshaw to Southgate, December 1, 1903, Trinity College Papers.

[62] Jacob Long to Southgate, November 20, 1903, Trinity College Papers.

Many students at Trinity also voiced support of their teacher and defended the principle of academic freedom. Mims felt a new spirit on the campus. "There is now," he wrote to Walter Page, "a spirit of dedication to a great and worthy ideal that is in every sense sublime. It is worth living many years to see a student body act with the poise and good sense and love of the right that this student body has manifested—and this without any pressure whatever from the faculty." Only one student withdrew from the college during the fracas. Their courage was in sharp contrast to the silence of the rest of the academic community of North Carolina. "Many men are with us in the fight," Mims confessed to Page, "but few will declare themselves. *Not a college man in the state has lifted his voice.*"[63]

Eleven trustees spoke at the meeting, with Furnifold M. Simmons leading the attack on Bassett. Simmons, one of the leading Democratic politicians in the state and one of the men who had engineered the disfranchisement campaign of 1898-99, had come to Durham to win, as he put it, "the last fight for white supremacy."[64] The final three speakers, whose remarks, unfortunately, the minutes of the meeting do not record, supported Bassett, with Southgate summing up the position of the defense. At the beginning of the session Southgate had made his own position clear by reading the various letters he had received in support of Bassett. When the vote was finally taken, at the end of a long wearying day, the count stood 18 to 7 to retain the errant professor.[65]

The opposition was constituted of Simmons, one businessman, and five preachers, thus giving a clerical tinge to the minority. Four preachers joined with Southgate, Duke, and the businessmen who supported Bassett. Earl Porter, whose study of the Bassett affair is the most exhaustive to date, concludes that "the majority was largely composed of Methodists from the business community in Durham and throughout the state. Most of them *at that time or*

---

[63] November 24, 1903, Page Papers.

[64] Quoted in Mims to Page, December 4, 1903, Page Papers.

[65] Porter, *Trinity and Duke*, p. 132.

in the past had business associations with the Dukes."[66] This point should be stressed because the intellectuals of Bassett's generation kept insisting that industrialization and the business community would ultimately bring a freer climate of opinion on all matters. Nevertheless, the board of trustees' statement concluded that "Professor Bassett does not believe in, nor does he teach social equality."[67]

The intellectuals' faith in the latent liberalism of the business community gains credence from the fact that most of the mail supporting Bassett also came from the business community. Moreover, following the Board's decision, Southgate received numerous letters of praise and congratulations from businessmen. One, a native of North Carolina and a graduate of the University at Chapel Hill, wrote from Georgia to praise the decision. Closer to home, the owner of the Fire and Life Insurance Company of Burlington said that the trustees' decision meant that "freedom of conscience must and shall have free sway in the 'Old North State.'" Similar letters came from Dred Peacock and J. Elwood Cox, prominent Tarheel businessmen.[68] And minds could change. The Reverend H. K. Boyer of Statesville admitted that although he had earlier joined those calling for Bassett's dismissal, he now realized that he had acted foolishly, and one J. A. Hornaday of Burlington wrote to Kilgo in 1909: "Six or seven years ago when Trinity was wrestling with the 'Bassett matter,' I 'butted in'; subsequently I found that I had 'played the fool' and decided to meddle no more with matters about which others knew so much more than I."[69] Immediately following Bassett's vindication, Mims described his frayed feelings to Walter Page: "For a month I have been in such a tension as I have never experienced before. And when the reaction came after the great victory, I was almost too

---

[66] *Ibid.*, p. 133.

[67] Quoted in Hamilton, *Fifty Years of the South Atlantic Quarterly*, p. 64.

[68] James P. Albright to Southgate, December 3, 1904; Dred Peacock to B. N. Duke, December 4, 1903; J. Elwood Cox to B. N. Duke, December 4, 1903, Trinity College Papers.

[69] H. K. Boyer to Southgate, January 12, 1904; J. A. Hornaday to Kilgo, December 27, 1909, Trinity College Papers.

nervous and exhausted to write."[70] William Garrott Brown, although elated, concluded that North Carolina still retained "blind prejudice and intolerance."[71]

As for the beleaguered Bassett, at first he was jocular and inclined to take a mildly amused and detached view of the whole matter—he had, after all, hoped to stir up something. Perhaps he was hoping for a successful, short "little war." "By the way," he wrote to his friend Frederick Bancroft in October, "I have done an article for the forthcoming *Quarterly*" which "will not please the Southern politicians. There is a statement in it to the effect that Booker T. Washington is the greatest man (save Lee) born in the South in a century. I forgot to except Lincoln. My friends tell me this will stir up some fires of its own accord in this part of the world. Wait and see, I may go North a little too soon."[72] At the height of Daniels' attack Bassett asked Bancroft whether he had heard of "the storm." "It did not seem to me a very extreme article—but a plain one." Maybe by being quiet, he wrote him in another letter, "and by taking some blows on my fat back," he could "break a hole in this crass Southern intolerance, and maybe I'll get my fat back broken instead." He closed in good humor: "Take my advice in regard to your own book and don't tackle these folks till you get all your material from this side of the line and till you are safely back on the North side of the good old Potomac."[73] He would say little, be quiet, and let the storm pass, as Walter Page had advised him to do.[74] He did consent, on the urging of friends, to an interview with a local reporter to explain that his reference to "equality" had never meant "social equality," but rather "equality of opportunity."[75] His explanation did not help much.

Bassett began to feel the pressure in mid-November. He wrote to Kilgo confessing to a great sense of guilt for having put the

[70] Mims to Page, December 4, 1903, Page Papers.

[71] Stanton [Brown], "The South at Work," Boston *Evening Transcript*, March 9, 1904.

[72] October 11, 1903, Bancroft Papers.

[73] November 9, 1903, Bancroft Papers.

[74] Bassett to Page, November 7, 1903, Page Papers.

[75] A copy of the interview is in the Trinity College Papers.

college in such a vulnerable position and thanking him for his supportive statement to the faculty and his confidence in the past. "We came together, possibly we may go together," he wrote. "If not that, we shall have a long trial together. If it shall be so that we remain to fight—and endure side by side—may I not have your ready confidence in meeting this enemy so that I may ward off some blows?" "They can never make the world forget that we were not afraid of them."[76]

Throughout the ordeal Bassett relied heavily on his many friends. Everyone at the college, he wrote Page, "stands like a rock on the question of liberty of thought. They have treated me like men and brothers, and I have no doubt they will do all they can."[77] All along, Bancroft remained a sympathetic listener. In late November Bassett confessed to him angrily: "If they knew how much I despise their little conclusions, and their narrow view of history, they would send me away."[78] Then his morale got an unexpected boost. William A. Dunning assured him in mid-November that Columbia University had a spot for him should he be forced to leave Trinity. But Bassett's highest regard was reserved for Kilgo. "You must not discount the fortitude and influence of Trinity's president," he wrote to Bancroft on December 3. "He is a man—every inch of him; and the way he stopped Simmons in this fight is worth putting down in history."[79] Today, a bust of John Spencer Bassett stands in the main quadrangle of Duke University.

The lasting effects of the ordeal on Bassett are difficult to estimate. Although he was a shy, rather retiring scholar, given to speaking softly about "objectivity," he was also capable of sharp, cutting remarks. He felt drawn to the quiet of the cloistered library, yet he fought with Josephus Daniels and Furnifold Simmons. Kilgo liked to fight; Bassett said he did not: "If my heart's inclinations were followed, I should run off to some quiet and unobserved harbor, if such a refuge could be had, and give myself

[76] November 19, 1903, Trinity College Papers.
[77] November 7, 1903, Page Papers.
[78] November 18, 1903, Bancroft Papers.
[79] December 3, 1903, Bancroft Papers.

to books and writing; for I cannot believe that nature made me to wage war, and there are a half dozen books dancing in my brain and begging me to write them."[80]

But for the moment a decisive victory had been won, and Bassett now had to make a number of decisions. What direction should the *South Atlantic Quarterly* take? (He was pleased to discover that the controversy had attracted over a hundred new subscribers, many from the South.[81]) Should Daniels be answered? As it turned out, Daniels decided to forgo further contest, Bassett decided that silence was his best course as well, and the matter disappeared from public notice. Soon Bassett had resumed his former pace: "Since I last wrote you," he said to Bancroft in 1904, "I have been crowded most damnably with work. I have got out my Magazine, taught school, written newspaper articles, written biographical sketches for money (but not for much of it), reviewed books, played tennis, and done something of most everything else but work on [Andrew] Jackson."[82]

* * *

It is to the magazine that we must turn to trace the progress of Bassett's mind. To Walter Page, who was eager for the journal to remain responsive to social questions, Bassett confided that he had Kilgo's continued support but that he did not want to cause needless controversies when there was so much constructive work to be done.[83] "I *don't* wish to abandon the critical spirit I have used, nor do I want to give them a chance at me on mere details."[84] He did not abandon that spirit, but his later writings never regained his former verve and insight. In the first issue following the controversy, he did speak pointedly and critically about the "Negro problem"[85] (he aligned himself squarely on the side of Negro intellectuals who denounced segregation and disfranchisement),

[80] Bassett to Page, November 7, 1903, Page Papers.

[81] Bassett to Page, December 8, 1903, Page Papers.

[82] October 27, 1904, Bancroft Papers.

[83] December 3, 1903, Page Papers.

[84] December 8, 1903, Page Papers.

[85] Review of Booker T. Washington et al., *The Negro Problem, South Atlantic Quarterly* 3 (1904):95–96.

but myths and stereotypes began to creep into his writing. In "The Negro's Inheritance from Africa" and "The Task of the Critic"[86] Bassett reiterated the common arguments about "stages" of evolutionary growth and the Negro's place at the bottom stage. The "mind" of the African turns on "animal emotions, expressing itself in impetuous fear, joy, or sorrow," readers learned from Bassett.[87] Missing was mention of the relationship of the white South to the African's "mind." "The Task of the Critic" lacked the intensity of his earlier writings. He did defend his friend William E. Dodd, who had come under attack for listing "Some Difficulties of the History Teacher in the South."[88] Truthseekers like Dodd, Bassett concluded, "have always existed in the South and they will always exist there. No unification of public opinion can destroy them."[89]

But in a sense public opinion had silenced Bassett. His defense of Dodd appeared in the issue which announced that his scholarly work required his resignation from the journal.[90] He was stepping down "reluctantly," while gratefully acknowledging that the magazine had succeeded because of contributions from Southerners—"the intelligent men." Every article in the current issue, he noted, was written by a native Southerner.

Bassett devoted the year 1905 to his scholarly work. In the spring of 1906 came an irresistible job offer from Smith College. It offered fewer teaching responsibilities, more money, nearby research libraries, and more time for writing.[91] He wrote to Page, whom he had tried unsuccessfully to see on his way to the interview in Northhampton, that he could do more scholarly work in a calm New England town with its good libraries and the peaceful atmosphere than he possibly could in the South. He was aware of Page's recent advice to Clarence Poe that he ought to stay in the South and continue spreading enlightenment through the *Progres-*

---

[86] *Ibid.*, pp. 99–104, 297–301.

[87] "The Negro's Inheritance from Africa," p. 101.

[88] *South Atlantic Quarterly* 3 (1904):117–22.

[89] "The Task of the Critic," p. 301.

[90] "Editor's Announcement," *South Atlantic Quarterly* 4 (1905):91.

[91] Stephenson, *Southern History in the Making*, p. 116.

sive Farmer, but, said Bassett, Poe "stands between the scholar and the general public and he is the man the South needs and the man whom it will encourage—it will be another generation before it will be ready for the scholar or the writer of serious books."[92] He reminded Page that when he had left, the South would not tolerate even a good editor, and now all that had changed. To Dodd (who himself left Randolph-Macon in 1908 for the University of Chicago) Bassett wrote in 1907, "It was the conviction that I could not write history and direct public sentiment too that made me willing to come North."[93]

The dilemma was a real one for Southern academics. Edwin Alderman caught its essence: "We, who are pioneers in constructive work in a region like this, have a hard time . . . to bear our public burdens and still reserve time for quieter work. The climate fights against us for five months and in the winter there is a certain fierceness in the activities of life that tend to sweep us away, in spite of ourselves, from reflective labor."[94] Bassett phrased the problem to his former student William K. Boyd, who replaced him at Trinity, this way: "it is very well in the South to be an antiquarian but difficult to be a historian in the cosmopolitan sense. It is easy to do the work of popular 'arousement,' but not that of mature and scholarly thinking. All the impulse to stir up something leads to a stage of achievement which a cultured community ought to have passed a generation ago."[95] Later Bassett confessed to Boyd that he had left Trinity not for more money, a lighter teaching load, or the cultural life at Smith (all "reasons" he had given himself and friends) but because "I merely wanted a peaceful atmosphere."[96] That sounds similar to his comment to Walter Page in 1903, quoted earlier, that his heart, if not his brain, wished for a "quiet and unobserved harbor."

* * *

[92] May 29, 1906, Page Papers.

[93] Quoted in Stephenson, *Southern History in the Making*, p. 131.

[94] Alderman to Charles W. Eliot, quoted in Malone, *Alderman*, p. 145.

[95] October 11, 1908, Bassett Papers.

[96] January 2, 1912, Bassett Papers.

Bassett left the South convinced that he had helped to liberate the Southern mind, and indeed few men have done more toward that goal. Like Cable, he had pointed out the gulf between the South's pretensions and its practices, and had done so with a power of expression equal to his ideas. Unlike Trent, he had achieved an explicit understanding of the South's problems and had moved steadily toward a more cogent presentation of that understanding. Sledd's outrage had exploded in one impassioned outburst, and he had returned to the South within a year after leaving Emory (he returned to Emory itself in 1914), but he ceased to be a social critic. "The Negro: Another View" proved to be his one outcry, while Bassett proclaimed his anger and outrage against injustice for several years. His departure was thus much more of a loss to the South than Trent's and Sledd's had been.

Although the Bassett affair, when lumped together with the criticisms leveled at Cable, Walter Page, Trent, and Sledd, seems to substantiate Wilbur J. Cash's fears, some features of the Sledd and Bassett incidents suggest that the attacks, as ugly as they were, may have been inspired by considerations other than those of censorship. Scholars who have examined the motives of Mrs. Felton and Josephus Daniels have been tempted to conclude that each was using racism as a subterfuge.[97] Possibly Mrs. Felton was evening her score with Candler, as he thought. As for Daniels, an ardent champion of public education, it was no secret that he had never forgiven Kilgo for attacking the state universities, nor had he, a Bryanite, forgotten that Kilgo and the faculty had been Gold Bugs at the height of the Free Silver fever of the 1890s.[98] Despite this animosity, however, the *News and Observer* had kept its hostility to Trinity College in check prior to the eruption of the Bassett affair.[99] Daniels had dealt lightly with Sledd, contenting himself with a denunciation of his article as a "slander" of the South.[100] Further, on earlier occasions when Daniels had

[97]See Warnock, "Andrew Sledd," pp. 264–71; Morrison, *Josephus Daniels Says . . .*, pp. 121–48.

[98]I am indebted to Joseph L. Morrison for this information and its interpretation.

[99]Porter, *Trinity and Duke*, p. 112.

[100]*Ibid.*, p. 112.

denounced Kilgo's views and the college's affinity for Republicanism and trusts, he had never gone to extremes. A proud man, he was not eager to suffer another public humiliation. One may well ask whether, had Bassett stayed in the South and continued to speak out, he might not have opened up the Southern mind as no one else had been able to do.

This conjecture gains plausibility from the fact that in each incident, including the Simms affair, the popular reaction included an element of moderate to liberal opinion.[101] The Savage Ideal was there, ready to be invoked by Daniels, Mrs. Felton, and their like, but there were also students, professors, businessmen, preachers, and other Southerners ready to defend those who spoke frankly; for instance, the independent-minded young men whom Bassett and Trent and Page had known in college would, by 1900, have been active in business and the professions. This "Silent South" (the expression is Cable's, coined in 1885) of informed liberals unprepared to accept the Savage Ideal could perhaps have been aroused to action if the sort of intelligent leadership, humane vision, and outraged conscience represented by Bassett had been available.

But this is, at best, speculation. We do know that after 1914 social criticism from the academy became less explicit, less noisy, and more committed to such issues as the value of literature, setting educational standards, the merits of road-building programs, and, in some quarters (namely, at Vanderbilt University, where Mims tried to keep the old optimism alive), a defense of conservative agrarian ideas. The careers of William K. Boyd and William P. Few typify the academic liberal who prevailed after 1914: dedicated teachers and able scholars, they worked quietly to build Trinity College into a first-rate liberal arts college and then into Duke University.[102]

[101] Warnock, "Andrew Sledd," pp. 269-71.
[102] Porter, *Trinity and Duke*, pp. 174-238.

Part II

REDEEMING THE SOUTH FROM THE SAVAGE IDEAL

INTRODUCTION

In spite of the intensity of the attacks on Sledd and Bassett, the intellectuals did not lose hope. To redeem the South they proposed, over the course of the decade, three "solutions," which they pursued ardently. Like Emerson, they wished to free men from the "prisons" that kept them from being good and reasonable. Schools, public and private, were to be built to save the people from ignorance and superstition, and a culture of learning was to be created. Many confidently announced that industrialism, which they identified with prosperity, would save the South by banishing poverty. To a segment of the intellectual community political reform, or more precisely, the destruction of the Solid South and the establishment of democracy, was another solution to the problems of the South. The faith of the intellectuals, at bottom, was an American one: educated, prosperous, democratic men are good men. Democracy, industrialism, and education were identified with moral regeneration and the redemption of man. As Edwin Alderman recollected in 1906, "Our institutions needed to be democratized; our thought to be nationalized; our life to be industrialized, and *the whole process was one of education*" (italics added).

5

EDUCATION AND FREEDOM

IN THE 1890S ILLITERACY prevailed in the South. Fully one-fourth of all Southerners lacked even the basic skills of reading and writing. Public schools were open only three or four months a year, and the teachers were ill prepared and underpaid. There were private preparatory academies but almost no public schools to fill the gap between the inadequate primary schools and the colleges and universities. Many of the latter were that in name only, and few of the better ones—Trinity, Sewanee, Emory, Vanderbilt—showed promise of a more distinguished future. Aside from Ellen Glasgow (and her novels won critical acclaim only in the 1920s) and Thomas Nelson Page, whose romances enjoyed a brief vogue, the South was a literary wasteland. Defenders of "our beloved Southland" ballyhooed the legion of lady writers and ex-Confederates who churned out novels and "true" histories; their efforts prompted John Spencer Bassett to remark that "men who have fought bravely with the sword are tempted to make asses of themselves with the pen."[1] No publishers of distinction existed to serve the needs of serious scholars, and the *Sewanee Review* and the *South Atlantic Quarterly* were almost alone as journals of critical thought. The libraries found in the colleges and universities were usually small and narrow in scope. Library

[1] Quoted in Stephenson, *Southern History in the Making*, 102.

shelves in church colleges abounded with theological tomes, while critical and historical works were scarce.

From the beginning the intellectuals gave priority to rebuilding and improving the schools and intellectual disciplines. Virtually the entire intellectual community involved itself in the "movement" for public schools that swept across the South in the 1900s. Whether as officials of the Southern Education Board or as interested bystanders, they publicized the South's plight and attracted numerous supporters. Most important, they succeeded in tapping two sources of power and wealth, Southern politicians and Northern philanthropists.

The older hands, educational missionaries like Atticus G. Haygood of Atlanta, a Methodist bishop, and J. L. M. Curry, a Georgian who had been working for the cause since the 1880s in Alabama and Virginia,[2] welcomed this fresh support. Knowing that they would be silenced if a freer climate of opinion were not created, the younger men proclaimed that intellectual freedom was not a luxury but a necessity, not only in the schools but in the marketplace, and that building schools would create such a climate.

This coalition of idealists made heady predictions. Education would produce both a literate citizenry and a democratic society, for through education the people would become not only literate and economically productive but racially tolerant. No educated man could be a bigot, a partisan Democrat, a religious reactionary, or a good-for-nothing idler. While arguing for competitive capitalism, they announced—without bothering about the contradiction—that education's great service to mankind was the promotion of economic cooperation and social harmony. Education, wrote one of their number in 1909, "is building up community life by making effective the cooperative principle," and concluded, "We look to the school to beget kindliness between neighbors, regard-

---

[2] For descriptions of Haygood and Curry, see Dabney, *Universal Education*, 1:123–28; Edwin A. Alderman and Armistead C. Gordon, *J. L. M. Curry, A Biography* (New York: Macmillan Company, 1911); Harold W. Mann, *Atticus Greene Haygood, Methodist Bishop, Editor and Educator* (Athens: University of Georgia Press, 1965), pp. 169–81.

less of color or creed."[3] In short, education meant nothing less then the ethical and moral regeneration of the South. Starting with an atomistic conception of the state, they deduced that the education of the individual meant social regeneration. Moreover, by identifying the state as the "folk" and assuming the basic goodness of man, they were able to impute goodness to the educated "state." Samuel Chiles Mitchell once boasted that the new schools would make the Southerner, and hence the South, lawful, humane, and rational.[4] Edwin Alderman knew that the New South needed "men with faith in education as a great agency for moulding social and economic forces."[5] Nowhere does one find an extended examination of how schools will remake men. For guidelines the intellectuals offered only high-flown defenses of reason and intellectual freedom.

Whenever defending or praising education, however, Alderman and his fellow educators habitually noted that the South needed new leaders. Their stress on "lack of leadership" and their attacks on the politicians, preachers, and planters (or their descendants) indicate not only dissatisfaction with the status quo but their own desire to become the voice of the South. This ambition is revealed in their preoccupation with "public opinion"—"the most majestic of all human agencies," said Alderman—and their constant praise of the "true South" or the "real South." They were willing to broaden the base of the new leadership to include like-minded Southerners ("men of the better sort," as William Garrott Brown put it), such as businessmen, college-educated clergymen, lawyers, and doctors.

The logic of this position was that if, by definition, the schools teach virtue, then teachers and educated men must be the most virtuous. Some men, like James H. Kirkland of Vanderbilt, even identified the school—"in its parental capacity"—with the state

---

[3] Samuel Chiles Mitchell, "The American Spirit in Education," *South Atlantic Quarterly* 8 (1909):256, 259.

[4] Samuel Chiles Mitchell, "The School as an Exponent of Democracy in the South," *Sewanee Review* 16 (1908):24.

[5] "Charles D. McIver of North Carolina," *Sewanee Review* 15 (1907):108.

itself.[6] To fellow-educator Charles A. Smith of the University of North Carolina, "the common school system must recognize its imperative to serve democracy" because, in the South, "the citadel of democracy is the school house and no longer the courthouse."[7]

The confidence born of these convictions was offset by an undercurrent of anxiety and pessimism, however, which surfaced now and then in troubled or angry outcries: "we need a few first-class funerals," said Walter Page; "we write as a people in the stage of crude animalism," said Bassett; "the South has gone insane," said Kilgo. In *The Southerner* Page had his protagonist lament: "We were and are disinherited, we who had no more to do with the Civil War than with the Punic Wars and no more to do with slavery than with the Inquisition, and yet we suffer the consequences of slavery and war."[8] During a visit to Mississippi in 1907 he wrote to his wife that all things conspire against the Negro: "I'm afraid he's a goner." Yet on the same day that he wrote these despairing words he also wrote to a fellow laborer for public education, "Well, the world lies before us. It'll not be the same when we get done with it that it was before; bet your last penny on that—will you!"[9]

Let us turn now from words to deeds to see how the intellectuals threw themselves into the Southern educational crusade. The idea of universal public education had triumphed in the North by 1900, but in the South it required careful cultivation throughout the 1880s and 1890s. In 1898, the year after Page's celebrated "forgotten man" speech, a small group of concerned churchman and Southern educators and a sprinkling of Northerners gathered at Capon Springs, West Virginia, to discuss ways to rescue the forgotten man of the South. The leading spirit of the Conference for Southern Education, as it was called, was Walter Page's friend

[6]"The School as a Force Arrayed against Child Labor," *Annals of the American Academy of Political and Social Science* 25 (1905):559.

[7]Pp. 18–25; for Smith's views see his "Our Heritage of Idealism," *Sewanee Review* 20 (1912):345.

[8]P. 75.

[9]Page to Alice Page, February 10, 1907; Page to Wallace K. Buttrick, February 10, 1907, Page Papers.

J. L. M. Curry, who had gained a thorough knowledge of Southern conditions through his work for the Jeanes Fund, a Northern philanthropic organization committed to Negro education. As a result of his labors on behalf of the black man, Curry, along with most other white intellectuals, had concluded that the education of the white man was the most urgent task confonting the South.[10] He called the Capon Springs meeting to bring the best thinking of the region to bear on the problem. Though the conference itself yielded meager results, there were already in motion forces destined to transform Curry's cause into a full-scale crusade.[11]

The first stirrings of life appeared in 1901, when the conference met again in Winston-Salem. In addition to the usual assortment of teachers and preachers from the nearby boroughs, the meeting attracted high-ranking Southern politicians and professors and Northern philanthropists. The last group included John D. Rockefeller and William H. Baldwin, the president of the Southern Railroad. A Southerner, George Foster Peabody, who had found Yankee finance friendly and profitable, was also present. Their attention had been drawn to Southern conditions by Charles W. Ogden, a department store magnate from New York who for several years had been escorting trainloads of Northern dignitaries through the South in private railroad coaches to show them how the other half of America lived. Ogden, a blend of self-aggrandizing piety, sincere humility, and a genuine sense of "service," got on well with Southerners who shared his brand of optimism and idealism. On board the special train he had hired for the Winston-Salem conference were millionaires, New York preachers of the stature of Charles Parkhurst, Lyman Abbott, the editor of *Outlook* magazine, and Walter Hines Page. On hand to meet the train were Curry, McIver, Alderman, at this time president of the University of North Carolina, Charles W. Dabney, president of the University of Tennessee and former member of the Watauga Club, and Governor Charles B. Aycock.

[10]Curry, "The Negro Question," *Popular Science Monthly* 55 (1899):177-85.

[11]See Dabney's two-volume work, *Universal Education*.

Aycock's presence was a sign of the times. Soon to become nationally known as the "education governor," he had swept to victory in 1900 on a platform of racism and educational reform. One of the chief architects of the White Supremacy campaign of 1898, Aycock, along with Josephus Daniels, had hit upon educational reform as a way of assuring the illiterate whites that they would not be disfranchised by the proposed literacy qualifications for the vote. Aycock's victory saved North Carolina from further "Negro domination" and assured a "white man's government."[12] The New South intellectuals were pragmatic enough to realize that they must work with Aycock and with politicians like Hoke Smith of Georgia and Braxton Bragg Comer of Alabama, the latter a wealthy Birmingham businessman whose successful blend of reform and racism is reminiscent of that of Progressive reformers elsewhere in the United States. Then too, as we shall see, since many Southern intellectuals shared the basic assumptions of White Supremacy, cooperation with the Aycocks involved only a minimum of discomfort. The notable exception was the faculty of Trinity College; none of them joined the movement in any official capacity.

Aycock gave the inaugural address at Winston-Salem. Adept at the stump rhetoric of Southern politics (William Garrott Brown frequently complained that Southern politicians knew nothing but stump rhetoric), he vividly outlined the dreary facts of Southern ignorance. His appeal powerfully affected men like the Reverend Mr. Parkhurst, who had toured the city's black ghettos to see what a "problem" the whites had on their hands.[13] Dabney augmented

[12] Edmonds, *The Negro and Fusion Politics in North Carolina*; and Oliver H. Orr, Jr., *Charles Brantley Aycock* (Chapel Hill: University of North Carolina Press, 1961), pp. 165–88.

[13] Dabney, *Universal Education*, 2:538–41; Woodward, *Origins of the New South*, p. 402. Lyman Abbott returned from Winston-Salem to conclude: "We have got to get rid of our more or less vague ideas that all men are created equal and that every man has the right to stand where everybody else does" (New York *World*, April 28, 1901); Reverend Parkhurst expressed a similar view: "I never had a right conception of the southern negro before. This visit changes my whole view of the question and of what must be done for them [the Negroes]. Now I can see that the southern people know far better than I how to train and prepare them for American citizenship. I understand now why they should never have been made full citizens before they were trained" (Dabney, *Universal Education*, 2:33).

the Governor's words with an equally frank and factual portrayal of the South's pressing need for money and education: "The Southern people are poor—many of them are extremely poor. Their schools are poor because they are poor; the converse is equally true—the people are poor because the schools are poor."[14] Dabney's speech, brimming with Jeffersonian idealism and the optimistic imagery of the Forgotten Man, was calculated both to arouse the Northerners and to allay any of their misgivings about working with Aycock or about redirecting their philanthropy to the Southern whites.[15] Ogden and Baldwin's original commitment had been to Negro education; Dabney and the intellectuals argued persuasively that the whites, once educated, would be tolerant toward blacks. They reasoned that education would eradicate the ignorance from which white racism stemmed. Furthermore, so the argument went in the hands of the intellectuals, efforts to educate blacks only increased the illiterate white man's hostility.[16]

Fortunately for the intellectuals, Aycock had pledged that his administration would oppose demands to restrict educational expenditures to the proportion of taxes paid by the two races, a scheme that would have wiped out the black schools. Moreover, compared to James K. Vardaman of Mississippi, who publicly referred to Booker T. Washington as "that coon," Aycock clearly represented the "conservative" wing of Southern politics.[17] Thus it was the Southern intellectual community which rechanneled the humanitarian impulse of the Northern business barons. By this means what might have become an irreconcilable split between the politicians, the professors, and the philanthropists was averted at Winston-Salem.

[14]*Proceedings of the Fourth Conference for Education in the South* (Winston-Salem: n.p., 1901), pp. 46-62.

[15]Edwin A. Alderman to Charles W. Dabney, September 30, 1901, Alderman Papers, University of Virginia Library.

[16]See, for example, Edwin A. Alderman, "Education in the South," *Outlook* 68 (1901):775-80; William Garrott Brown, "Of the North's Part in Southern Betterment," *ibid.*, 78 (1904):418; Curry, "Negro Question," pp. 177-85; Dabney, *Universal Education*, 2:4-20.

[17]For the fullest expression of this view, see Edwin A. Alderman, "Charles Brantley Aycock—an Appreciation," *North Carolina Historical Review* 1 (1924):243-50.

Once there was general agreement on the goals of the conference, the next step was to create the machinery to carry out plans for state-wide publicity campaigns. The most important agency set up was the Southern Education Board, an organization of Northerners and Southerners which sought to unify the movement through publicity and propaganda and to serve as a clearinghouse for new ideas. Indirectly, the Board helped to create an intellectual community by bringing like-minded men together.

The list of the original Southern members of the board sounds like a roll call of the Watauga Club: Page, McIver, Alderman, and Dabney, along with Curry and Ogden, who served as president. In 1902 Edgar Gardner Murphy assumed the office of executive secretary, one of the few paid positions. Numerous others joined in the next few years, including Samuel Chiles Mitchell, James Hardy Dillard, and James H. Kirkland.[18] These young, educated Southerners could observe at close range the workings of Northern philanthropy. The largest benefactor, John D. Rockefeller, contributed over $53 million to various programs in Southern education, including the endowment of a school of education for the University of Virginia; Andrew Carnegie fulfilled Murphy's request for a library and Y.M.C.A. building at Montgomery, Alabama.[19]

Both as official board members and as willing partners in the new venture, Southern academicians and writers made a major contribution to the movement. With a grant from Rockefeller, Dabney helped establish a Bureau of Investigation and Information on the campus of the University of Tennessee and made it into the movement propaganda center. Included in the bureau's massive output was a thorough study of the South's poverty and educational backwardness. In 1903 Dabney persuaded the Southern Education Board to underwrite a summer school for teachers at the Knoxville campus. Dabney offered free dormitories and built "Jefferson Hall" to house the new school. More than eleven thousand teachers participated in the program in the next six

---

[18]Dabney, *Universal Education*, 2:60.

[19]*Ibid.*, pp. 123-24; Allan Nevins, *John D. Rockefeller: The Heroic Age of American Enterprise*, 2 vols. (New York: Charles Scribner's Sons, 1940), 2:463-98.

years. To make the work of the summer school permanent, Peabody endowed the George Peabody College for Teachers in Nashville and chose as its first president Bruce R. Payne, a graduate of Trinity College with a doctorate from Columbia University. As a boy in North Carolina, Payne had come under the influence of Alderman and McIver, so that intellectually the line runs from the Watauga Club through Trinity College and Jefferson Hall to the George Peabody College for Teachers.[20]

In Tennessee Kirkland assisted the cause with speeches and organizational work. McIver continued his personal evangelism in North Carolina, preaching to larger and larger crowds throughout the state on the value of education. He admitted that schools cost money but pointed out that "only the savage pays no tax" and that "education is the salt of democracy and prosperity."[21] Mitchell in South Carolina, Murphy in Alabama, and President Walter B. Hill of the University of Georgia campaigned in their states. Annually the crusaders convened in a Southern city to publicize their solidarity, invoke Jefferson's name, and hear "philosophical addresses" on such subjects as "local taxation."[22] Alderman and Walter Page were frequently on hand as speakers and organizers. The following quotation from Page illustrates his enthusiastic pace:

I send you this while I think of it—for no use but only for your personal information, if it should at any time, or in any way, turn out that I can serve the Board on any of these trips, or through any of these channels, by getting specific information, or by doing anything else.

June 13th—I shall address the North Carolina Teachers' Association of Wrightsville, on Education Towards Freedom of Speech. I am going to roast alive certain old preachers that have been scaring the courage out of these teachers—an old Praise-God-Barebones crowd.

[20]Dabney, *Universal Education*, 2:82-85, 106-22.

[21]Quoted in Louis R. Harlan, *Separate and Unequal: Public School Campaigns and Racism in the Southern Seaboard States, 1901-1915* (Chapel Hill: University of North Carolina Press, 1958), p. 91.

[22]See, particularly, *Proceedings of the Seventh Conference for Education in the South* (Birmingham: n.p., 1904).

June 17th—I am going to deliver the Commencement Address at the Jacob Tome Institute at Port Deposit, Maryland.

Later (in July) I am going to Dabney's summer school at Knoxville to speak about a week on

> Whatever else you Do, for the Love of Heaven
> write the English Language as well as you can.

I shall soon have off the press a little volume of addresses and magazine articles by me, called "The Rebuilding of Old Commonwealths"; all about the *Necessity of Free Public Education in the South by Taxation, because both the Old Aristocratic System of Education and the Ecclesiastical System Failed to Reach the People.* This is printed at my own expense to give away to anybody who will read it.[23]

* * *

The ideas and actions of two other zealous servants of public education suggest further dimensions of the mind of the New South. Though differing in temperament and personality, Edgar Gardner Murphy and Samuel Chiles Mitchell shared a common faith in education. Mitchell, a native Mississippian whose academic training included a Ph.D. in history from the University of Chicago, became president of the University of South Carolina in 1908 at the age of forty-four, following several years of teaching in small Southern colleges. He repeatedly promised that even the problems of the South could be alleviated through education. Murphy, while no less energetic or committed, tended to take a more somber view of human nature, perhaps as a result of his early religious upbringing and training in Episcopal theology. Nevertheless, his faith in education prompted him to devote himself to education and social reform, following his resignation from the ministry in 1901.

From the moment Murphy joined the Southern Education Board in 1902, his calm temperament and gentle exterior, combined with inner toughness, made him a valuable addition. His message was a familiar one to the intellectuals: the school is indispensable for democracy, prosperity, and individual development.

[23] Page to Wallace K. Buttrick, April 11, 1902, reprinted in Hendrick, *Training of an American*, pp. 407–9.

"The modern school," he once said, has a duty "not only to culture, but to citizenship. The state-supported school must give the state support—support as it teaches with a healing wisdom and an impartial patriotism the history of the past."[24] To the farmer or millhand who cast a wary eye on those who would keep his children in school at harvest time, Murphy reiterated his generation's views: "The farmer or the laborer who can read or write finds in that power the enlargement of his market."[25]

Despite his extensive duties for the board, however, Murphy did not neglect Alabama and its white children. He spoke often in the state, coordinated its educational campaign, and, through such pamphlets as "Alabama's First Question," won the support of businessmen, politicians, and the state teachers' association. He helped to persuade Braxton Bragg Comer to include educational reform in his platform when he made his successful bid for the governorship in 1906.[26]

Murphy's zeal for education resulted in part from fear of the illiterate Southern whites, who had been emancipated politically and economically after the Civil War. He feared the ignorant, uncouth ways of the newly enfranchised poor whites who were streaming into the cities from the countryside and the mountains, there to be pandered to by politicians. "The new world which has resulted from our political and industrial reorganization," Murphy said in 1904, "has brought into power vast multitudes of the unlettered and the untrained, a white population possessing all the pride, all the energy, all the assertiveness of the older order, without its experiences or its culture."[27] Such a turbulent social order, Murphy warned, needed intelligent leadership.

Partly as a result of his class-consciousness Murphy adopted the "educate the white man first" theme. He used the prestige and publicity of the Southern Education Board to assert the Southern

[24] *Problems of the Present South: A Discussion of Certain of the Educational, Industrial and Political Issues in the Southern States* (New York: The Macmillan Co., 1904), pp. 48-50.

[25] *Ibid.*, p. 55.

[26] Dabney, *Universal Education*, 2:396-97; Hugh C. Bailey, *Edgar Gardner Murphy: Gentle Progressive* (Coral Gables, Fla.: University of Miami Press, 1968), pp. 163-64.

[27] *Present South*, pp. 169-70.

attitude toward school segregation and the importance of concentrating money and attention on the whites. On several occasions he publicly justified the expense of maintaining two separate and unequal school systems: the South was poor, but not too poor to keep the races apart in the schools. "No man now living, no child of any man now living, will ever see at the South these two races taught together in the same institution. These races must be educated apart. The South . . . is not ready to discuss that question with anybody. It is a closed question."[28] Murphy's pronouncements echoed the private and public decisions being made inside the Southern Education Board and the movement. Now and again some of the Northern philanthropists felt the urge to "do something for the Negro," but Murphy along with Alderman and Dabney—who once threatened to resign if the Southern view was abridged—dissuaded them from embarking on new crusades for black education or rights.[29] Murphy's public defense of school segregation and his promise that educated whites would one day become tolerant helped quiet Yankee fears. "I feel 'like a dog' to have to say these things," Murphy confessed to Ogden, after cautioning him to remain silent about the blacks, "but I *know* our people."[30] Ogden in turn worked to mollify Northern public opinion when it was aroused by lynchings or riots in the South. Though a trustee of Hampton Institute, he avoided Negro schools during his travels in the South and urged black leaders to adopt an attitude of patience.[31] Southerners also changed the mind of men like Baldwin and Lyman Abbott of the *Outlook*.[32] Through it all the Southerners offered sincere, well-intentioned, "logical" advice to their Northern friends, while still keeping to the bargain struck at Winston-Salem by defending some education for blacks and criticizing the radical wing of Southern racism.

---

[28]Murphy, "The Task of the South," an Address before the Faculty and Students of Washington and Lee University, December 10, 1902, Murphy Papers, University of North Carolina Library.

[29]See Harlan, *Separate and Unequal*, pp. 92–96.

[30]Murphy to Robert C. Ogden, April 4, 1904, *ibid.*, p. 95.

[31]*Ibid.*, p. 96.

[32]William H. Baldwin to Murphy, n.d., 1904; Lyman Abbott to Murphy, December 31, 1906, Murphy Papers.

In 1908 his failing health forced Murphy to leave the board. The progress made in the decade since the Capon Springs meeting gratified him. Everywhere, even in the deep South, the states were taxing themselves for education; expenditures more than doubled in the first decade of the twentieth century.[33] In recognition of his service, the newly created Carnegie Foundation for the Advancement of Teaching departed from its practice of granting pensions solely to retiring teachers and awarded Murphy an annual pension of three thousand dollars. "In spite of your precarious health," Samuel Chiles Mitchell wrote him, "you have done a far greater service to the cause of truth and humanity than any of the rest of your fellows."[34]

Though Mitchell's criticisms of the South could be as caustic as those of Trent and Bassett, his belief in rationality and the innate goodness of man was as great as Walter Page's faith in man. Educated leaders, he knew, would guide the people to their better impulses. He was a thorough Jeffersonian: "Confidence in the capacity of the average man," he announced in 1909 for the Southern Education Board, "is the creed of this crusade," and the following year, "the public school implies faith in the capacity of the average man."[35]

Mitchell hoped that schools would revolutionize Southern society. Educated people would be freed from the tyranny of the corrupting ideas of caste, reaction, and particularism inherited from the Old South. The average man would think critically about politics, and that would mean death for the Solid South. He would make more money, whether as a farmer or businessman, and prepare the way for progress.[36]

Implicit in all of Mitchell's hopes was an unmistakable rejection of the present South. Like his contemporaries, he found the cause of the South's problems outside of natural man, in his ignorance, his prejudice, his history. "The cruel circumstances of history," he

[33] Murphy to Ogden, January 9, 1909, Harlan, *Separate and Unequal*, p. 249.

[34] Mitchell to Murphy, July 19, 1909, Murphy Papers.

[35] "The School as an Exponent of Democracy," p. 19; "American Spirit in Education," p. 257.

[36] "American Spirit in Education," p. 259.

said in 1904, had isolated the South from the three great influences of the modern day—slavery had choked liberalism, secession had smothered nationalism, and cotton had starved industrialism. The past, he said pointedly rejecting the mythology of the antebellum South, was "an instance of arrested development," but now education would change all that.[37]

Whereas Murphy yearned to believe that the best thought of the present day was but an extension of the aristocratic mind of the Old South, Mitchell would have none of the rosy, romantic view popularized by his contemporary Thomas Nelson Page. In the New South, Mitchell announced proudly, if prematurely, in 1910, "a community has taken the place of the old plantation. And that spells progress."[38] Part of the progress, of course, was his own generation's awareness that the white masses, though forming into a community, needed educated leadership.[39]

Few agreed more heartily with this point of view than John C. Kilgo, whose career in education helps us to understand the Southern mind. He stayed outside the formal organizations of the educational crusade, but as president of Trinity College from 1894 to 1910 he aligned himself and the school—in the Bassett affair, for example—with the new critical spirit. Yet Kilgo showed little sympathy for those who believed that public education could solve the Southerner's problems. All education was a fine thing, he held, and he applauded the movement for better public schools, but he believed that higher education belonged to the church colleges, where "Christian education" could serve the whole man. Soon after coming to Trinity he joined other preachers and sectarian officials in denouncing as "socialistic" and "unfair" to the church colleges proposals to provide tuition for students at the University of North Carolina.[40] Combative and deeply concerned for Trinity's future, Kilgo believed that secular education could

---

[37]Samuel Chiles Mitchell, "The Educational Needs of the South," *Outlook* 76 (1904):417.

[38]Samuel Chiles Mitchell, "Do Our Colleges Pay?" *South Atlantic Quarterly* 9 (1910):219.

[39]Mitchell, "Educational Needs of the South," pp. 417-18.

[40]Porter, *Trinity and Duke*, pp. 64-70.

not or would not ask the questions that must sooner or later be asked and answered if education were to be "complete."

The South, Kilgo often charged, was getting as much education as it wanted. Southerners countenanced "woefully inadequate" schools and underpaid teachers; rural Southerners, in particular, saw no need for book learning. Couple that fact with the Southerner's propensity to brag about everything "Southern"—Kilgo and the Trinity faculty had observed that trait long before Wilbur J. Cash pointed it out—and one found, said Kilgo, the cause of the section's backwardness. Furthermore, the Southern soil is the best breeding ground for "emotionalism" on the face of the earth, and "it is a well-known law of psychology that thought and emotions are in inverse ratio to each other." The charge that the South was too emotional, too sentimental, or too romantic—Cash's charge— was frequently made by Kilgo's contemporaries, as was the placement of responsibility for the South's failure to produce any greater thinker or "sound body of ideas to influence people"[41] on those who fostered this atmosphere. Like many of his contemporaries, however, Kilgo was sustained in hope by the belief that there was a "real South" (he preferred Cable's phrase, the "Silent South") behind the ignorance, the emotionalism, and the prejudice. He found that South in the professions, among the teachers, within the educated clergy, among the businessmen who were unafraid of men like Josephus Daniels and who would, he hoped, speak and lead.[42]

Kilgo's experience as a circuit-riding minister in South Carolina and as financial agent for Wofford College did not suggest an academic career (he held an undergraduate degree from Wofford plus a year of "graduate" reading with one of his professors), but when he became president of Trinity he set to work to transform it into a top-flight college serving scholarship, the South, and the church. Through a series of improvements in the school's academic and financial status he won the confidence of the faculty. In 1896

[41] John C. Kilgo, "Some Phases of Southern Education," *South Atlantic Quarterly* 2 (1903):143-45.

[42] John C. Kilgo, "The Silent South," *ibid.*, 4 (1907):202, 205, 208, 210, 211.

he proudly announced that his small group of teachers had, in two years, made over a hundred addresses and prepared forty papers for publication.[43] In John Spencer Bassett, Edwin Mims, and Jerome Dowd, professor of political economy, all hired in 1893, Kilgo found three bright and energetic young men who responded to his idealism. When the new Methodist president made good on his promises to respect intellectual freedom and to raise academic standards by hiring only professionally trained men, not retired clergymen, the morale of the faculty rose to the point where several professors, including Bassett, joined Kilgo in his attack on secular higher education. Although Bassett complained that Trinity was a "narrow and uninspiring place to work," he praised Kilgo lavishly even before the president supported him in establishing the *South Atlantic Quarterly*.[44]

Kilgo had a further success when he persuaded the wealthy Duke family to make a long-term financial commitment to Trinity. Although he knew from his Wofford days that Southern Methodists were unwilling or unable to support higher education, he did solicit funds from North Carolina churches. But when his treasurer returned to the campus in the fall of 1894 from a fund-raising summer with scarcely enough money to cover his own travel expenses, Kilgo knew that he would have to tap other sources. Luckily for him, Washington Duke, the patriarch of the family, took a liking to Kilgo's blend of old-time religion and up-to-date goals for Trinity. For some years Duke had been making small, sporadic gifts to the school, but in 1896 he and his sons, James (Buck) Buchanan and Benjamin, began a serious philanthropic program. Their gifts culminated in 1925 with an enormous bequest from Buck Duke, which changed the college into Duke University.[45]

Kilgo tried other methods of leading Trinity into the modern world as well. To raise entrance requirements he and the faculty

---

[43] Porter, *Trinity and Duke*, pp. 75-76.

[44] Bassett to Herbert B. Adams, January 16, June 31, 1896 (photocopy), Bassett Papers.

[45] Porter, *Trinity and Duke*, pp. 62-63, 140-68. The president of Trinity at the time was William P. Few, whom Kilgo hired in 1896 as a professor of English.

compiled lists of high schools and academies whose standards met Trinity's. In 1898 the college opened its own college preparatory school on the campus. When Kirkland of Vanderbilt started the Association of Colleges and Preparatory Schools of the South to help the denominational schools standarize their entrance requirements, Kilgo and Mims worked out the arrangements for Trinity's participation.[46] These steps were praised by the faculty but violently criticized by those who feared that Trinity would become inaccessible to poor boys. The criticism mounted when Kilgo made it clear that even young men preparing for the ministry would have to meet Trinity's academic standards. To some, merely hearing "the call from the Lord" qualified a young man to enter Trinity College, but to Kilgo, following his father's lead, ministers needed education as much as anyone else, or more. "Somehow or other the notion is getting abroad that fools are competent to preach the gospel, and the Lord doesn't need any other sort," he said. On the contrary, "God never called a man to preach whom he did not first call to get ready." "If he gets a divine call to go to Trinity, let him understand that it is to study hard and get ready."[47]

Kilgo next undertook, with characteristic vigor, to augment the library's meager holdings. He compared the Trinity library of ten thousand books to Vanderbilt's twenty thousand and Chapel Hill's thirty thousand and announced that some day Trinity must have one hundred thousand books.[48] Under his guidance and with the help of the Duke money, a new library building was built and Walter Page was invited to give the inaugural address when the library opened in 1903. When he traveled through the state conducting preaching missions (or "protracted meetings," as extended visits of a guest preacher were commonly called), he would ask his audience to buy a book for Trinity or to search through their bookshelves for something that might prove valuable to the college. He often got off the train at the Durham depot, his Bible and luggage in one hand and a box of old discarded books in the other.

---

[46] *Ibid.*, pp. 72-73.

[47] Newsom, *Chapel Talks of John Carlisle Kilgo*, pp. 122-24.

[48] Undated MS, Trinity College Papers.

Another part of Kilgo's program was to add a woman's college and a law school to the campus. Like a number of his friends, including McIver, Alderman, Mitchell, and Walter Page, Kilgo was free of the traditional Southern hostility toward education for women, and when the Methodist Female College of Greensboro temporarily closed its doors in 1903 Kilgo made a direct and successful appeal to Benjamin Duke for an added endowment for a women's college.[49] At about the same time he appealed to the Dukes for funds to establish a law school. The funds were again forthcoming, and the new school opened its doors in 1906.

Kilgo's eagerness to expand and improve Trinity College sprang from his religious assumptions. After education had made man prosperous, democratic, and tolerant, it must consider what he called the fundamental questions: the existence of God, the meaning of life, history, and love. "If God is not," he said, "the belief in Him is a superstition that should be cured; if He is, faith in Him is a truth that should be strengthened. State schools should make positive utterances concerning divine existence as well as private and church schools" (Kilgo knew very well, of course, that secular schools could neither ask such questions nor make such pronouncements). Christian education, he wrote in the *South Atlantic Quarterly*, sought "to go beyond mere conclusions of a material logic and ascertain the higher spiritual conclusions of life and history."[50]

God, he said in one sermon which sought to reconcile faith and reason, "sets no limits upon the rights of men to know the truth, but rather stirs them with the energies of His spirit to search it out. God, of all beings, has little patience with, or tolerance of, a timid search for truth." Thus Trinity College was to be no haven for those whose faith was unexamined. "Young men," Kilgo charged in a sermon which opened the school year in 1899, "it is the province of Christian education to make you lovers of, and searchers after truth, and if it fails in this it has no other ground

---

[49] John C. Kilgo to B. N. Duke, June 30, 1903, Trinity College Papers.

[50] John C. Kilgo, "How Does Religion Concern Education?" *South Atlantic Quarterly* 2 (1903):219.

upon which to defend its cause. The Christian college must be a place where truth, all truth, must feel at home and have supreme authority."[51] To his theologically conservative friends who wished to limit the search for truth in the church colleges, Kilgo replied, "In every moment of the world's notable advances the most stubborn resistance has been a creed. Science had to halt at altars and thrones, philosophy has stood fettered at ecclesiastical tribunals, civic progress has been impeded by traditional teaching, and truth has made its way on the earth by hard contentions and tedious advances. It is a horrible treason against the throne of God and the mission of the Holy Ghost to set any limits upon the rights of the sons of God in their efforts to find the truth."[52]

One final quotation reveals the extent of Kilgo's commitment to "truth." The occasion was the beginning of the 1898 academic year, and he set the tone in his annual sermon. As was his practice, he extolled all the maxims of the Protestant Ethic, but his theme was truth. The Spanish-American War had just ended, but this sermon was no paean to peace: "Peace at any price! Give us peace! No Sir, we want truth, we want truth if it brings war, we want truth if it brings destruction, if it splits the old world to pieces. My God, give us truth if it tears the very stars out of the heavens and makes the very throne of God Himself to shake." Those who did not share these feelings, he concluded, had no business starting the school year at Trinity College.[53]

To dismiss Kilgo's words as the bombastic rhetoric of a preacher would be to miss the point. Kilgo understood that the emerging scientific attitude which dismissed from serious consideration everything except the observable or provable was a serious threat to Christian beliefs, or truths, as he said. But more than that, he could also see, as William James saw more clearly, that rationality itself was a way of thinking—a "sentiment," said James—about man and knowledge that presupposed (or accepted on faith) an

---

[51] MS entitled "I Have Kept the Faith," n.d., Kilgo Papers, Duke University Library.

[52] "Opening Sermon," September 17, 1899, Kilgo Papers.

[53] Sermon preached to student body and faculty, Main Street Methodist Church, September 18, 1898, Kilgo Papers.

orderly, knowable world. Kilgo sensed that the academic world was being captured by those who demanded that "every proposition of his faith be tested in the light of scientific assumptions or physical laws.[54] Kilgo could not, as James in fact could not, build a theory of man's knowledge which would encompass and accommodate both reason and faith equally—a theory which would do more than prove the legitimacy of faith by showing the limitations of rationality—but he had perceived what the fundamental epistemological problem of the twentieth century would be.

Paradoxically, Kilgo's brand of Christian education did not convert Trinity into an anti-intellectual "Bible" college. In fact, his actions did not diverge greatly from those of such contemporaries of his as Alderman and Kirkland. Like them, he hired the best men he could lure away from the secular eastern graduate schools. Though he hoped that they would be religious men, he did not require it. In fact, in 1906 he appointed a Jew, Samuel Fox Mordecai, to be the first dean of his new law school. When disgruntled Methodists objected, he told them, "I am not hunting for a churchman, but for a lawyer,"[55] and there the matter rested. He did bemoan secularization (he lamented that "education has come to be wholly an academic affair, and the academicians have consented to the monopoly, if indeed they have not labored to bring it about and to have professional pride in their exclusive control"[56]), but he actively supported his own professionally trained professors. At Trinity formal Christian education consisted of completion of a one-hour Bible course taught by Kilgo himself— one of his innovations—and attendance at weekly chapel services.[57] All in all, he seems to have shared more of the secular faith of his time than he realized. As he put it in one of his chapel talks, "For a college to show a selfish indifference to the problems of human progress is an act of treason to the interest of mankind. . . . One should find in colleges the most serious spirit of labor as he should find the most earnest type of patriotic faith."[58]

[54]Sermon on John 20:26, n.d., Kilgo Papers.
[55]Porter, *Trinity and Duke*, p. 144.
[56]MS on "the meaning of education," n.d., Kilgo Papers.
[57]Porter, *Trinity and Duke*, pp. 64–70.
[58]Newsom, *Chapel Talks of John Carlisle Kilgo*, p. 68.

The men who were struggling to free the Southern mind from prejudice held biases—some apparent, some hidden—that clouded their vision. William E. Dodd, of Randolph-Macon College, already established in scholarly circles as a bright young historian, irritated many of his friends by repeatedly calling attention to the fact that these partisans of freedom had so completely absorbed the ethic of capitalism that they did not think "freely" about capitalism—to be specific, about the way capitalists like Rockefeller had achieved their wealth. Why, he asked, had the Southern Education Board members and the faculty of Trinity College—men who had denounced racists and demogogues and insisted upon discussions of local taxation and the need for better schools—not spoken out on the need for discussing the politics and economics of the trusts? Dodd charged, moreover, that the Southern Education Board had interfered with free speech by refusing to grant funds to probe political and economic questions.[59] To test the Board, Dodd applied for a grant allowing him to establish such discussions. His request was denied in a noncommittal reply. When Dodd suggested making economics the subject of an annual conference, Ogden refused. Then Walter Page refused to publish an article by Dodd of the sort he usually welcomed for the *World's Work*, "The Status of History in Southern Colleges."[60]

Dodd made his criticism public in 1907, one year before he moved on to the University of Chicago, recently established by a munificent grant from Rockefeller. He went so far as to single out Ogden and Rockefeller by name. Reviewing his arguments in "Freedom of Speech in the South," Dodd wrote that no issue should be immune to discussion, not even "the scandalous bribery and tyrannical conduct of certain great corporations." The failure of the Southern education movement to confront economic issues was

distinctly discouraging to those who have hoped still for better things, who even now wage a steady war against backwardness and deeply entrenched tradition. How can we ever bring our people to the highest level of civilization, to real productivity in statesmanship, in letters and the arts, when a great field of activity is closed

[59]Dodd, "Freedom of Speech in the South," *Nation* 84 (1907):383-84.
[60]Harlan, *Separate and Unequal*, pp. 100-101; Page to Dodd, May 23, 1902, Dodd Papers, Library of Congress.

against investigation on the part of the college men, when colleges unanimously decline to entertain any opinions on these subjects. If one great theme is tabooed why not the others? And if Southern colleges fear to speak their minds or fail to find their voices, who will take the lead toward the complete and more perfect freedom? [61]

No one, however, not even Dodd himself, took up the great theme of capitalism. That aspect of the Southern mind is discussed in the following chapter.

[61] Dodd, "Freedom of Speech in the South," pp. 383-84.

6

PROGRESS AND PROSPERITY

With patience and with the rapidly increasing educational and industrial quickening of the South, there is arising within her public life a clearer outlook, a saner Americanism, a freer and juster civic sense."[1] These optimistic hopes, voiced by Edgar Gardner Murphy, sounded reasonable to his contemporaries, who believed factories and schools to be avenues to a richer and better future. They stressed the prosperity sure to be reaped from industrialism and castigated the debilitating attitudes inherited from the plantation South. As early as 1907 Walter Page observed, after one of his trips south, that Southerners had become cheerful, optimistic, and industrious. "They are, of course," he explained, "like the people of the North, or the people of the West, and they needed only the touch of industrial prosperity to reveal not only their kinship but their essential identity."[2]

On economic issues, Page and his friends, with their backgrounds of rural and small-town Protestantism and the Puritan ethic, raised the doctrines of work and self-help to the level of moral absolutes. They became open champions of the South's own

[1] *Present South*, p. 200.
[2] Walter H. Page, "A Journey through the Southern States," *World's Work* 14 (1907):9010.

"middle class"—the capitalists, industrialists, and New South entrepreneurs who shared the bourgeoisie's self-congratulatory image and equated their own good fortunes with the progress of humanity. Southern men of letters became doctrinaire defenders of laissez-faire capitalism (though they raised no objections to government subsidies and tax exemptions for the businessman) and denounced all those who expressed doubts about the sanctity of competitive capitalism. With the exception of Dodd (and even he was orthodox on economic issues most of the time), they contemptuously dismissed as "Bryanesque" any viewpoint to the left of that of Grover Cleveland. Populism was an anathema, and they rarely mentioned socialism and communism at all. For the most part, they were silent about glaring economic problems like farm tenancy and sharecropping. Only one or two mentioned the notorious "convict-lease" system whereby the state leased its prisoners to businessmen or factory owners for a pittance, although the surviving records suggest that these men were cruelly treated. Several courageous voices were raised against child labor, but few gave special attention to the poor of the South. Instead, the intellectuals—even those who fought for child labor legislation—sang the praises of capitalism and the captains of industry—North and South—who steered the treasure ships.

* * *

The explanation of this love affair with middle-class capitalism at a time when intellectuals elsewhere were exposing the "robber barons" and starting to rebel against middle-class values and assumptions lies in the particular history of the South. The young Southerners had seen the factory and the machine introduced into an atmosphere of poverty and defeat. The first signs of a brighter day came in the 1880s, with the advent of cotton mills, touted by their owners and self-appointed publicity men as the salvation of the South. The mills were built, they said, not for mere profit but to bring work, and ultimately prosperity, to the white Southern laborer. Following that patriotic venture (and historians will grant the entrepreneurs a measure of patriotism along with self-interest) came great leaps forward in the tobacco, steel, iron, and coal industries. By the 1890s Danville and Burlington, bolstered by rising cotton prices, were competing with the New England textile cities, Lowell and Waltham. Durham was the home of the Dukes' American Tobacco Company, a colossus duplicated in Winston-Salem by the factories of R. J. Reynolds and his sons. Farther south, through Alabama and Tennessee, smaller-scale Southern entrepreneurs tapped the soil for its coal and iron ore and blasted their way to wealth in iron and steel.[3]

Another manifestation of the changes taking place was the growth of towns and cities. Durham, only a railroad station in 1865, had a population of 6,679 by 1900; Birmingham, a corn-field in 1870, had grown into a major industrial city of 38,415 by 1900. Its blast furnaces belched so much smoke and soot, William Garrott Brown noticed in 1904, that well-dressed businessmen ordered their shirts with detachable collars and cuffs.[4] Birmingham's astounding metamorphosis sent reverberations throughout the South; cities like Wilmington and Spartanburg vied for the title of *the* New South town.[5]

However, the smoke from the foundries, the smell from the tobacco sheds, and the roar of spinning machines were welcome as a sign of life in a land that had known its share of death and dead ideas. Wealth for some would mean wealth for all, schools, hospitals, libraries, roads, parks, homes, clothes—everything the Yankees had. The South, as Woodward reminds us, has had "a long and quite un-American experience with poverty."[6] As Brown put it in 1904, "a proud and pleasure-loving people," Southerners had had the "best of nothing." "Southerners are tired of the threadbare, the makeshift, the second-best," he said. "Sheer hatred of poverty is as common a ruling passion among them as anywhere on earth."[7]

---

[3] These changes are outlined in Philip A. Bruce, *The Rise of the New South* (Philadelphia: George Barrie and Sons, 1905); Broadus Mitchell, *The Rise of the Cotton Mills in the South* (Baltimore: Johns Hopkins Press, 1921); and Woodward, *Origins of the New South*, pp. 107-41, 291-320.

[4] Stanton [Brown], "The South at Work," Boston *Evening Transcript,* April 1, 1904.

[5] Woodward, *Origins of the New South*, pp. 136-37.

[6] *Burden of Southern History*, p. 17.

[7] Stanton [Brown], "The South at Work," Boston *Evening Transcript*, February 25, 1904.

In addition to their first-hand experience of poverty, the intellectuals also could observe the workings of a generous and constructive philanthropy. The beneficence of the Rockefellers, Carnegies, Peabodys, and Dukes in favor of education and public causes was taken as proof of the robber barons' good intentions. Wanting "to do something for the South," as one of the Dukes said to Walter Page,[8] the millionaires bequeathed huge sums and token favors to their chosen causes with equal readiness.[9] For example, in 1904 James B. Duke personally paid for a much-needed vacation in Europe for a weary Kilgo.[10] In 1902, when Bassett complained about his low salary, Benjamin Duke added three hundred dollars to it from his own pocket. The grateful Bassett responded in terms that reveal much about the middle-class mind of the New South:

It is worth being a drudge and taking some hard knocks from your enemies when you realize at last that there are men of sense who appreciate your efforts. Your action brings me that consolation; may there be reason for you to feel abundantly the same consolation for what you have planned for the rebuilding of the intellectual life of the South. I feel more and more that it is a privilege to work in this cause, and I know that the efforts made in Durham are being more and more appreciated everyday by the world of scholars in the North. The work is good work and will live.
There is no other institution in the South which is so well known for its progress in the educational world. Its influence will be greater in the future than it is now.[11]

Despite Bassett's gratitude, however, no one at Trinity could match Kilgo's faith in industrialism or his reverence for the masters of finance. Despite an earlier flirtation with Populist radicalism of the Tillmanite variety in South Carolina, when he settled in Durham he became a staunch defender of trusts, particularly the

---

[8] Walter H. Page to Alice Page, February 17, 1899, Page Papers.

[9] Edwin A. Alderman was moved to say "thank God for Andrew Carnegie" when commenting on the industrialist's aid to the education movement (Alderman, "The Achievement of a Generation," *South Atlantic Quarterly* 5 [1906]:245).

[10] B. N. Duke to John C. Kilgo, December 19, 1904, Trinity College Papers.

[11] Bassett to Duke, January 27, 1902, Trinity College Papers.

tobacco trust, and of Trinity's intimate relationship with the Duke family. Many small tobacco farmers cursed the titans and their high-handed ways, but Kilgo allied himself with arch-conservatives in North Carolina—men like J. R. Caldwell, editor of the *Charlotte Observer*, and Daniel A. Tompkins, a self-made man, cotton mill owner, unrelenting foe of child labor reform, and part-owner of the *Observer*. Both Caldwell and Tompkins were given to decrying the "radical spirit" (read Progressivism) that was "capturing" America and the South.[12] In the *Observer*, which echoed Tompkins' hostility toward all reformers except Prohibitionists, Kilgo defended laissez-faire capitalism and warned of creeping "mobocracy."[13]

Kilgo's economic views reached full expression in 1909 in a panegyric to the American Bankers' Association on "The Democracy and Fraternity of American Industrialism."[14] "In its freedom from class distinctions and the rule of caste," Kilgo began, linking capitalism with the basic freedoms of the Western world, "our American industrialism is the finest triumph of democracy to be found in any part of the world." He recited the capitalist's creed: the great captains had made their way to the top by work, by hard work. Every boy in America has the same opportunity, nothing keeps a man in his place in America but his industry or lack of it, all doors are open to men. "In the fields of our industry each man is to a larger degree the master of his own destiny than he is in any other sphere of American life." To Kilgo's mind, the much-publicized "rags-to-riches" theme of capitalism was not only true, it was proof of capitalism's essential humanity. Capitalism, by rewarding personal diligence and hard work—who in America works harder than Mr. Morgan?"[15] Kilgo asked—was the outward social expression of the Protestant Ethic. Believing that, he regarded capitalism as a spiritual absolute, moral and benevolent, not evil and ruthless toward men, as some had said. He did con-

---

[12] J. R. Caldwell to Kilgo, August 12, 1907, Kilgo Papers.

[13] H. E. Seeman to Kilgo, September 3, 1906, Kilgo Papers.

[14] *South Atlantic Quarterly* 7 (1909):338–46.

[15] *Ibid.*, pp. 339–41.

tend that labor had a right to organize, but he softened his words by assuring the bankers that if labor had such rights then so did capital.[16] Such talk aroused the ire of Josephus Daniels, Kilgo's long-time enemy. If Kilgo "ever had any radicalism in South Carolina," Daniels fumed, "he packed it up and threw it into the Pee Dee River before he crossed into North Carolina, for from the time he arrived, he associated himself with influences that could not have had any sympathy with Tillman or with tillers of the soil."[17]

The fact was that few Southern intellectuals beyond the walls of Trinity sympathized with the "tillers of the soil"; the majority, like Kilgo, put their faith in the fraternity of American industrialists. When William Garrott Brown, on tour for a Boston daily, visited the Carolina Piedmont in 1904, he found tangible support for his notions about the benevolence of capitalism. Durham, he wrote, unlike nearby Hillsboro or Chapel Hill, could boast new roads, better buildings, modern hospitals (one for the whites, another for the blacks), and Trinity, a good college that was rapidly becoming better. What had happened to Durham was the Dukes.[18] To Brown, whose own father had made a success in real estate after the Civil War, the story of Washington Duke's climb from obscurity to wealth suggested the possibilities awaiting other hard-working Southerners. The Dukes were living embodiments of the Puritan ethos, in their personal lives as in their philanthropy. Brown's conclusion was typical of the thinking of his generation; the Dukes represented the "true South," whose "true leaders . . . are the masters in business, the men at the head of the various professions, the strong, capable, thoughtful men in every city and town and country neighborhood." Men like the Dukes had awakened "liberal impulses" everywhere; they were the "guardians of the plain man's opportunity."[19] Brown was not totally

---

[16] *Ibid.*, pp. 334–35.

[17] Daniels, *Editor in Politics*, p. 104.

[18] Stanton [Brown], "The South at Work," Boston *Evening Transcript*, March 3, 1904.

[19] *Ibid.*

ignorant of the steps taken by the plain man's guardians to amass their fortunes, such as rebates, "kickbacks," from shippers, and price and cost manipulations, but he looked to the future, to ends, not means, and dreary, dreamy Hillsboro seemed irrelevant beside Durham's factories, schools, and hospitals.

Publicists like Brown did all they could to make the way smooth for the course of Southern industrial capitalism. They assured their readers that the new day would not spell the end of the South as a land of charm, manners, hospitality, warmth, and sense of place and tradition. The South was entering the machine age relatively late, and so it could reap its benefits while spurning "crass commercialism" and other Yankee imperfections, they said. No one explained how the South was to go about the business of getting rich while avoiding the grosser excesses of the acquisitive instinct. The intellectuals were convinced that a wealthy society based on competition would become a cooperative culture. As Perry Miller suggested about Americans of an earlier age, their dream was that unity would result from the diversity of individualism and American life. Literature and Southern culture would not perish in a machine economy because industrialism was not synonymous with "materialism" or "utilitarianism." "These are theories of life," one professor explained in the *World's Work*, "while industrialism is a means of living."[20] Could a "cultivated man" live in an industrial society, Walter Page asked in 1904. His answer was an unqualified yes. In fact, he predicted that in the new day the number of cultivated men would multiply, for "the most impressive social fact in modern history is the industrial development of the United States."[21] Southerners, to quote him once more, "needed only the touch of industrial prosperity to reveal not only their kinship but their essential identity."[22]

There was one obstacle keeping the South from attaining its share of industrial prosperity. It needed labor, or so its leaders

---

[20] Charles A. Smith, "Does Industrialism Kill Literature?" *World's Work* 4 (1902):2102–4.

[21] "A Cultivated Man in an Industrialised Age," *World's Work* 8 (1904):4980–82.

[22] Page, "A Journey through the Southern States," p. 9010.

thought. Everywhere one heard the lament that the labor supply was not keeping pace with the South's expanding economy.[23] This anxiety sprang in part from a notion widely shared among whites that the Negro was becoming an indifferent and inefficient worker. A wave of hostility toward blacks spread across the South in the 1890s and early 1900s, and many intellectuals helped to give currency to the notion that, whether because of their inherent laziness, biological inferiority, or physical weaknesses, the Negro workers did not measure up to the new demands. Some echoed Alfred Holt Stone, a Mississippi planter and author, who contended that with the restraining hand of slavery lifted, the blacks were reverting to their true lazy natures. At cotton-picking time they could not be relied on. On his own plantation Stone had turned to immigrant labor, such as Chinese, and he urged others in the South to follow suit.[24]

Stone's solution was not new. For years—as early as 1865 in some places—there had been an attempt to lure immigrants southward. By 1900 the industrial revival had aroused new enthusiasm for immigration.[25] Southern writers, including Walter Page and William Garrott Brown, argued that the South should follow the Northern example and try to attract immigrants, particularly northern Europeans, who were similar in attitude to Southern whites. In addition to presenting these arguments directly to the South, Southerners also stated their case in Northern publications.[26]

William Garrott Brown adopted this view as early as the 1890s, and a long trip through the South in 1904 reinforced his position.

[23] See, for example, Walter L. Fleming, "Immigration to the Southern States," *Political Science Quarterly* 20 (1905):276–94; Emily Fogg Meade, "Italian Immigration to the South," *South Atlantic Quarterly* 4 (1905):217–33; Bert James Lowenberg, "Efforts of the South To Encourage Immigration," *ibid.*, 33 (1934):377–84; and Rowland T. Berthoff, "Southern Attitudes toward Immigration, 1865–1914," *Journal of Southern History* 17 (1951):328–60.

[24] Alfred Holt Stone, "The Italian Cotton Grower: The Negro's Problem," *South Atlantic Quarterly* 4 (1905):42–47.

[25] Berthoff, "Southern Attitudes toward Immigration," pp. 329–31.

[26] Fleming, "Immigration to the Southern States," pp. 276–94; Stone, "The Italian Cotton Grower," pp. 42–47; William Garrott Brown, "The White Peril: The Immediate Danger to the Negro," *North American Review* 179 (1904):824–34.

From January to June he traveled as a special correspondent for the Boston *Evening Transcript* and sent back twenty lengthy travel accounts to his newspaper. His accounts, entitled "The South at Work," reflected most of the sentiments common among New South intellectuals. His trip began in Washington, D.C.; from there he went through Virginia and the Carolinas into Florida, and then across the lower South, a section whose history he had recently popularized in his lively book *The Lower South in American History*, through Alabama, Mississippi, Louisiana, and across Texas. In the factories of Birmingham and the plantations of the Delta, Brown found the working South replete with optimism and with jobs to be filled. In Rotarian fashion he announced, in his first dispatch, that the region now realized "as never before what wealth means in the modern world. Along with the craving for it comes the awakening to the possibility of acquiring and creating it, if only her industrial methods can be somewhat improved."[27]

No reader of Brown's articles could fail to see that the South was a land of opportunity. Although he did mention racism[28] (most Southern writers found the subject irresistible), child labor,[29] and the causes of intellectual intolerance,[30] he maintained a respectful distance from these subjects and made only perfunctory references to farm tenancy and sharecropping. He was no "objective" reporter: his job was to find a working South, and he did so. Virginia's fallow land offered farmers "untrod avenues to wealth," he said.[31] South Carolina had cheap and abundant land for "intelligent white farmers"; the cotton mills also offered work.[32]

Alabama and Mississippi had jobs even for non-white immigrants. In the steel mills Brown discovered unions organized and committed to their men. Despite opposition from owners, the

[27]Stanton [Brown], "The South at Work," Boston *Evening Transcript*, February 25, 1904.
[28]*Ibid.*, March 9, April 4, April 7, 1904.
[29]*Ibid.*, March 14, 1904.
[30]*Ibid.*, March 9, 1904.
[31]*Ibid.*, February 25, 1904.
[32]*Ibid.*, March 14, 1904.

unions were growing, Brown admitted.[33] The plantations, like the factories, needed hands, and Brown noted that groups of Germans and Chinese had already arrived and established themselves in some rural areas.[34] They succeeded because unlike the Negro—and Brown wrote that he heard this often—they were willing to work and to be frugal. The Negroes were simply unreliable, the governor of Virginia told Brown, and Aycock echoed his sentiments. Brown was pleased to learn that in Durham the blacks worked well in the tobacco plants; however, he reported, the cotton mill owners refused to hire them because of their "inefficiency." He himself believed that it was a question of work habits, not race.[35] Alfred Holt Stone continued his theme: he and others wanted good, "clean" immigrant workers from the North or northern Europe. Brown transmitted this call to his New England readers wherever he heard it.[36]

Brown's willingness to accept the views of such men as Aycock and Stone reflected his own high level of tolerance for racist pronouncements and his enthusiasm for prosperity, but it also reflected his hope that imported workers would drive Southern whites, particularly the "poor whites," out of their traditional sloth, so that they would become the factory workers of the South. He hoped to see the factory tap, as the plantations never had, the long-dormant energies of these shiftless shanty farmers and hill people, known variously as rednecks, clay-eaters, and white trash. In South Carolina he was pleased to discover this emancipation under way. The poor whites were proving themselves dependable in the mills, coming to work on time and working hard. This was also the case in Louisiana: "It is possible now to live in New Orleans as free from any dependence on the service of negroes as one could in New York or Boston."[37] Though Brown later lamented the fact that the white masses' combination of new-found aggressiveness and traditional racial antip-

---

[33] *Ibid.*, April 1, 1904.
[34] *Ibid.*, April 4, 1904.
[35] *Ibid.*, March 1, March 9, 1904.
[36] *Ibid.*, April 4, April 7, 1904.
[37] Brown, "The White Peril," p. 829.

athies had resulted in discrimination against the Negro in the labor market, his pleasure over the new dynamism of the poor whites did not abate. They are "the South's great unutilized reserve," he said in 1910. Though their "ignorance, inertia, and prejudice had strengthened into a Chinese wall of hopeless conservatism" during slavery days, industrialism had broken down that wall.[38]

Brown's dreams did not stop here: he looked to the day when the South's prosperity would mean a better life for everyone. But he and his friends never questioned the bourgeois dream or doubted its values. Their desire to put people in the factories came only indirectly from a concern for the poor, trapped in their own despair and their debts to planters and mill-town paternalists. In all Brown's travels in the rural South he apparently never talked to tenant farmers or sharecroppers, white or black, nor did he understand the problems of the dirt farmers. It was typical that when he did discuss the "agricultural situation," it was with a group of Birmingham bankers.[39]

* * *

There were some blemishes on the face of Southern capitalism, however, that not even Brown's generation could excuse or ignore. One of the more glaring abuses was child labor in the cotton mills. While not unique to the South, child labor was deeply entrenched there. By 1900 one-fourth of all mill operatives were under sixteen years of age; in many mills children as young as six or seven worked from sunrise to sunset. Upon learning of the extent of the practice, several intellectuals spoke out fearlessly against it.[40] Leading the fight were Edgar Gardner Murphy and a Presbyterian clergyman, A. J. McKelway of North Carolina. They were aided by hundreds of other citizens and were publicly supported by Walter Page, James H. Kirkland, Clarence Poe, and Jerome Dowd (Dowd

[38]William Garrott Brown, *New Politics for the South* (Boston: Houghton Mifflin Co., 1914), p. 114.

[39]Stanton [Brown], "The South at Work," Boston *Evening Transcript*, March 26, 1904.

[40]Irene Ashby, "Child Labor in the Southern Cotton Mills," *World's Work* 2 (1901):1290–95.

was the only person from Trinity College who publicly denounced child labor).[41] A reform sentiment was aroused that eventually affected the national conscience.

Those who battled against child labor were indeed morally outraged at the exploitation of children, even for the sake of prosperity, but it must be admitted that they were distressed because the children being exploited were white. Blacks, including black children, were excluded from most mills. As the reformers said on many occasions, child labor was morally reprehensible and ultimately socially wrong because the South's future citizens were being demoralized or, in some cases, destroyed as effective participants in society. There is little evidence that any of the reformers, particularly Murphy and McKelway, would have been as concerned had the children been black. Black children worked just as hard and just as long on the plantations, but the reformers seldom mentioned them. Moreover, as a later chapter will show, both Murphy and McKelway were apologists for Southern racism.

* * *

The Reverend Mr. Murphy seemed an unlikely candidate for a crusader's role.[42] Rector of a fashionable Montgomery church, St. John's Episcopal, he proclaimed biblical and universal themes in his sermons without pointing to the sins in the city around him.[43] Yet, as a result of his missionary work in the slum sections of Montgomery, he had become aware that in the mills women and

[41] See, for example, Walter H. Page, "The Worst Crime of Civilization," *ibid.*, 4 (1902):2475-76; "Progress in Child Labor Legislation," *ibid.*, 5 (1903):3264-65; Jerome Dowd, "Child Labor," *South Atlantic Quarterly* 1 (1902):41-43; James H. Kirkland, "Ethical and Religious Aspects of Child Labor," *Annals of the American Academy of Political and Social Science* 32 (1908):62-96; Clarence H. Poe, "The South: Backward and Sectional or Progressive and National?" *Outlook* 114 (1916):328-31.

[42] For biographical information on Murphy, see Maude King Murphy, *Edgar Gardner Murphy* (New York: by the author, 1943); Hugh C. Bailey, *Edgar Gardner Murphy: Gentle Progressive* (Coral Gables, Fla.: University of Miami Press, 1968); Daniel Levine, "Edgar Gardner Murphy: Conservative Reformer," *Alabama Review* 15 (1962):100 - 116; and Allen J. Going, "The Reverend Edgar Gardner Murphy: His Ideas and Influence," *Historical Magazine of the Protestant Episcopal Church* 25 (1956):391 - 402.

[43] Edgar Gardner Murphy, *The Larger Life: Sermons and Essays* (New York: Longmans, Green and Co., 1897).

children were working long hours in crowded, unsanitary conditions. In the summer of 1901 Irene Ashby, representing the American Federation of Labor, came to Alabama to investigate mill conditions. She brought her facts to Murphy, who she had heard would offer sympathetic advice and effective help. Her findings, published in the *World's Work*,[44] shocked Murphy. Children as young as six and seven were working twelve or more hours a day—or night, as was often the case. The work brutalized women and children; poor ventilation and flying lint frequently caused pneumonia and other throat and lung diseases. "I am familiar with the slums of two continents," she concluded, "but I can say I have never seen a more pitiful sight than the mill children, nor known little ones for whom the outlook was more hopeless." She went on, "It is not only that they are pale, shrunken and bowed—they look as if their brains were hypnotized and their souls paralyzed."[45]

Murphy responded by conducting his own investigations of these revelations. They convinced him that only a full-scale attack would save the children. He decided to resign from the ministry and became an activist.[46] At the opening session of the Alabama legislature he appeared at the head of a coalition of women's groups which had been campaigning against child labor. They came to lobby and testify on the need for legislative action. At first, Murphy's presence must have been both amusing and irksome to the lawmakers, but he soon convinced them that he was an unrelenting reformer. The mill lobbyists and Bourbon politicians, in league with the mill men, were able to block passage of the proposed legislation and labeled the reformers misguided "female humanitarians" who would destroy the Southern mills and allow New England to win the "textile war."[47] They attacked Murphy, but he only redoubled his efforts. He led the formation of a per-

---

[44] Ashby, "Child Labor in the Southern Cotton Mills," pp. 1290-95.

[45] *Ibid.*, pp. 1294-95.

[46] Murphy, *Murphy*, pp. 43-46.

[47] Elizabeth H. Davidson, *Child Labor Legislation in the Southern Textile States* (Chapel Hill: University of North Carolina Press, 1938), pp. 36-42; Davidson, "Early Development of Public Opinion against Southern Child Labor," *North Carolina Historical Review* 14 (1937):230-50.

manent Alabama Child Labor Committee in 1901. As the committee prepared for the next session of the legislature, scheduled for
1904, Murphy enlisted the support of many prominent Alabam-
ians, including Booker T. Washington.[48]

Murphy knew from Irene Ashby's study of twenty mills that a
large part of the solution to child labor in Alabama lay in New
England. Fully half of the major mills in Alabama were owned
outright by New England capitalists and employed twice as many
children as home-owned mills. In fact, Yankee power was so
strong that one Massachusetts financier had been able to secure
repeal of Alabama's one child labor law in 1893 by promising the
state a new mill.[49] Murphy made an "Appeal to the People and
Press of New England" in the Boston *Evening Transcript*. In New
England it was met with silence. At home officials of the New
England-owned mills responded with insults. One official
attempted to discredit Murphy's case by saying that since he had
relied on a "skillful, female labor agitator" his "grossly exaggerated" charges could be ignored. The attack, he said, was a covert
attempt to weaken the plants and allow labor agitators to unionize
the industry. Child labor reform, while perhaps necessary in some
instances, was but the "entering wedge" for the unions.[50] The
reformers also had to contend with the argument that Alabama
should not act until Georgia and other states did lest it find itself
with prohibitive labor costs while others cornered the market.
Even some Northern carpetbaggers protested that Alabama must
not lead the South to defeat in the textile war with the Yankees,
who did not work children because they had a cheap immigrant
labor supply. Some officials admitted the need for reform but
demanded compulsory school attendance laws first, to ensure that
the unemployed children would not be idle. Others portrayed protection of children as a socialistic infringement upon their "right"

[48]Murphy shared the speaker's stand with Jane Addams in Atlanta in 1903. His
speech is reprinted in *The Present South*, pp. 129–49. See also his pamphlets, "The Case
against Child Labor," "The South and Her Children," and "Child Labor and Politics," in
the University of North Carolina Library.

[49]Ashby, "Child Labor in the Southern Cotton Mills," p. 1293.

[50]Bailey, *Murphy*, p. 72.

to work and to enter into contracts and upon the right of their parents to allow them to work.[51]

These arguments determined the way in which Murphy was forced to plead his case. Since he had a taste for abstractions and believed that even millowners would ultimately listen to reason and morality, he would have preferred to argue on a high moral plane. But circumstances forbade it. He felt compelled to point out the absurdity of assuming that children knew anything about contracts or their "right" to work. He reminded those who talked of "rights" and condemned reform as "paternalistic" that earlier many of them had defended long hours, even for children, and communal mill villages as a paternalistic way of insuring work for the irresponsible poor whites and at least a subsistence standard of living for people who might, left to themselves, live in squalor. "To hear some of our opponents dwell upon the mill as a philanthropy you would suppose that the average child could find in the average cotton mill a comprehensive educational equipment—a sort of institutional civilizer:—a kindergarten, grammar school, high school, university, and a trip to Europe, all in one."[52] Do not believe a word of it, he warned.

When his detractors accused him of being misinformed, he marshaled a wealth of documents, one such being his booklet *Pictures from the Mills*, a collection of damning photographs he had taken in the mills of the city. When critics countered by calling him a sentimental visionary, he told of seeing a small girl, scarcely eight years old, who had been maimed for life in a mill accident. Such injuries resulted from the carelessness of the children operating the machines, he was told, but to Murphy children were supposed to be careless—carelessness was part of childhood. Get the children out of the mills, he demanded, get them into the open air where they can grow into adulthood with sound minds and bodies.[53]

Murphy's Alabama Child Labor Committee circulated petitions and pamphlets, reorganized local pressure groups, and met with

[51] Murphy, *Present South*, pp. 129–49.
[52] *Ibid.*, pp. 138–39.
[53] *Ibid.*, pp. 110–24, 143.

politicians and businessmen. The year 1903 was crucial because the legislature would not meet again until 1907, and Murphy felt it imperative to secure legislation as soon as possible. Hoping to make their pleas as persuasive as possible, the reformers, at Murphy's urging, continued to insist that they wished neither to further unionism nor to harm the mills. Though Murphy publicly admitted that the union leaders had consistently taken the "moral" side of the controversy, and though he questioned the sincerity of those who clamored about the "entering wedge," he insisted that Irene Ashby, Samuel Gompers, and other union officials keep out of the fight in Alabama.[54]

Being conciliatory toward businessmen was not difficult for Murphy. For years he had praised capitalism and its promise for American life and had been a supporter of Southern industrialization even during the height of the child labor dispute. The factory, he said, in one speech against the evil of working children, has become one of the benevolent forces creating civilization; its rightful place is beside the school, the church, and the home.[55] As such a force it dare not ruin itself and society, Murphy argued, and urged the transgressors to do the right and moral thing, to return to "honest" competition. Like Woodrow Wilson, he never seemed to wonder whether ruthlessness and winning by any means was not inherent in the capitalist competitive ethic. He moralized capitalism by urging sportsmanship and other old-fashioned values on the millowners. He had no quarrel with the profit motive: he yearned to harmonize profit and human welfare—which was, after all, the very thing that the capitalists had promised would happen.

Murphy had a pragmatic side to his personality as well, however—it was evident in the educational crusade—which aided the reform cause. Reactionary New South organs like the *Manufacturer's Record* of Baltimore denounced him as "Bryanesque," a "demagogue," and a "hysterian of the masculine gender."[56] But in Birmingham several mill men, fearing radical reform, approached

[54] Bailey, *Murphy*, p. 84.
[55] Murphy, *Present South*, p. 102.
[56] Bailey, *Murphy*, p. 80.

Murphy with a compromise measure to present to the legislature. Upon hearing that Braxton Bragg Comer, a millowner and rising star in the Democratic Party, would participate in their proposal, Murphy agreed. With powerful men presenting it as a sensible reform, the proposal passed. Its major achievement was to establish twelve years as the minimum age (for orphans the limit was lowered to ten years) and sixty as the maximum number of weekly work hours. The first step, Murphy sighed with relief, had finally been taken.[57]

With this victory Murphy emerged as a nationally known champion of human rights. He personified courage and moral conviction and as a speaker radiated integrity. That, along with his growing reputation as a propagandist and planner, tended to obscure his fundamental conservatism, and progressives everywhere looked to him for support and ideas. Northern professors and pundits saluted him as the voice of the "real South," and he was asked to appear in Atlanta with Jane Addams as a principal speaker at the National Conference of Charities and Corrections in 1903. The following year he joined with various Northerners, including Felix Adler, to form the National Child Labor Committee and served as its national secretary for the next two years. He advocated moderate measures and persuaded the leaders of the Committee to gather information before they voiced complaints.[58]

Unfortunately, the reformers fell out among themselves, and Murphy must bear much of the blame. His intractable opposition to federal child labor legislation on the grounds of States' rights conflicted with the Northerners' view that only national legislation could abolish child labor. The clash came to a head in 1906, when a majority wanted to support the Beveridge Bill, which would have made fourteen the minimum age for workers producing goods for interstate commerce. Murphy publicly called for defeat of the bill and urged his friends to follow his example.[59] So powerful was his reputation that the other NCLC members acquiesced in silence.

[57]*Ibid.*, pp. 102-6; Murphy, *Murphy*, pp. 47-50.
[58]Murphy, *Present South*, pp. 129-49.
[59]Bailey, *Murphy*, pp. 94-96.

147

One story has it that President Roosevelt, whose support was considered crucial, was so moved by the force of Murphy's States' rights arguments against the bill that he abstained from supporting it adequately.[60] By helping to block the bill Murphy was partly responsible for delaying federal action for years.

After leaving the national NCLC organization, Murphy turned his attention to Alabama and the forthcoming legislative assembly of 1907. Governor Comer had won his support in 1906 by standing for public education but lost it again in 1907 when he failed to support child labor legislation. Murphy wasted no time. He revived the Alabama Child Labor Committee, made numerous speeches, and poured forth pamphlets on the subject. His pamphlet *A Plea for Immediate Action* demanded a minimum working age of twelve, with a minimum of sixteen for night work, and compulsory school attendance laws. He sent a copy to each member of the Legislature and appeared on opening day to lobby. This time he was successful. A bill incorporating each of his demands passed both houses and received Comer's signature.

For the moment, the fight in Alabama had been won. Murphy knew that not all laws were enforced, but he was justifiably proud and elated. When his old friends of the National Child Labor Committee asked him to return, he seriously considered it, especially when they assured him that they would study conditions in each state before making a decision as to whether to support federal legislation. But failing health forced him to decline. As his replacement, Murphy recommended A. J. McKelway, who had joined the national organization in 1904 as assistant secretary for the Southern states.[61]

Like Murphy, McKelway was an experienced reformer with a first-hand knowledge of child labor.[62] A brusque, energetic man with a penchant for polemics, McKelway joined numerous reform causes, ranging from prohibition to penal reform and anti-gambling laws. By the end of his embattled career, he had moved to

[60] *Ibid.*, pp. 96–97, 107.

[61] Herbert J. Doherty, Jr., "Alexander J. McKelway: Preacher to Progressive," *Journal of Southern History* 24 (1958):179.

[62] For events in North Carolina, see Elizabeth H. Davidson, "Child Labor Reforms in North Carolina since 1903," *North Carolina Historical Review* 14 (1937):109–34.

the North and allied himself with Northern liberals, including Amos Pinchot, Frederick C. Howe, and Walter Lippmann, who yearned for what Lippmann called mastery over drift. During his career, he fought for public education, women's suffrage, the initiative, referendum, and recall, and welfare programs for the poor and unemployed. He was the only major Southern intellectual of his day to denounce the convict-lease system, though he never took an active interest in the issue.[63] All in all, he was, except on the matter of race, one of the most liberal men ever to come out of the South.

Born in Pennsylvania, McKelway was brought to the South when he was a year old, and he grew up as a Southerner. After graduating from Hampden-Sydney College and Union Theological Seminary in Richmond, Virginia, he held pastorates in North Carolina. In 1897 he moved to Charlotte to edit the *Presbyterian Standard*, and there, in the mill country, he came to know child labor. Murphy's writings helped convert him to reform, and by 1901 McKelway had converted the *Standard* into a militant protest sheet. Soon opportunities arose for him to work in more active ways. During the legislative session of 1903, he lobbied for new laws and helped to focus public opinion on the politicians and their promises. That year North Carolina enacted a mild child labor law, establishing twelve years as a minimum age, with a maximum work week of sixty hours for minors. It was a victory of sorts, perhaps a first step. Its chief weakness, thought McKelway, was the absence of provisions for enforcement.[64] The victory was sufficient to convince Murphy that McKelway would be a valuable member of the National Child Labor Committee. When asked to become assistant secretary for the Southern states, McKelway accepted immediately, quit the *Standard*, and resigned his ministry.

Taking Murphy's advice, he spent the next few years touring New England mill towns, boning up on the English history of child labor and reform, and discussing the Southern situation with Mur-

---

[63] A. J. McKelway, "Convict Lease System in Georgia," *Outlook* 90 (1908):67–72.

[64] Davidson, *Child Labor Legislation*, pp. 118–20; Doherty, "McKelway," pp. 177–78.

phy and others.[65] In the summer of 1905 he was back home preparing for the North Carolina legislature's meeting. Josephus Daniels, who opened the pages of the Raleigh *News and Observer* to him, and Governor Aycock provided information and helped him draft a proposal to raise the minimum age to fourteen, particularly for girls, and to outlaw night work altogether for those under sixteen. McKelway was practical enough to heed Murphy's advice to seek a compromise with the millowners. Murphy had high hopes that Daniel A. Tompkins, Kilgo's old friend, might take the lead (Tompkins, although a millowner, was one of Brown's "guardians of the plain man's opportunity" and logically belonged to the intellectuals' "true South"). But Tompkins was contemptuous of all reformers and rejected McKelway's overtures, leaving him with almost no support among the business elite. His words and proposals were ignored. Daniels advised him to give up, but he went into the mills, when he could gain entrance (Tompkins refused to allow McKelway to enter either of his two mills, even without a camera[66]), and took photographs for his pamphlets.

But some gains were being made. The public was becoming aroused, and the mill men (including Tompkins) decided in 1907 that a compromise would take the wind out of the reformers' sails. Led by Tomkins, the mill men proposed a minimum age of twelve years, with the proviso that twelve- and thirteen-year-olds be allowed to work only four months a year. This would allow them to attend school for six months. The proposal included a sliding scale: thirteen- and fourteen-year-olds could work five months a year and have five months of schooling; fourteen- and fifteen-year-olds, seven months of work and three months of schooling; fifteen- and sixteen-year-olds, ten months of work and two months of schooling. With the support of the millowners the legislative process worked smoothly, and North Carolina inched into the twentieth century.[67]

---

[65] A. J. McKelway, "The Child Labor Problem," *Annals of the American Academy of Political and Social Science* 28 (1906):312-26.

[66] Davidson, "Child Labor Reforms in North Carolina since 1903," p. 112; Doherty, "McKelway," pp. 178-80.

[67] Davidson, "Child Labor Reforms in North Carolina since 1903," pp. 115-17.

McKelway's willingness to compromise his principles for concessions did not make him immune to criticism from the mill men. Unable or unwilling to forgive him, they called him a traitor; one of their sheets, the Charlotte *Textile Bulletin*, branded him a "scalawag," a turncoat bought with Northern money. (Men of McKelway's generation often had to endure this particular slander.) At first McKelway ignored the charge, even though Murphy urged him to point out the Southern origins of the NCLC and the number of Southerners in the national organization. By the time he finally replied, the accusations had been widely circulated and had seriously undermined his effectiveness.[68] So thorough and malignant was this character assassination that Wilbur J. Cash, who was the son of a mill superintendent in Gaffney, South Carolina, recalled that "to this day he is remembered in North Carolina, by most people who remember him at all, with angry contempt."[69]

McKelway fared better elsewhere. In Georgia, with the aid of Governor Hoke Smith, another progressive whose political posture was a mixture of racism and reform, McKelway revitalized the reformers and helped them push a compromise measure through in 1906. Next year he was in Alabama helping Murphy. On the national scene his star ascended as Murphy's declined. Senator Beveridge applauded his work and praised his writings,[70] and in 1907 the NCLC brought him to Washington to replace Murphy. His appearance in the capital reflected the dominant attitude within the organization. Though still willing to concentrate on the states and forgo direct agitation for a federal law, the committee leaders leaned toward supporting Beveridge's proposals. In McKelway they had a fighter who had concluded that the mammoth sprawl of America's interstate corporations signaled the emergence of a national economy that no state, or group of states, could hope to control.[71] Murphy now found McKelway such a zealot for federal legislation that he could not discuss the matter calmly with

---

[68] A. J. McKelway, "Child Labor in the Southern Cotton Mills," *Annals of the American Academy of Political and Social Science* 27 (1906):264–65.

[69] *Mind of the South*, p. 229.

[70] Doherty, "McKelway," p. 181.

[71] A. J. McKelway, "The Evil of Child Labor," *Outlook* 85 (1907):360.

him. To anyone who would block federal legislation on the basis of the constitutional case for States' rights, McKelway retorted, "I would deplore the making of any such issue as shall put the rights of the state over against the rights of the child, because the child will win."[72]

However, it was a decade before the children won. When they did, it was with the support of another Southerner whose career outside the South had isolated him from Southern conditions. Woodrow Wilson's years in the North may explain why he did not respond immediately to McKelway's pleas to speak out for child labor reform. As early as 1912, when Wilson was attracting the admiration of educated Southerners, McKelway urged him to broaden his New Freedom to include welfare programs for the poor and the unprotected.[73] Though Wilson remained silent on the need for child labor legislation and vetoed a measure McKelway had supported tirelessly, McKelway retained confidence in him. Wilson finally justified his faith by supporting the Keating-Owen bill, which prohibited interstate commerce in goods produced by workers under fourteen years of age. Wilson signed the bill into law on September 1, 1916. Such was part of the history of what Arthur Link has called the "most significant victory of the social justice movement before the New Deal."[74]

[72] A. J. McKelway, "The Awakening of the South against Child Labor," *Annals of the American Academy of Political and Social Science* 29 (1907):17.

[73] A. J. McKelway, "The Impressions of an Eyewitness," *Outlook* 13 (1913):556.

[74] Arthur S. Link, *American Epoch* (New York: Alfred A. Knopf, 1967), p. 71.

7

AN AMERICAN POLITICS
FOR THE SOUTH

N O GENERATION of Southerners raised on Jefferson and the yeoman ideal could have looked with equanimity upon the South's politics. In the 1890s the last threat to the supremacy of the Democratic Party collapsed with the demise of Populism. Though the South had been solidly Democratic since 1877, when the party had "redeemed" it, there had been various agrarian challengers—the Greenbackers, the Independents, and the Alliance Movement, forerunner of the Populists. Populism, with its radical plans for forging dispossessed blacks and whites into a political coalition, posed such a serious threat that the Redeemers dropped all pretense of maintaining their traditional paternalism and raised the cry of White Supremacy. Let white men gather together to protect themselves from another Negro domination, said men like Aycock. The strategy worked. In the process of vanquishing the Populists, the Democratic chieftains disfranchised the Negro, raised legal walls to segregate him, and emerged as the guardians of the Southern way of life. To question the Democratic Party now meant to question White Supremacy, a heresy tantamount to questioning the South itself. The ideal had become solidarity, not democracy.[1]

[1] Woodward, *Origins of the New South*, pp. 235-63; *The Strange Career of Jim Crow*, pp. 49-96.

The intellectuals were scandalized by all this. To them a closed mind was detestable: they were the heirs of Jefferson, Mill, and Arnold and believed that the political order was simply a larger arena of human affairs, an extension of individuals, which should foster democracy among men by being itself democratic. Instead, they found what William Garrott Brown called the "politics of uniformity," in which the Solid South exalted the prejudices of the masses by calling their narrowness and bigotry patriotism.[2] Most of the intellectuals of Brown's generation despised the idea of the Solid South but remained silent in public. Some, particularly those in powerful positions, aware of the intricate links between politics and racism and mindful of the Savage Ideal, spoke vaguely about the need for "manliness" and political "independence." They reminded their countrymen that Jefferson had been a democrat and that democracy was the American tradition. Angrier men directly attacked racists and politicians. Some went even further, and focused their attack on the Solid South and the demagoguery and climate of ideas that sustained it.

Leading the critics were William Garrott Brown, the ubiquitous Walter Hines Page, William P. Trent, one of the first to speak out, the historian James W. Garner, and John C. Kilgo and Samuel Chiles Mitchell. They mounted their attack from all sides, but their main arguments can be reduced to two: the moral argument that sought to demonstrate the inherent virtue of democracy, and the contention that one-party politics, while ostensibly preserving political power for the South, actually robbed it of any effective voice in national politics. The South's solidarity allowed both major political parties to ignore it, on the assumption that it belonged securely to the Democratic Party.

* * *

The moral argument listed the ruinous consequences of losing political freedom: the people lose control over their society; voting and political debate become meaningless. The people, as Wil-

---

[2] Brown, "The South in National Politics," *South Atlantic Quarterly* 9 (1910): 103–15.

liam P. Trent charged, are at the mercy of the politicians, who keep them under the "despotic sway of party principles."[3] As Brown summed it up, the Solid South "is bad because of its effect on public opinion in reference to our own affairs. It makes for narrowness and bigotry, and against candor and independence. It has frequently caused, and may still be causing, persecution for opinion's sake." The depressing result is that good men, "men of freedom and independent minds," find politics repellent and choose other, more dignified professions, thus leaving the way open for men who, "being themselves without real independence and manliness of mind and temper, have freely invoked bigotry and prejudice and intolerance to overwhelm manliness and independence in others." The South has thus "been depriving itself of the leadership of its best and strongest minds and giving itself over to cheap men: cheap demagogues, cheap machine politicians, cheap partisan journalists."[4]

Not surprisingly, along with this argument went extravagant promises about the results of political "independence." Samuel Chiles Mitchell knew that such independence would bring the South back into national affairs and would encourage good men to enter politics.[5] Edwin Alderman reasoned that an "American" politics would bring the Southerner into the mainstream of national and world opinion.[6] Let nationalism take root, as it had in the North, Mitchell promised, and everything would be improved.[7] "It will mean far more than the liberating of genius," Trent had predicted in the 1890s. The collapse of the Solid South would mean "the checking of political corruption, and the uplifting and ennobling of every citizen who has a vote to cast. It will mean a freer play of mind that will affect advantageously every industrial, educational, and social interest. It will mean that the

---

[3]Trent, "Dominant Forces in Southern Life," p. 52.

[4]"The South in National Politics," pp. 110-11.

[5]"The Nationalization of Southern Sentiment," *South Atlantic Quarterly* 8 (1908):110.

[6]Alderman, "The Growing South," p. 10382.

[7]Mitchell, "Nationalization of Southern Sentiment," pp. 111-13.

South's cry for capital and more laborers will be fully responded to, that in wealth and culture its people will soon be abreast of those of other sections, that they will contribute in ample measure to the glory of the Union, and that they will grapple with their own peculiar problems with confidence and enthusiasm."[8]

In all these pronouncements about democracy, certain assumptions were made. Democracy was identified with freedom—an equation highly cherished by the intellectuals of the New South—and the two terms were used interchangeably. As society was regarded as the sum of individuals, democracy was the rational way for individuals to live together. This high regard for democracy was but another expression of a set of assumptions about the goodness of natural man: a free man is a good man, and men living in a democratic society will therefore be good—if they have proper leadership. Thus the duties of politicians were regarded as seriously as those of teachers and other groups on whom the "real South" was thought to depend.

The contrast between these assumptions and the reality of the South around them forced the critics to say that the South had yet to try "democracy." Many turned to history to prove that although the South had known democracy once, in Jefferson's day, slavery had extinguished it. Most of them believed, like Trent, that slavery had caused the South to turn to reactionary, insular politics. Then came war and Reconstruction, each with its pressures for uniformity of opinion, then the frustrations of defeat and poverty, compounded by ignorance and fear of the black man. The resulting narrow, unyielding, sentimental, and anti-democratic spirit romantically identified the Solid South with virtue. Through it the white man had enslaved himself and deadened his best impulses. "Independence" was truly Southern, the argument ran, and the Southerner ought to exercise this birthright. No party, not even the "white man's party," stood above freedom. Freedom meant voting one's mind rather than one's fears.

By "independence," the intellectuals actually meant the freedom to vote Republican. They did not for a moment mean the

[8]Trent, "Dominant Forces in Southern Life," p. 52.

right of Southerners to vote for any and all political parties—the Populists, for example, or some other left-wing party. For them "democracy" was synonymous with mainstream American politics and capitalism, while Populism, with its demands for free silver, government regulation of the economy, and, in some cases, nationalization, was an aberration, a mixture of agrarian foolishness and poor-white hostility toward respectable government. It was a "class movement" aimed at advancing, by whatever means, the fortunes of a particular economic class at the expense of the general welfare. The notion that Southern Populism offered a concrete example of political disagreement among Southerners over basic issues, that Populism could have given the South a two-party structure and hence an "American" politics, did not occur to them. A rich opportunity to explore deep social and economic ruptures of Southern society was thus lost.

This very blindness tells something more about these middle-class social critics, however. In the decade following Populism's collapse—when criticism of the Solid South peaked—the intellectuals attempted to destroy the myth that political solidarity was the Southern way, always had been and always would be. But in attempting to document their case that independence was Southern, they invariably pointed to the South before the Civil War, at a time when the main political conflict was between Whigs and Democrats. No intellectual ever publicly pointed to the recent past, the 1890s—an era their audience knew from personal experience—as an example of true "independence." In 1910 James W. Garner, an expatriate Mississippian who held the chair of history at the University of Illinois, traced the history of independent political thought in the South in an article for the *Annals of the American Academy of Political and Social Science*.[9] He lashed out at racist politicians, denounced the Solid South, and urged the "intelligent men of the South" to lead the way. He offered an argument from history: "In the old days, *before the civil war* [italics mine] . . . the white people were pretty evenly divided

[9]"A New Politics for the South," *Annals of the American Academy of Political and Social Science* 35 (1910):172–83.

among themselves on all political questions upon which a mutual difference of opinion was possible." Yet since then, "while the material and intellectual progress of the south during the last quarter of a century has been extraordinary, politically it has remained stationary. Its political thought has been absolute and undisputed. During this time the southern white people have exhibited little difference of opinion on the great political issues that have divided the people of the rest of the country."[10]

To understand Garner and the others one must keep in mind that Populism violated their value system. It proposed a coalition between blacks and whites and stressed the common interests of the two races. Although white Populists were not entirely unprejudiced or equitable in their treatment of black Populists, still they came together for political rallies, picnics, and songfests; whites and blacks shared the speakers' stands and preached unity. In Populism the South had a genuine example of an indigenous attempt at racial cooperation, an attempt to lift massive numbers of Southerners of both colors out of poverty. It offered an alternative to the paternalistic racism of the Democratic Party, which kept itself in power by controlling black votes.[11] In spite of their repeated calls for "racial cooperation," the white intellectuals were psychologically unprepared to accept Populism's challenge to White Supremacy and could not believe that all blacks should be allowed to vote.

The intellectuals' reaction to the disfranchisement of the blacks and their eagerness to believe that disfranchisement would help destroy the Solid South is further evidence of this attitude. The disfranchisers threw back the Populist challenge and insisted that the Democratic Party had blocked any future "Negro domination"; they promised that, with the Negro removed from power, whites could divide without fear of being conquered by an ignorant bloc of blacks. Some reformers, like Bassett, Brown, and Walter Page, grew alarmed at the authoritarian and violent methods used by the Democrats in accomplishing this "reform,"

[10]*Ibid.*, pp. 172-73.
[11]Woodward, *Strange Career of Jim Crow*, pp. 49-96.

but the majority agreed with the principle of disfranchisement.[12]
Edwin Alderman summed up the majority position when he called
it one of the "most constructive acts of Southern history."[13] To
understand the belief that disfranchisement could be a step toward
bringing democracy to the South, it may help to look at the
reverse of this assumption. On the other side of the coin of
"Negroes are inferior" was "whites are fundamentally good and
rational." Disfranchisement, then, was an end which justified the
violent and brutal means.

In the decade following the "reform" of Southern politics it
became a standard contention of the critics of the Solid South
that with the Negro excluded whites could and should exercise
their new freedom and vote for "real" issues. They appear amaz-
ingly naive. First of all, many urged that the new laws be enforced
fairly—by which they meant that such suffrage qualifications as
literacy tests and the payment of a poll tax be applied equitably to
both blacks and whites. Yet most admitted that disfranchisement
was racial in intent: how else could one explain the grandfather
clause that gave the vote without restriction to anyone who had
fought, or whose grandfather had fought, in the Confederate
army? Only Bassett and a few others could see that the whole
concept was fraudulent and thus could never be applied in a moral
or ethical manner. As conceived by the politicians, it had nothing
to do with equality or ethics. Such notions existed only in the
minds of those for whom it was an article of faith that the leaders
of the South would be moral. Second, the argument that whites
should vote for "real" issues betrays a radical overestimation of
the rationality of Southern whites and a concomitant failure to see
racism as an overwhelming concern of the white masses. The intellectuals had no everyday contact with blacks and knew little of
the psychological gratification provided for poor whites by racism.
They could not see that when voting ritualistically for the "white

---

[12] Walter H. Page, "The Grim Humor of the Alabama Election," *World's Work* 3
(1902):1585; "The Suffrage in Virginia and Alabama," *ibid.*, 2 (1901):799; "The
Supreme Court and the Suffrage," *ibid.*, 6 (1903):3491–92.

[13] Alderman, "The Growing South," pp. 10377–78.

man's party" white Southerners were expressing, in a very "real" way, the central resolve of the white South—to keep the Negro subservient.

* * *

Of the critics who contended that the South's impotence in national affairs stemmed, ironically enough, from its very solidarity, none probed that irony or castigated the Solid South as bluntly as William Garrott Brown. In the South, Brown charged, even schoolchildren know that both Democrats and Republicans could ignore the South at election time, the Democrats because it was safe, the Republicans because they considered it hopeless for one of their candidates to win there. As the nation voted Republican and elected presidents and congressmen, the South elected Democrats who had to hold out their hands respectfully in Washington to receive small political plums. For fully half a century, Brown wrote in 1910, "the South has had, except for poor Andrew Johnson's incumbency of an office whose powers he was not permitted to exercise, no President, no Vice-President, no Chief Justice of the Supreme Court."[14] Neither party, within memory, had nominated a Southerner as its presidential candidate; except for Cleveland's Cabinet, Southern politicians were virtually ignored; of twenty-eight Supreme Court justices only five had been Southerners. Compare these facts with the South's great political power during the first seventy-five years of the republic, said Brown, and the South's current plight was evident: "The change is therefore very great, one of the most striking to be found in the history of any country. Indeed I am not sure that in any country there ever did occur such a shifting of power across geographical lines." He pointed out that this loss was more than one of political power alone: the South no longer leads the nation, or even contributes significantly to its leadership: "If for fifty years there has been a single great general law or policy initiated by Southerners or by a Southerner, or which goes or should go by any Southerner's name, the fact has escaped me."[15]

[14]Brown, "The South in National Politics," pp. 105–6.
[15]*Ibid.*, p. 106.

Since the early 1890s this sort of criticism had been emanating from the Southern colleges, particularly the private ones, safe in their independence of state financing. William P. Trent and his colleagues at Sewanee openly condemned political uniformity and insisted that it was democracy, not political parties, which deserved one's loyalty. In 1896 Burr J. Ramage, prompted more by youthful optimism than by facts, predicted that a growing spirit of nationalism and rationality in the South had doomed sectionalism and political solidarity.[16] In 1902, when President McKinley was assassinated, both Ramage and John Bell Henneman, speaking at a college memorial service, said that McKinley's national attitude revealed to the South how its politics had kept it isolated from the main currents of American life.[17] Neither, however, could match Trent's outspokenness. The Solid South had not only undermined political life (the region had not produced a "thoroughly great statesman since Jefferson") but had also corrupted its own citizens, Trent charged in 1897. "It has rested like a black cloud over every schoolhouse and college, has enfeebled and diverted to wrong ends the power of the press, and has hampered or thwarted the genius of every youth of lofty aspirations."[18]

After 1900, the year Trent moved north, Trinity College overshadowed Sewanee as a source of political criticism, just as it did in scholarship and literature. Nestled in the Piedmont, where the drama of race and politics shoved all other issues from the stage, and nurtured by the Dukes' Republican money, Trinity College became a cradle of independent thought. Its leading spirit was Kilgo, who loathed the Democrats for their racism and their "unsound" economic ideas. The Solid South, to his mind, was an anachronism. From the chapel pulpit he exhorted students and faculty to view politics critically, to stand above petty political considerations, to exercise independent judgment, and to be in all things national-minded. He celebrated McKinley's election in 1896 with the admonition: "If we are true Americans, if we know the

---

[16] "Dissolution of the Solid South," pp. 493–510.

[17] Burr J. Ramage, "President McKinley," *Sewanee Review* 9 (1901):483–88.

[18] Trent, "Dominant Forces in Southern Life," pp. 51–52.

real meaning of citizenship, if we have in us genuine patriotism, we know it is the duty of each to do all within his power to make Mr. McKinley a great president." "No man's party is bigger than his country," he went on. "Learn that! Stand up in the line for your nation. Be an American above anything else."[19] On other occasions Kilgo warned that "bossism" and "graft and impudence" were the logical results of an unchallenged, uncriticized political party which thought of itself as the government.[20] Not even the sleepiest undergraduate could have missed the meaning when Kilgo thundered one day in chapel, "I say frankly to you this morning, I belong to no political party, I exercise that much freedom. I go as a quarry slave under no political lash."[21]

Several of Kilgo's colleagues said amen to his political preachings. As we have seen, Bassett directed his fury at the racism of the people and their politicians. In a more gentle fashion, Edwin Mims shared Bassett's and Kilgo's passion for independence. An early admirer of Theodore Roosevelt, in 1905 Mims tried to refute the notion that T. R. was unsympathetic to Southern problems: "Mr. Roosevelt has the highest possible appreciation of the Southern people . . . he has done all in his power to maintain pleasant relations with them, and . . . he has an evident desire to do them service."[22] Like others who pleaded with Southerners to change their ways, Mims from time to time half-consciously appealed to their racism, as when he argued that Roosevelt did not favor social equality. He agreed with the "best thought" of the South, with the editors of "an increasing number of newspapers, the presidents of the best Southern colleges, and the substantial business men of various States." "There can be no doubt," continued Mims, "that he is one of the most interesting and forceful men of the world today."[23]

He is the sort of Republican, said Mims the following year, whom Southerners should like.[24] At the same time, William P.

---

[19] Quoted in Newsom, *Chapel Talks of John Carlisle Kilgo*, pp. 47–48.

[20] *Ibid.*, pp. 95–98.

[21] *Ibid.*, p. 114.

[22] "President Theodore Roosevelt," *South Atlantic Quarterly* 4 (1905):58.

[23] *Ibid.*, pp. 50–51, 59–62.

[24] "The Independent Voter in the South," *ibid.*, 5 (1906):1–7.

Few discovered a new independence among Southern voters.[25] When Taft was elected in 1908, Few commended the new President's interest in the South. There was a new nationalism in the White House, he said, which signaled the death of "sectionalism" in the Republican Party. Now it was time for the funeral of Southern sectionalism as well.[26]

Walter Page prematurely sent flowers to its funeral. His antagonism toward the racism of the Southern Democrats was matched by his commitment to democracy and a revived Republican Party. Characteristically, Page argued that the Democratic Party, in spite of its claims, did not represent the real South. James K. Vardaman, Page wrote in 1903. was only "one type of man who has lived in isolated ignorance."[27] Ben Tillman, South Carolina Democrat and race-baiter, Page was confident, would be swept out of office as industrialism and education, the factory and the school, created a culture of independent and truly Americanized voters.[28]

Page's optimism allowed him to find numerous indications that Southerners were daily being converted to an independent stance. He was greatly encouraged in 1900, for instance, when Senator John L. McLaurin of South Carolina refused to support Bryan or free silver.[29] When McLaurin threatened to join the Republican Party in protest, Page took up his cause. The *World's Work* portrayed the senator as a national-minded man who had put principle above party, yet was not crucified by the Southern press.[30] Later the Senator's speech "Breaking Up the Solid South" appeared in the *World's Work*.[31] Though he subsequently found action more expensive than words and remained a Democrat, Page continued to hope that some day the McLaurins of the South would have the courage of their convictions.[32]

[25] William P. Few, "Southern Public Opinion," *ibid.*, 4 (1905):1–12.

[26] William P. Few, "President Eliot and the South," *ibid.*, 8 (1909):184–91.

[27] "How the Negro Rules in Mississippi," *World's Work* 6 (1903):3941–42.

[28] Page, "Barbarism and Heroism in the South," *ibid.*, 2 (1901):1250–51; "The Meaning of Tillman," *ibid.*, 3 (1902):1912–15.

[29] Page, "Is the Solid South To Yield at Last?" *ibid.*, 2 (1901):797–99; "The Secession of Senator McLaurin," *ibid.*, p. 798.

[30] Walter H. Page, "The Democratic Split in South Carolina," *ibid.*, p. 910.

[31] *Ibid.*, pp. 985–86.

[32] Page, "Commercialism to Divide the South," *ibid.*, pp. 910–11.

Like the others, Page was most hopeful about Southern politics during the Roosevelt-Taft years. He warmed to T. R. immediately. Southerners, he said, could identify the Rough Rider with such romantic figures as Jeb Stuart and Stonewall Jackson. When Roosevelt toured the South in 1905, Page hailed the visit as "one of the best acts of his presidency." Now everyone would know that the President was an American above sectionalism.[33] Later that year, Page's enthusiasm had increased: "His winning of the South has, at least for the time and let us hope for all times, rid us of sectionalism and of the hideous indecencies of Southern personal abuse as a political weapon or pastime."[34] Later, a more subdued Page merely called Taft another friend of the South.[35]

* * *

Most Southerners who found the Solid South unsavory had to content themselves with grumbling about the "dominance of a single party" or the "despotic sway of party principles." As literary men they were far from the seats of political power, and knew that Southerners seldom read books or learned journals. They also feared that the public protests they did make had little effect on the politicians and less on the white masses, who voted Democratic as regularly as they attended Sunday services—in some places being a Republican was as dangerous as being unbaptized.

But, as the crusades for education and child labor suggest, the critics had a practical, activist bent. William Garrott Brown's political activities provide a case in point. Off and on during the last years of Roosevelt's administration and the first years of Taft's presidency, Brown was living in Asheville, North Carolina, in order to recuperate from tuberculosis. He wrote regularly for national weeklies and from 1905 on supplied weekly editorials to *Harper's Weekly.* In addition to providing him with good copy on the state's political turmoil, his enforced stay in Asheville brought him into contact with several young Republicans who intended to

[33]"The President and the South," *ibid.*, 9 (1905):5783–84.

[34]"The President and the Southern People," *ibid.*, 11 (1905):6917–18.

[35]"Republican Party in the South," *ibid.*, 15 (1908):10060–62; "Can Mr. Taft Break the Solid South," *ibid.*, 16 (1908):10516–17.

create what Brown called a real party instead of a machine which existed mainly to dispense federal patronage and to send bribed delegates to national conventions. Brown liked his new adventures. Given a free hand by George Harvey, owner of *Harper's Weekly*, Brown attended party caucuses and state conventions, interviewed the reformers, and waged an editorial campaign to persuade Roosevelt, and Taft, and other high-ranking Republicans to disavow "corrupt" machine-dominated parties and to encourage "honest" men.[36]

Aside from Woodrow Wilson, Brown was probably the most politically minded Southern intellectual of his generation. From his earliest years Southern politics had both fascinated and repelled him. When he graduated from Howard College in the 1880s he harbored political ambitions, and tradition more than justified his hopes. His family, successful in business, had at one time been moderately well-to-do black belt farmers—some called them planters. Physically he was rather imposing, tall (six feet six inches) and lanky, had a deep, drawling voice, and excelled in debating. He epitomized the traditional Southern gentleman whose logical province would be politics. But in the new world of Southern democracy, where race- and Yankee-baiting garnered more votes than manners and family, one had to hustle and woo the masses. (One may suspect that Brown's own experiences provided the basis for his frequent assertion that the South's best young men shunned politics.)

Brown chose, instead, to be a writer. After graduate work in history at Harvard he wrote histories, biographies (including, of course, one of Robert E. Lee), and other pieces, including an unsuccessful novel. However, he maintained his interest in politics. He organized Harvard's first Southern Democratic Club, where he frequently debated Republicans. An early admirer of Grover Cleveland, Brown campaigned for him throughout Massachusetts and Rhode Island in 1892. Though Cleveland offered him a minor position in his administration after the election, he regretfully

---

[36] Bruce Clayton, "An Intellectual on Politics: William Garrott Brown and the Ideal of a Two-Party South," *North Carolina Historical Review* 42 (1965): 319–34.

concluded that his poor health incapacitated him for the job. When Harvard offered him a library position, he settled down to make his name as a historian instead. He loved history, and his style was readable and lively: his *Lower South in American History* was received with admiration by both historians and literary critics.

He continued to be attracted toward the more robust world of American politics, however,[37] and his enforced stay in North Carolina gave him a chance to observe at first hand the workings of democracy in the South. In the election of 1908 the Republican vote increased significantly everywhere, particularly in Georgia, Texas, Tennessee, Kentucky; in North Carolina, the increase was more than 32,000. "Independence" it would have been, Brown chortled in *Harper's*, had North Carolina gone for Taft.[38] Shortly after Taft's inauguration he predicted that "it is only a question of time until a majority in southern states will favor the Republican party."[39] He soon found, however, that Southern Republican parties were often mere outlets for distributing patronage and that Taft's nomination had depended on the votes of Southern Republican delegates. He concluded that the situation could never be remedied until national party leaders stopped dealing with the machines, and, accordingly, he set out to expose the machines and to persuade Taft to help "respectable" Republican parties.

Brown had hit upon a vital political link. Since the South supplied one-third of the national convention delegates, control of the Southern machines was crucial for Republican presidential aspirants.[40] Roosevelt had killed Mark Hanna's presidential ambitions in 1904 by controlling the Southern Republican machines.[41] Four

---

[37]Stephenson, *Southern History in the Making*, pp. 27–51.

[38]"The New Republican Party in the South," *Harper's Weekly* 53 (1909):5.

[39]William Garrott Brown, "President Taft's Opportunity," *Century Magazine* 78 (1909):252–59.

[40]Dorothy G. Fowler, *The Cabinet Politician: The Postmasters General, 1829–1909* (New York: Columbia University Press, 1943), pp. 291–96.

[41]John Morton Blum, *The Republican Roosevelt* (Cambridge, Mass.: Harvard University Press, 1954), pp. 43–48.

years later he instructed Frank Hitchcock, his Assistant Postmaster
General, to line up the South for Taft, and Hitchcock then became
Taft's Postmaster General.[42]

At the invitation of a small but vocal group of reform-minded
Republicans, Brown attended the North Carolina state Republican
convention in the summer of 1908. There he got an introduction
to patronage politics. Shortly afterward he confided to a friend,
"I felt that Taft, though perhaps a fit man, was not fairly named,
and democracy may require us to vote for Bryan."[43] But not even
democracy could induce him to do that. Brown voted for Taft, in
spite of his attitudes toward Hitchcock, and then set out to convince them to disavow the Southern machines.

There was good reason for Brown to hope that Taft might
cooperate. In 1906, speaking in Greensboro, he had declared that
in states where no "respectable" party existed federal patronage
should be given to Democrats.[44] This was a policy Brown and
Walter Page had been urging for some time, the theory being that
white Southerners would thus learn to trust the Republicans,
while the local parties, bereft of patronage, would be forced to
reorganize. (That such a policy would also greatly strengthen the
White Supremacy Democrats was never explored by Brown or any
other critic of the Solid South, nor did they acknowledge that the
machines were racially mixed holdovers from Reconstruction days
and thus represented at least some blacks.) The intellectuals were
elated that Taft seemed to be moving toward a new Southern
policy. In 1908 he broke Republican precedent by campaigning in
the South, announcing as he traveled that as president he would
represent every American, North and South.[45] Brown's reaction
was one of delight: Taft showed "a general interest in the South-

[42] Henry F. Pringle, *The Life and Times of William Howard Taft*, 2 vols. (New York:
Farrar and Rinehart, 1939), 1:347.

[43] Brown to Charles W. Thompson, June 23, 1908, Brown Papers.

[44] Daniels, *Editor in Politics*, p. 488.

[45] William Garrott Brown, "Mr. Taft, the South, and the Negro," *Harper's Weekly* 53
(1909):4. It is not known how influential Brown may have been in Taft's decision to
come South, but Brown wrote that he had "set a number of influences at work to induce
Taft to come South" (Brown to J. Elwood Cox, November 14, 1908, Brown Papers).

ern question as we have not seen matched in any President since Lincoln."[46]

Following the election Brown arranged for Walter Page to meet Taft in order to persuade him to speak before the North Carolina Society of New York and to announce his Southern policy.[47] In that speech Taft recalled the South's past glories and insisted that he was not going to "rehearse the painful history of Reconstruction" nor to quarrel with the new racial order. He valued "respectable" Republicans in a white man's democracy. The Constitution was not "inconsistent with the South's obtaining and maintaining what it regards as its political safety from the domination of an ignorant electorate.[48] Soon after, Taft returned to the South hoping to attract its support. He again attacked the Southern political machines and reiterated these racist views.[49]

Nevertheless, throughout 1909 Brown kept a close eye on Hitchcock and patronage and frequently warned him to remember Taft's promises. The President's first appointments in the South seemed proof of his sincerity: he chose a conservative Southern Democrat for a federal post in South Carolina and gave Democrats federal judgeships in Alabama. As Brown saw it, Taft's attitude and his appointments had "fairly knocked the breath out of more than one Southern Republican machine."[50]

However, there was more to be known about Southern Republicanism and the promises of national leaders. Through his friend Thomas Settle, who had originally brought him into the party in North Carolina, Brown met various other Republicans bent on taking over the state organization. He liked Congressman John M. Morehead, of a distinguished and philanthropic family, and industrialists J. Elwood Cox and Daniel A. Tompkins (whose opposition to child labor legislation was discussed earlier). They seemed to be

[46]"Mr. Taft, the South, and the Negro," p. 4; William Garrott Brown, "To William Howard Taft: Greetings," *Harper's Weekly* 53 (1909):6-9.

[47]Brown to William R. Thayer, November 13, 1908, Brown Papers.

[48]Taft, *The South and the National Government* (n.p., n.d.).

[49]Woodward, *Origins of the New South*, p. 468.

[50]William Garrott Brown, "He Means What He Says," *ibid.*, p. 4.

good men who symbolized a "growing spirit of independence."[51] At the convention of 1910 the reformers gained control of the platform committee and turned over the writing of the platform to Brown. "We renew our allegiance to the Republican policy of protection," Brown wrote, though he himself was a free-trade man, because "the Southern states, and North Carolina in particular, have profited by that policy in the past, and have every reason to expect increased benefits from it in the future." The platform ended with the declaration that the party did not exist merely as a "machine for distributing federal offices and electing delegates to national conventions."[52]

Among these reformers Brown found a significant number of influential Southerners who had been converted to Republican tariff policies and who would some day, if they were encouraged, vote their economic convictions rather than their fears. Still, the overall outlook was bleak. From Morehead, Brown learned that three-quarters of the Republican Party members were committed only to patronage. By 1910 Brown was convinced that Taft had no interest in reforming the machines and that federal appointments were going almost exclusively to machine men. It was in this mood that he sought to bring new pressures on the President and the machines.

Late in 1910 he began a series of interviews about the South with Taft's personal secretary. In these Brown argued that Taft had a strategic opportunity to foster Republican sentiment in the South. He could do this with political safety because he would surely be renominated in 1912. The real fight would come in the election, in which Southern electoral votes might be important. Brown pointed to several signs that the South was ready to convert to a respectable Republicanism: the growth of the iron and textile industries in Louisiana and Alabama would mean a growing commitment to tariff protection. He foresaw a revolt of Gold Democrats from the Bryanized party (Morehead, Tompkins, and

---

[51] John M. Morehead to Brown, March 8, July 2, 1910, Brown Papers.
[52] Copy in the Brown Papers.

others like them had already joined the Republicans, he pointed out, and others would follow). He reminded the President that with disfranchisement the whites would feel free to divide, but the administration's appointments were shoring up the corrupt parties which made "a disgusting mockery of representative government."[53] Taft replied that he agreed completely,[54] but no policy changes occurred as a result.

In May 1911 Brown returned to Taft, in a letter suggesting a presidential pronouncement that no one in the administration was to trade patronage for Southern delegates. The President's popularity would be enhanced, Brown admonished, because "the step is demanded, as it has for years been demanded, by every consideration of fairness and square dealing." Furthermore, "it is right in itself, because the practices aimed at are wrong and mean and dangerous to our institutions."[55] To aid his appeal, Brown sent copies of his letter to Taft's friends, including Senator Henry Cabot Lodge, who replied, "I well know not only the character of the Southern delegates but the part which they have played." Taft's secretary replied that the President was indeed pleased with the showing his party had made in the South.[56] However, no such public statement was forthcoming. Taft, with an eye to the nomination in 1912, realized that he needed the Southern delegates. From Roosevelt's corner came words that sounded suspiciously like campaign talk, and though Roosevelt had given him the Southern delegates in 1908, Taft was in no mood to return the favor. Brown understood the situation in mid-1911, when he learned that Taft liked his proposals but did not want at the moment to commit himself to any specific changes.[57]

In the meantime, Brown tried to convince some newspaper or magazine to investigate the Southern Republican parties. First he approached the New York *Times*, explaining that while he himself

---

[53] Brown to Charles W. Norton, October 13, 1910, Brown Papers.

[54] Taft to Brown, November 3, 1910, Brown Papers.

[55] Brown to Taft, May 29, 1911, Brown Papers.

[56] Henry Cabot Lodge to Brown, June 1, 1911; A. Piatt Andrew to Brown, June 18, 1911, Brown Papers.

[57] Andrew to Brown, June 18, 1911, Brown Papers.

could not do the required leg work, he would put a reporter in touch with informed Southerners and write the introduction and conclusion. The reporter would be a Southerner, with Washington experience, though "not a muckraker."[58] When the *Times* rejected the offer, Brown proposed the plan to *McClure's Magazine*, then to *Harper's Weekly*.[59] Both turned him down, but he kept pressing the matter in his weekly editorials for *Harper's*.[60]

Brown knew North Carolina politics personally, and acquaintances of long standing kept him informed of the party's doings in Alabama. Alfred H. Stone, who had publicly criticized Roosevelt's handling of patronage in Mississippi, kept him posted on events there. From Texas, Colonel Edward M. House, later destined to share Woodrow Wilson's friendship and burdens, reported that one man had controlled the patronage in his state under both Roosevelt and Taft.[61] Brown's anger increased. In May 1912 he said of the newly chosen Southern Republican delegates: "The mass of Southern Republican delegates chosen this year are not merely products of the same old methods employed in 1908. They are . . . the very same men or the same kind of men that have been coming up to the Republican conventions and naming Republican candidates for something like forty years. This scandal has been flagrant for decades, but this year it is so very flagrant that one cannot help hoping something will, at last, be done about it."[62]

* * *

But by the summer of 1912 Brown and the other critics of the Solid South had their attention diverted from democracy and machine politics to Woodrow Wilson's ascending star. Though Wil-

[58] Brown to Charles W. Miller, January 3, 1911, Brown Papers.

[59] Brown to Edward S. Martin, November 27, 1911, Brown Papers.

[60] William Garrott Brown, "The Tariff and the Southern Republicans," *Harper's Weekly* 55 (1911):4; "Alabama's Insurgents for Taft," *ibid.*, p. 4; "The Insurgents and the Southern Postmasters," *ibid.*, p. 5.

[61] Alfred Holt Stone to Brown, January 1, 1912; Edward M. House to Brown, December 14, 1911, Brown Papers.

[62] William Garrott Brown, "The Scandal of the Southern Delegates," *Harper's Weekly* 56 (1912):5.

son's drive toward the White House had sputtered in 1911, after his reforms had alienated New Jersey political bosses, he regained momentum in 1912 when he fashioned a new ɔrganization headed by Southerners, including William G. McAdoo and Walter Hines Page.[63] The second echelon of this group included Edwin A. Alderman, William E. Dodd, and A. J. McKelway. An early admirer of Wilson, Page was stressing his "vision" and "statesmanship" in the *World's Work* as early as 1911. In May of that year he wrote, "The figure of Woodrow Wilson is rapidly taking on national proportions."[64] In 1912 the *World's Work* serialized Wilson's "New Freedom";[65] William Bayard Hale and others contributed admiring articles and biographical sketches.[66] Page and Alderman kept an eye on Wilson's chances throughout the summer of 1912 and kept each other informed of new developments. When Wilson won the Democratic nomination by dislodging Bryan, Alderman acknowledged his excitement "that the mortar board instead of the slouch hat has become the symbol of democratic leadership."[67]

Unlike Page and Alderman, Brown did not know Wilson personally. As a writer for *Harper's Weekly* he could not ignore him, as its owner, George Harvey, was a supporter of Wilson as early as 1906 and praised him to everyone he knew.[68] At first Brown was not impressed: "By the way," he wrote to his editor, "can't you coax the Colonel down off the moribund Wilson hobby? I know President Wilson, and admire him, But . . . ! You and I are in the running if he is."[69] Brown did admire Wilson's Manchesterian economic notions and his corresponding hostility toward Bryan's "radicalism," but when Wilson started to temper his criticism of

[63] Arthur S. Link, *Wilson: The Road to the White House* (Princeton: Princeton University Press, 1947), pp. 313–16, 329–37.

[64] Walter H. Page, "The Ending Month," *World's Work* 23 (1911):14293.

[65] Seven installments of the "New Freedom" appeared in *ibid.*, 25 and 26 (1912).

[66] William Bayard Hale, "Woodrow Wilson: Possible President," *ibid.*, 22 (1911): 14439–52.

[67] Alderman to Page, July 12, 1912, Page Papers.

[68] Link, *Wilson: Road to the White House*, p. 359.

[69] Brown to Edward S. Martin, May 19, 1909, Brown Papers.

Democratic bosses and political corruption and to speak menacingly of the "money power," Brown grew alarmed. He admonished Wilson: "Don't, we beg of you,—I will be old fashioned and *implore* you—don't throw away what Cleveland kept, what Roosevelt lost—the confidence of men of your class."[70] For whatever reason, Wilson did return from economic issues to issues of political reform, which pleased Brown.

During the campaign, Brown said little about Wilson, leaving the singing of his praises to Walter Page and Colonel Harvey. He concentrated on Taft and Roosevelt, the Bull Moose candidate. Throughout the summer of 1912, during Roosevelt's unsuccessful attempt to win the Republican nomination, Brown attacked Roosevelt for his new-found radicalism. "I am not a Republican," Brown confided to a friend, "but have thought the most pressing duty of the moment was to smash Roosevelt, and have contributed my editorial mite chiefly to that end."[71] He also contributed his mite toward smashing Taft and the Republicans. Perhaps Brown's general disappointment with Taft's Southern policy explains his attacks on the Republican Party during the campaign. A typical editorial, "The Scandal of the Southern Delegates," castigated the Republicans for having "striven ignobly among themselves for the personal profits" of the machines: "If their strife has at last aroused and disgusted the country, they have themselves alone to thank for their own and their party's shame."[72]

Wilson's victory exhilarated Brown and most Southern intellectuals. "We have a new deal," Page wrote excitedly to a friend.[73] McKelway interpreted Wilson's election as a victory for progressive politics over "privilege."[74] The stalwart democrat William E. Dodd, of the University of Chicago,[75] was equally elated, as were David T. Houston, Thomas Nelson Page, and Clarence Poe. But none

---

[70] Brown to Woodrow Wilson, October 30, 1911, Brown Papers.

[71] Brown to Jeremiah Smith, May 5, 1912, Brown Papers.

[72] Brown, "The Scandal of the Southern Delegates," p. 5.

[73] Page to Henry Wallace, November 8, 1912, Page Papers.

[74] McKelway, "Impressions of an Eyewitness," p. 566.

[75] Dallek, *Democrat and Diplomat*, p. 70.

could match Page's enthusiasm. "I have a new amusement, a new excitement," he wrote to Alderman, "a new study, as you have and we all have who really believe in democracy—a new study, a new hope, and sometimes a new fear; and its name is Wilson." Page's excitement sprang in good part from the fact that in Wilson he and Alderman had "a man somewhat like us," a man "whose thought and aim and dream is our thought and aim and dream."[76] He was everything the intellectuals summed up in their image of the good man: Southerner, gentleman, moralist, professor, author, administrator, Christian, and Democrat. He, like them, honored competitive capitalism and sought through reforms and appeals to conscience to protect it from radical schemes that would destroy the profit motive and private property. In his celebration of the "little man," the "man on the make," the hardworking, thrifty, God-fearing, uncomplaining solid citizen, the theme of "The Forgotten Man" resounded.

Wilson in turn recognized the Southern intellectuals as kindred spirits. He welcomed Page's advice and sought his views on possible Cabinet appointments. For Attorney General, Page suggested Andrew J. Montague, the former governor of Virginia whose advocacy of public education and good roads had won him the admiration of many Southern intellectuals. He represented, said Page, "the old (genuine) Southern gentleman and statesman class."[77] When Wilson asked what he thought of Josephus Daniels for a Cabinet appointment, Page reminded him that Daniels had been "the vicious mouthpiece of the inquisition" in the Bassett affair and that he was a narrow-minded reactionary on race issues and a neo-Populist as well. "Josephus Daniels is a most industrious and ambitious man with the good quality of being able yet to learn as readily as in youth," Page admitted, but added, "he had few chances to learn in his youth." Daniels was anybody's man, Page said, definitely "not of Cabinet size."[78] What Wilson thought of Page's advice is unknown, but Daniels became his Secretary of the Navy.

[76] Page to Alderman, December 31, 1912, Page Papers.
[77] Page to Wilson, undated memorandum, Page Papers.
[78] Ibid.

For a time, Wilson considered Page himself for a Cabinet appointment. His interest in America's natural resources made him a possible candidate for Secretary of Agriculture, and various men, including Clarence Poe, recommended him for the job.[79] Page, doubting his own qualifications, supported David F. Houston, who got the post.[80] Wilson then considered Page for Secretary of the Interior, but his Northern advisers vigorously opposed a white Southerner in that position. Wilson finally decided to give Page an ambassadorship.[81] Though Page was at first undecided, he did accept the offer, sold his controlling interest in the *World's Work*, and departed for the Court of St. James.

The election of Woodrow Wilson signaled the end of the South's isolation from national politics. Everywhere in Washington, as C. Vann Woodward has observed, one heard a softer accent and noticed Southern Democrats in powerful places usually filled by Northern Republicans.[82] Wilson's Cabinet included at least five Southerners, and his closest adviser was Colonel House of Texas. In Congress Southern Democrats chaired nearly every important committee and held top positions in both houses. Chief Justice White, of Louisiana, presided over the Supreme Court. Thomas Nelson Page joined his cousin Walter in the diplomatic corps as the American ambassador to Italy.

And what of the Solid South? After 1912 one hears little about it. When events invalidated the realistic argument, it may have been less noxious to the intellectuals' sensibilities than it had earlier, at least this was doubtless the case for some, whose hostility toward Southern politics was primarily based on their sense of political impotence. William Garrott Brown did continue to attack it. However, his declining health prevented him from enjoying the South's new power and from carrying on his battle. He interpreted Wilson's election as a challenge to the South and warned that if

---

[79] Poe to Page, December 20, 1912, Page Papers. Poe told Page that he was running editorials in his behalf in the *Progressive Farmer*.

[80] Page to Clarence H. Poe, December 24, 1912, Page Papers.

[81] Arthur S. Link, *Wilson: The New Freedom* (Princeton: Princeton University Press, 1956), pp. 18–19.

[82] Woodward, *Origins of the New South*, pp. 480–81.

Southern Democrats did not act "responsibly" and in a "national manner," they could not hope to stay in power: "Let the South through its newspapers and other organs of public opinion, sustain its representatives in that attitude, and the country will not regret what it did election day."[83] He further stressed the South's need for a second party. In January 1913 he castigated an Alabama newspaper for saying that there were not enough Republicans in Alabama to "hold a state convention in a big hall." Such talk, he said, was a defeatist acceptance of the Solid South. Both Democratic politicians and partisan editors wanted to keep their hold "on a too unanimous public"—"we are tempted to use Grant's language and say 'a too damned unanimous public.'" "Little cliques and machines" still controlled the Republican parties, he said, and "no well-wisher of the South can be content to see its political life unhealthily different from the rest of the Union."[84]

Nor did the mere presence of Southerners in Wilson's administration mollify Brown. The Cabinet was "the weakest in my recollection," he confided to a friend—too many Southerners were being appointed.[85] When Colonel House protested that Wilson was having difficulty finding good Democrats in the North and West, Brown replied that he knew of many qualified Democrats in Massachusetts alone.[86] He thought Walter Page a "good man" but perhaps unduly radical on some subjects. He had done some good work but was simply not qualified for such a position. As Brown put it to House, Page was "an expert hatcher of other birds' eggs."[87]

Early in April 1913 Brown complained that *Harper's Weekly* was not severe enough in its criticism of the new administration. "In my judgment," he wrote to the editor, "we ought to live up to our promises and treat it just as we have others."[88] Shortly after

[83]William Garrott Brown, "The South and the Election," *Harper's Weekly* 56 (1912):4.

[84]William Garrott Brown, "The Republicans and the South," *ibid.*, 57 (1913):4.

[85]Brown to Edward S. Martin, March 2, 1913, Brown Papers.

[86]*Ibid.*

[87]Brown to Edward M. House, December 3, 1912, Brown Papers.

[88]Brown to Edward S. Martin, April 3, 1913, Brown Papers.

this, however, the *Weekly* changed hands and its format was radically changed. Brown died in 1914, and his death marked the end of an era of political criticism in the South.

* * *

As it proved, the intellectuals were wrong: schools and factories were built long before the Solid South collapsed. Looking back, it is clear that all along its critics were too optimistic—perhaps "naive" would be a better characterization of their prophesies about the fate of Southern Democrats. But one suspects that, in part at least, their frequent farewells to the politics of uniformity were rhetorical, uttered in the hope of changing men's minds. Perhaps, too, as publicists they exaggerated the redemptive powers of democracy.

Part III

THE CENTRAL THEME OF SOUTHERN HISTORY

INTRODUCTION

Southern history since 1914 reveals the failure of the intellectuals to redeem the white South from the Savage Ideal. They can hardly be blamed for failing to solve vast and deep-rooted social problems far beyond the power of their words or acts. They were trying to change and shape that elusive thing called public opinion and cannot be held responsible for Southern history. Yet one must acknowledge the racist way in which they interpreted and pursued their ends. From the building of public schools to the attempt to alter the South's economic and political structure, they were all too willing to sacrifice or ignore the Negro. From the perspective of the black Southerner the public school movement meant that his schools would be isolated and inferior; the achievement of industrial prosperity depended upon a continuing supply of cheap labor, black and white; the movement to democratize Southern politics rested on an explicit acceptance of disfranchisement; the education crusade and the intellectual rationale for White Supremacy permitted only a token concern for black schools and black voters. America's great commitment to equality was deferred in part because of the actions of Southern intellectuals: they helped to increase the gap between blacks and whites, helped to intensify fear and prejudice through their advocacy of rigid separation of the races, and, ironically, thus helped nourish the Savage Ideal.

The intellectuals did not realize the consequence of their words and actions (though they were aware of their immediate racial effects) because they trusted the white South. They were, in Reinhold Niebuhr's phrase, "children of light," who foolishly underestimate the tenacity of evil and who, thinking themselves good, are blind to their own corruption. Their identification of "the South" with white Southerners obscured the central theme of Southern history: the enduring presence of the Negro. As black man, slave, former African "savage" converted to the white man's religion and to Anglo-Saxon ways, the Negro has been the South's one great absolute, through slavery, secession, war, defeat, Reconstruction, and all that has happened since. Dismiss him, and the very idea of the South becomes meaningless. This one fact the intellectuals could not grasp.

All of which brings us to John Spencer Bassett, who came close to understanding the central theme of Southern history and whose clash with the Savage Ideal seemed to his contemporaries the epitome of all that was wrong with the South. Bassett exposed the fraudulence of disfranchisement and of trying to found a democratic society on White Supremacy. He sensed that the white South was sacrificing the Negro to its own political and psychological needs. His words were scathing; he paid no homage to shibboleths, racial fears and myths. Here was a man who had begun to see the South from the vantage point of the black Southerner. And then he was silenced. Though they "won" at Trinity in 1903, in reality the intellectuals and the South had lost.

No one will ever know what effect the incident had on Southern thought, but never again in Bassett's time did a white Southerner question or attack white racism with his insight and passion for exposing its evil. Perhaps his colleagues held their tongues for fear that irate words might add to the black man's burden. This much is clear: after Bassett, white Southern racial thought was expressed in a subdued, abstract way. The prevailing image of the white Southern intellectual became that of a scholarly, benign man who felt "concern," not outrage, over the Negro's plight. Far too often that concern, compelling enough in some men to give them an insight into the psychological damage racism inflicts on master and slave, obscured the fact that the intellectuals' prinicipal concern was for the whites who were "forced" to live with Negroes.

Such a climate was unhealthy—Wilbur J. Cash, for instance, had to struggle against this subtle form of racism—because it created the illusion of innocence in the intellectual community and allowed some of its members to air blatantly racist sentiments. Had Bassett's approach prevailed, such men might have been discredited in intellectual circles. As it was, however, the majority accommodated themselves to the racists in their midst and sought, as a middle road between overt racism and a diatribe on the scale of Bassett's, to convert institutions and the public to a humane and benevolent attitude toward the oppressed race. However questionable this approach appears in the light of Southern history, at the time it had the advantage of being sane, reasonable, and, given the circumstances, feasible. But a price was paid for such an attitude, however reasonable it may have been. The black man lost the support of the intellectuals, and they forfeited the opportunity of cutting through the trappings of racism to attack the Savage Ideal.

8

THE INTELLECTUALS AND
SOUTHERN RACISM

ONE SPRING DAY in 1897 W. E. B. Du Bois was walking down an Atlanta street on his way to meet Joel Chandler Harris, the editor of the Atlanta *Constitution* and creator of the Uncle Remus tales. Harris, so Du Bois had been assured, represented the better sort of white Southerner, a man with the interests of the Negro at heart. But the slender, intense young Du Bois, a black man from Massachusetts with a doctorate from Harvard, never kept his appointment. "Walking to his office," Du Bois recalled years later, "I passed by a grocery store that had on display out front the drying fingers of a recently lynched Negro." Then and there he was convinced that the enormity of the white South's racial crimes made it a matter of little importance to blacks whether they could trust even the better sort of Southerner.[1] That silent hand pointed to a deep-rooted sickness in the souls of white folks.

* * *

Du Bois's decision was fully justified. Lynchings, particularly the violent, brutal ones of the sort which enraged Andrew Sledd, disgraced the South. Lynchings combined with race riots, racist poli-

[1] Ralph McGill, "W. E. B. Du Bois," *Atlantic Monthly* 216 (1965):78.

ticians, a scurrilous press, and a racist literature to imprint White Supremacy on the Southern mind.[2] Newspapers, often the official organs of the avowedly racist Democratic party, regularly referred to blacks as "niggers," "coons," and "sambos" and luridly described Negro crime.[3] The disfranchisers discovered that race-baiting was the best issue they had yet found. Even after disfranchisement and segregation were complete, this abusive and violent language continued from patricians like John Sharp Williams of Mississippi as well as from such figures as Ben Tillman and Cole Blease of South Carolina, whose exploitation of racism embarrassed even Wade Hampton and the original disfranchisers.[4] Senator Tillman, a popular Chautauqua speaker, repeatedly defended racism and, frequently, lynchings as well. Following Theodore Roosevelt's celebrated dinner with Booker T. Washington in 1901, described by one newspaper as the "most damnable outrage which has ever been perpetrated by any citizen of the United States,"[5] Tillman said, "The action of President Roosevelt in entertaining that nigger will necessitate our killing a thousand niggers in the South before they will learn their place again."[6] This racism in politics frequently spilled over into violence. All four of the major race riots of the period occurred after elections in which racism had been the major issue. Each riot left Negroes dead and Negro

---

[2] *Origins of the New South*, pp. 350-51.

[3] See, for example, the editorials and articles in the Richmond, Virginia, *Dispatch* for July 16 and 27, 1890, March 3, 1891, September 1, 1892, April 27, 1893, August 29, 1899, and May 21, 1900.

[4] Here is an example of John Sharp Williams' thoughts on the subject: "You could ship-wreck 10,000 illiterate white Americans on a desert island, and in three weeks they would have a fairly good government, conceived and administered upon fairly democratic lines. You could ship-wreck 10,000 negroes, everyone of whom was a graduate of Harvard University, and in less than three years they would have retrograded governmentally; half of the men would have been killed, and the other half would have two wives apiece" (quoted in Rayford Logan, *The Negro in the United States* [New York: Van Nostrand Co., 1957], pp. 50-51). For Tillman's views, see Francis B. Simkins, *Pitchfork Ben Tillman* (Baton Rouge: Louisiana State University Press, 1944), pp. 394-404. According to Simkins, Tillman's justifications for lynchings were "merely emphatic repetitions of words heard wherever Southerners forgathered" (p. 404).

[5] Quoted in Dewey Grantham, Jr., "Dinner at the White House: Theodore Roosevelt, Booker T. Washington, and the South," *Tennessee Historical Quarterly* 17 (1958):116.

[6] *Ibid.*, p. 117.

property destroyed. "It is evident," commented one Southern newspaper in 1900, "that the grand idea of white supremacy has become the stalking horse of anarchy in this part of the Union."[7]

In the summer of 1908, Georgia completed the disfranchisement of its blacks. It was less than two years after the notorious Atlanta race riot and represented the political triumph of White Supremacy in the South. When Edwin Alderman surveyed the Southern scene for the *World's Work* from his vantage point as president of the University of Virginia, he wrote that the South's future had never seemed brighter.[8] The growth of the public school movement heartened him; so did the achievements of industrialism. And the Negro question, while admittedly a difficult one, was being satisfactorily answered—since the white Southerner was developing "a certain scientific-mindedness in intellectual approach and mental habit." He admonished his readers, most of whom were Northerners, that on the race issue "the best Southern thought on this matter is neither optimistic nor pessimistic, but watchful and steady."[9]

Alderman misrepresented "the best thought." Southern intellectuals were anything but watchful and steady; his words ignore or deliberately conceal the racism of the white Southerners. Several men of his generation whom he knew and respected eagerly defended racist politicians, explained away lynchings, and blamed the blacks for "provoking" brutality from the whites. Of these racist intellectuals, the most prominent was Thomas Nelson Page, a Virginia aristocrat whose picturesque novels of magnolias, verandas, and contented, faithful darkies were highly popular.[10] In the 1890s, before racial attitudes had hardened, Page had helped prepare the way for White Supremacy. In fiction and essays he portrayed Negroes as hopelessly degenerate, especially freedmen, a menace to democracy as long as they voted, and an unwanted,

---

[7]Quoted in Woodward, *Origins of the New South*, p. 351.

[8]Alderman, "Growing South," pp. 10373-83.

[9]*Ibid.*, p. 10378.

[10]See particularly *In Ole Virginia* (New York: Charles Scribner's Sons, 1887); *Red Rock* (New York: Charles Scribner's Sons, 1898).

alien race among the Angle-Saxons. "What of value to the human race has the negro mind yet produced?" Page asked in 1896. Negroes of distinction, he announced, had white blood in their veins, and even they had "in no single instance, attained a position which in a white man would be deemed above mediocrity." No white Southerner would consent to being "ruled" by the ignorant, vicious, brutish blacks.[11]

Page remained reactionary throughout the next decade. To him disfranchisement was an act of statesmanship quite in keeping with the South's oldest tradition, slavery. To be fair, however, it must be admitted that he never sought to delude himself or his Northern readers that disfranchisement was not really aimed at Southern blacks.[12] His apology for lynchings was a bit more artful. Though he conceded that Southern lynchings were a "barbarity" which had to be stopped, and that only about one-fourth of those lynched were real or suspected rapists, he went on to defend them as a righteous response of a public determined to convince the Negro that he could not rape white women and go unpunished.[13] Let the blacks stop committing "the crime," Page wrote, and the white South would abandon the punishment. Negroes had to be taught, as they were in the days of slavery, to keep their places—or feel the wrath of their masters. Some social organization as effective as slavery must be established, he concluded, because "the negro had the same animal instincts in slavery that he exhibits now."[14]

Page had a plan to reestablish this sort of social control. He had rejected the idea of deporting the race—a solution advocated by his friend and cousin Philip A. Bruce, the historian, as early as 1889[15]—as "impractical." Amalgamation Page found "utterly

[11]Page, *The Old South: Essays Social and Political* (New York: Charles Scribner's Sons, 1896), pp. 306-20, 343-44.

[12]Page, "The Disfranchisement of the Negro," *Scribner's* 36 (1904):15-24.

[13]Page, "Lynching of Negroes," pp. 34-37.

[14]*Ibid.*, pp. 44-48.

[15]L. Moody Simms, "Philip A. Bruce and the Negro Problem, 1884-1930," *Mississippi Quarterly* 19 (1966):356.

wrong." In 1904 he proposed that the "good" Negroes be put in charge of "all the rest" and held accountable for their conduct. "It might even be required," Page went on, "that every person should be listed and steadily kept track of."[16] Ten years later, this line of thought found expression in Clarence Poe's proposal that the white South arbitrarily "relocate" the Negro population into specific defined areas in the South. Segregated from the whites, the blacks could then be "controlled."[17]

Bruce, like Page a Virginian, though less caustic in his public pronouncements about the Negro, expressed notions similar to Page's in his early writings. His major work, *The Plantation Negro as a Freedman*, laid down what would become the givens of the next decade's racists: Negroes were immoral, unethical, childlike, and "naturally" given to thievery.[18] He advocated disfranchisement a year before the movement began in Mississippi. Over the next twenty years, he continued to urge measures that would keep Negroes in their place: since the Negro harmed the South and, besides, was losing out in the "struggle for survival," he should be deported to Africa.[19] Bruce knew almost nothing about Africa but frequently discussed the "savages" there and the potential role of American "Africans" (a pejorative term for him) in helping them. His deportation proposal fell on deaf ears, however, and by the turn of the century he had given up the idea. By this time the triumph of White Supremacy, he thought, made repression or deportation unnecessary.

In 1911, looking back over the Negro problem for the *Sewanee Review*, Bruce praised the great enactments of Southern statesmanship. These were the disfranchisement of the Negro, prohibition of racial intermarriage, racial separation in education and public conveniences, and residential segregation in the cities. If these

[16] Page, "Lynching of Negroes," pp. 47–48.

[17] Poe, "What Is Justice between the White Man and the Black in the Rural South?," *Publications of the University of Virginia Phelps-Stokes Fellowship Papers* (Charlottesville: University of Virginia Press, 1915), pp. 44–48.

[18] *The Plantation Negro as a Freeman* (New York: G. P. Putnam's Sons, 1889), pp. 77–79, 86–92, 129–33, 144–59.

[19] Bruce, "The Negro Problem of the South," *Conservative Review* 2 (1899):278–80.

rules were strictly enforced, Bruce assured his readers, the Negro would slowly but inexorably "revert back to the original pure African type."[20] What this scary prediction portended for "the South" he neglected to say. At this point he lost interest in the Negro problem—as did most men of his generation—and turned to writing history.

The most insensitive of the intellectuals, however, was not a conservative Virginian of the old order, like Bruce, but A. J. McKelway, the preacher and reformer. The reason for his attitude is unknown, but he paraded his racism as boldly as he denounced child labor and other injustices. He was the first to defend publicly outbursts of racial violence which he feared might outrage Northerners, but his were not the usual genteel "explanations" of Southern racism that readers had come to expect from men like Alderman. Using racist language, he accused Negroes of being the cause of violence and murder by whites. Even after the notorious Wilmington riot of 1898, McKelway assured readers of the *Outlook* that, though it ended with eleven Negroes dead and hundreds more injured, it was justifiable in the light of the Negroes' refusal to accept their disfranchisement gracefully.[21] Far from being a purposeless, irrational mob, the rioters were reacting to a situation no decent white man could tolerate. The "riot achieved its purpose," he said, and "business has resumed its normal conditions."[22] Two years later, when North Carolina completed the legal arrangements for White Supremacy, McKelway reassured his Northern readers that no rights had been violated. "Good government" would return to North Carolina, he promised.[23]

Later, when his reform battles carried him into the Deep South, McKelway seized other opportunities to defend Southern racism. He was in Georgia in 1906 at the height of Hoke Smith's successful White Supremacy campaign. In a series of articles for the *Out-*

[20]"The Evolution of the Negro Problem," *Sewanee Review* 19 (1909):386, 390.

[21]"The Race Problem in the South: The North Carolina Revolution Justified," *Outlook* 60 (1899):1057–59.

[22]*Ibid.*, p. 1059.

[23]"North Carolina Suffrage Amendment," *Independent* 53 (1900):1955–57.

look, McKelway portrayed the new governor as a "statesman" and praised his part in disfranchising the Negroes.[24] As before, he attacked the blacks. After Smith's campaign was over, there was a riot in Atlanta in which white mobs "looted, plundered, lynched, and murdered for four days," to quote a recent historian.[25] McKelway defended the riot for restoring the South to the whites. It "has taught the negroes a good lesson," he wrote, and demanded to know, if a Northern city such as New York were inundated by a wave of "Chinese brutes," what "understanding" the North would seek from the white South.[26] One may ask, at this point, whether McKelway, Page, and Bruce did have the best wishes of both races at heart, as they claimed.[27]

* * *

Yet the McKelways were far to the right of the majority of their contemporaries, whose compassion for the black man prompted their attempts to dilute white racism. It is to these moderates that one must turn in order to place Southern racial thought in perspective and to understand the racial assumptions of even the best educated, most intelligent, and most articulate Southerners.

In his own day, few such men were more articulate than William Garrott Brown. He concluded, fully three decades before U. B. Phillips popularized the notion, that the Negro and the white South's "way of dealing with him" was the "central theme of Southern history."[28] At bottom, Brown was an old-fashioned paternalist whose insights sprang, in part, from his experiences as a boy in the Alabama black belt. He never found reason to question

---

[24]"Atlanta Riots," *Outlook* 84 (1906):557-62; "The Suffrage in Georgia," *ibid.*, 87 (1907):63-66; "Hoke Smith: Progressive Democrat," *ibid.*, 94 (1910):267-72.

[25]Woodward, *Origins of the New South*, p. 350.

[26]McKelway, "Atlanta Riots," pp. 557, 559.

[27]McKelway, speaking of the North Carolina Red Shirts who terrorized and killed Negroes, commented: "It is difficult to speak of the Red Shirts without a smile. They victimized the negroes with a huge practical joke, the point of which was the ridiculous timidity of the black advocates of *manhood* suffrage" ("North Carolina Suffrage Amendment," p. 1956).

[28]Brown made this argument many times, but its fullest expression came in *The Lower South in American History*, pp. 26-65.

the orthodoxy of Negro inferiority, but at the same time his patrician biases kept him from glorifying all whites. Somewhat as
Murphy and others had done, he both feared and resented the
white masses. But his fears of the uneducated whites went deeper
than those of most of his contemporaries and led him to examine
the assumptions of white racism—even his own. Time and time
again he attempted to rethink the stock racial mythologies of his
day. He became convinced that, in the course of the white South's
relations with the Negro, particularly since 1865, a final and
irrevocable decision had been made to keep him, as the saying
went, on the bottom rail. If you grasp that, he said, you understand the South.[29] Racism bore a high price, he wrote in
1910, and payment of that price had kept the South "from entering more fully and potently into the life of the republic."[30]

Though Brown was forever telling Southerners to put aside the
race issue and consider matters "on their own merit," he himself
found it impossible to divorce the Negro from any matter that confronted the South.[31] He saw disfranchisement as a "reform," the
work of "good men," but wondered whether, judged against the
best of English or Jeffersonian standards, it was a victory for good
government. And how could White Supremacy be a victory for
free government—particularly when the basic antagonism between
the two races remained and whites were forced to be "solid"?
"The trouble is not in laws and institutions; it is in the men,"
Brown wrote in 1902, "not in the organization of the body
politic, but in its composition."[32] He could not take the next step,
however, and see that the new laws might ensure further antagonism by institutionalizing racism.

[29] For reviews of *The Lower South in American History*, see *American Historical
Review* 10 (1904):192-94; *American Journal of Sociology* 9 (1903):140; *Political
Science Quarterly* 17 (1902):701-2. William H. Glasson reviewed it for the *South
Atlantic Quarterly* (1 [1902]:293-94). For a favorable view of Brown's writings by
editors, see Frederick C. Howe to Brown, November 18, 1903; J. Henry Harper to
Brown, September 25, 1905; Hamilton Wright Mabie to Brown, June 3, 1903; Alexander
Jessup to Brown, December 8, 1903, Brown Papers.

[30] "The South in National Politics," p. 107.

[31] This was the burden of his "The South in National Politics."

[32] *The Lower South in American History*, pp. 265-68.

He did see, as did several others, the gravity of the Negro's economic plight. Beginning with a question that was rather common among whites—"are the two races of equal capacity for accumulation?"—he offered evidence in 1902 and again in 1904, that in landholding and the accumulation of other forms of wealth the Negro was falling behind the white man.[33] He admitted that Negroes lived in a caste society, with all its debilitating effects: "Life does not offer to them the same inducements to endeavor which it offers to the white man about them. . . . In the struggle for the things of this world, the negro is not lured on, as the white man is, by the visions of the kingdoms of this world, and the glory of them. . . . Black men, I suppose, cannot help feeling that what they can win from life is always short of what they might win if they were white." At this point Brown changed his course: "The caste arrangement which has succeeded slavery is of necessity . . . deadening to ambition. On the other hand, it does give the white man, as slavery did, the power, and the individual selfish motive to make the negro work."[34] To make the Negro work— that imperative overwhelmed his perceptions.

Brown's conscience was somewhat relieved by his belief, which was commonly held, that the South still offered the Negro his best chance for employment, that Northerners allowed Negroes to vote but did not want to work next to them. The Southerner, on the other hand, was long accustomed to working side by side with Negroes. After all, he reasoned, as Booker T. Washington had, the chance to earn a decent living was far more important than the right to vote.[35]

Brown had an opportunity to act on these principles when workers of the Georgia Railway went on strike in June 1909. White enginemen refused to work because black firemen had been given regular runs; they demanded that regular runs be reserved for

---

[33] Stanton [Brown], "The South at Work," Boston *Evening Transcript*, February 27, 1904.

[34] Brown, *The New Politics*, pp. 139-40.

[35] Stanton [Brown], "The South at Work," Boston *Evening Transcript*, February 27, 1904; "Of the North's Part in Southern Betterment," pp. 415-18; "The White Peril," pp. 824-34.

them exclusively and that the railroad stop hiring Negro firemen. Alarmed, Brown brought the strike to public attention in *Harper's Weekly*.[36] Surely, he argued, the solution need not be drastic action against the blacks. If that should happen, the South's reputation for economic equality would be seriously impaired. "If such reasoning is applied to Southern industries as a whole, where will it end?" he asked,[37] and pointed out the "grave menace to the negro's industrial future which the episode discloses."[38]

One other incident in which he was concerned involved what he acknowledged to be racial paternalism. In the winter of 1911, while he was in an Asheville sanitarium suffering from tuberculosis, he learned that Robert F. Campbell, a young clergyman, had attacked the city's white citizens for allowing prostitutes driven out of a white neighborhood to resettle directly across the street from a Negro school. Brown contacted Campbell and offered his assistance.[39] Campbell, a writer who knew Brown's work, asked him to make a direct appeal to the local whites. Brown complied, with a long open letter in the Asheville *Citizen* which appealed to Southern paternalism, or, as he called it, the "highest and finest in the Southern character."[40] This time Brown won, and he celebrated in *Harper's Weekly*. "We are gradually learning," he said, that if the race "situation is ever going to be better materially it will be in ways like this of Asheville's, where white people have out of their own hearts and consciences resolved that negro men and women shall have an equal chance with themselves to bring up their children in decent surroundings." "It sometimes happens," he went on, "that by a few convincing examples decency can be made, to towns as to men, the imperative fashion."[41]

But Brown was wrong. More than a "few convincing examples" of decency were needed to change men's ways, even his own. As

[36] Brown, "The Georgia Race Strike," *Harper's Weekly* 53 (1909):5.

[37] Brown, "The Georgia Strike," *ibid.*, p. 4.

[38] Brown, "The Georgia Strike Arbitration," *ibid.*, p. 5.

[39] Brown to Campbell, January 3, 1912, Brown Papers.

[40] Asheville *Citizen*, January 11, 1912.

[41] "Race Problem and the 'Social Evil' Combined," *Harper's Weekly* 56 (1912):5.

he said in 1908 to his old friend Charles W. Eliot of Harvard, "My own intense sympathy with men like Du Bois and Booker Washington has led me to rebel against this [caste system] in many ways that proved afterwards intensely painful to me and to those dear to me; but after going through countless moods and opinions on the matter I find myself settling into a conviction that the race instinct is rather salutary than hurtful—cruel as it seems and often is—to great permanent interests of society."[42]

Brown and men like him identified the white South with the "great, permanent interests of society." One could not be intensely sympathetic to Du Bois and continue to be a white Southerner in good standing, either with oneself or with one's friends. A society of two, separate, unequal races was being created, one dominant, the other powerless. Their hopes and aspirations in the new order would be, as Brown admitted, antithetical, and his final loyalty, for all his doubts, was to the white South.

* * *

Edgar Gardner Murphy, of all the intellectuals of Brown's generation, would seem most likely to come to an understanding of racism. Intelligent, widely read, and compassionate, he was of an abstract, moral turn of mind. He was trained in Christian theology but, in keeping with the secular trend of the times, seldom mentioned St. Paul or the Sermon on the Mount in his writings. His texts were the eminent Victorians and the best of recent history and sociology. And yet, like Brown, he could not free himself from Southern history. In fact, his writings constitute the most imposing intellectual apology for White Supremacy in Southern literature.

In 1899, the year that Murphy settled in Montgomery, there was a lynching in Georgia, involving finger chopping and other mutilations, which he described in the *Outlook*[43] as "a sickening and excuseless orgy of torture." Nothing could excuse "the dis-

---

[42] Brown to Charles W. Eliot, February 2, 1908, Brown Papers.

[43] Earlier, in the 1890s, when he held a pastorate in Laredo, Texas, he had organized a mass meeting to protest a lynching of a Negro (Murphy, *Murphy*, pp. 1-11).

gusting animalism of these Georgia executioneers," he said, but cautioned Yankees that such lynchings were the work of the rednecks and did not represent the new South that was emerging.[44] In the following year he founded the Southern Society, a discussion group, and called a Southern Conference of Race Relations in Montgomery.[45] To his disappointment, the organization collapsed after the first meeting, when no other city offered to host the second one. It was all just as well, Murphy concluded, because the speakers in Montgomery had been overwhelmingly pessimistic and had few positive plans.[46]

Racial events in Alabama soon diverted him from such theoretical discussions. In April 1901 the legislature called a convention to write White Supremacy into the state constitution. The intent, said officials, was to reform politics by purging illiterates from the voting rolls, but party leaders also told whites explicitly that they would not be disfranchised.[47] When the party chairman appealed to the clergy for support, Murphy did not, as he admitted in a lengthy and widely read open letter, oppose the "general intent" of the reform, but he did object to the advance assurances given the whites—this obvious fraud violated the principles of honesty and good government.[48] (Murphy's distrust of the white masses was visible on a number of occasions throughout the campaign in Alabama.[49])

Even in those counties in which blacks were a majority, there was an overwhelming vote for the disfranchisement convention. The politicians quickly "reformed" Alabama politics and, following the lead of other states, wrote a "grandfather clause" into the constitution. Murphy objected to the clause, but, being a practical

[44]"The Georgia Atrocity and Southern Opinion," Outlook 62 (1899):178–80.

[45]Murphy, The White Man and the Negro at the South (n.p., 1900), Murphy Papers; Booker T. Washington, "The Montgomery Race Conference," Century Magazine 40 (1900):630–32.

[46]Murphy, Murphy, pp. 30–31.

[47]William A. Mabry, "The Disfranchisement of the Negro in the South" (Ph.D. diss., Duke University, 1933), pp. 321–46.

[48]Montgomery Advertiser, April 19, 1901; clipping in the Murphy Papers.

[49]See Murphy, Present South, pp. 153–201, and his letters in the Montgomery Advertizer for June 26 and July 12, 1901, signed, respectively, "A Jeffersonian Democrat" and "Old-School Democrat," clippings, Murphy Papers.

man, bowed to the course of events (even though he knew that a great amount of fraud had been necessary in the black counties to get the "people" to vote themselves out of politics). Alabama's whites, he said, were not about to set their faces against a movement that was sweeping the whole South.[50] He even accepted the post of convention chaplain and, as such, gave the benediction that adjourned Alabama's White Supremacy constitutional convention.

In the meantime, Murphy attempted to reassure the public in the North. In the *Outlook* he admitted that disfranchisement was aimed at the Negro, that the new laws would probably not be applied equally to all, and that almost no defense could be made for the grandfather clause.[51] However, he urged crusaders for Negro rights to remember that actions or pronouncements from the North would only make matters worse for the blacks, that the whites had spoken and were in no mood to accept criticism, as seen in the lynchings, riots, the movement to reduce appropriations for Negro education even further, and the sporadic efforts to displace the Negro in the labor market. But he softened his argument by urging Northerners to remember that the black man could still work and prosper only in the South. Blacks, he said, receive "the sympathetic and practical co-operation of the Southern white man." "The real South—the South of the businessman, the educator, the churches, the schools, the homes—is helping the negro today as never before since the moment of emancipation." Just how the "real South" was doing so Murphy did not say, though he did admit that the Negro "may not be getting much aid from the politician."[52]

In the next few years, though he became involved in other causes, the race issue never left his mind for long. Like Brown, he discovered that he could not divorce the Negro from other issues, even though he had admonished the South to do so. His first major book, *The Problems of the Present South*, surveyed various social problems but is pervaded throughout by a sense of the

[50]"The Freedman's Progress in the South," *Outlook* 68 (1901):721-24.
[51]*Ibid.*, p. 722.
[52]*Ibid.*, pp. 722, 724.

importance of the racial issue. In this highly regarded work,[53] he instructed whites in what amounted to the proper attitudes and practices of a master race.

The key words in what Murphy called racial ascendancy were "co-operation" and "repression." By the latter he meant lynchings, race riots, and racist politics: these destroyed the Negro, whether by killing him or by driving him into a state of abject servility. Yet his primary argument against racism stemmed from his conviction that "repression" was self-defeating for the whites because it corrupted the dominant race by fostering violence and hate. By cooperation Murphy meant paternalism, benevolence, toleration, and charity toward the "weaker race." He urged whites to work together to "lift up" the Negro. His justification for this was a familiar one: the whites must lift the Negroes up or the Negroes would drag Southern civilization down.[54]

Murphy's argument, which he made many times, might be considered humane and realistic, given the racism of his day. He was openly contemptuous of politicians who exploited racism. Southerners who were honest had to admit, as he himself did in 1905, that disfranchisement laws were not being administered fairly—that whites were allowed to vote indiscriminately while Negroes, educated or not, were excluded in wholesale fashion unless the registrars thought that they would vote "correctly."[55] Such fla-

---

[53] For favorable reactions from white Northerners to Murphy's book, see *Outlook* 76 (1904):967-69; *Nation* 78 (1904):317; *Current Literature* 37 (1904):19-22. For reactions from white Southerners, see Josiah Bailey, *Biblical Recorder*, undated clipping, Murphy Papers; Mrs. John D. Hammond, "The Growth of Democracy in the South," *Methodist Review* 54 (1905):28-38; A. H. Shannon, *ibid.*, 56 (1907):189-92. I have been able to find only one unfavorable review from a white Southerner, that of Walter L. Fleming in *Political Science Quarterly* 20 (1905):161-63.

[54] Only two chapters of Murphy's book, *The Present South*, ignore the race issue.

[55] "Should the Fourteenth Amendment Be Enforced?" *North American Review* 180 (1905):109-33. Murphy's rationale for allowing even illiterate whites to vote is interesting: the poor white "represents a sturdy rural population which is unlettered and untrained, by reason of its isolation rather than because of his [sic] economic exhaustion or social degeneracy. He has listened, as his fathers have listened for generations before him, to the debate of political issues, and he has been trained by long experience in the clear and rigorous decision of public questions. He excels the negro voter by the genius of his race, by inherited capacity and by political training which has formed part of the tradition of his class. He is narrow, crude, assertive, and sometimes violent, but he is superior, as a factor in the electorate, not only to the negro, but to any other illiterate population of our country" (pp. 124-25).

grant violations of the law must be stopped: "It is in the interest of democracy itself that an injustice shall find redress, and that every properly qualified voter should be fairly accorded his political status in the impartial light of his legal qualifications. The moment the law is given the twist or the squint of race or class or party, it ceases to be law. It becomes the despotism of race or party. This despotism has at times been necessary. It is often benevolent. It is sometimes wise. One thing, however, it is not; nor can it be. It is not democracy."[56]

In an article called "The Task of the Leader,"[57] a favorite topic of his generation, Murphy again stressed the consequences of racism. Southern life was in danger of being totally corrupted by the hate generated by the disfranchisers. "A sincere effort for an indispensable reform has been captured by the demon of racial animosities," he concluded. Yet his opposition to federal enforcement of the Fourteenth Amendment was unwavering. The "real South" would simply have to redouble its efforts to persuade the white South to forsake repression for cooperation.[58]

It was in this mood that he wrote *The Basis of Ascendancy*, which he saw as his major contribution to helping the white South work out a rational way of dealing with the Negro.[59] He felt compelled to convince his fellow white Southerners that their path was one of ruinous repression, not cooperation, and that they must change their attitude or be destroyed.

One of his major arguments against what he called repression was that it violated democracy, which was the spirit of the age. The "modern spirit" would not long tolerate a system of caste and bondage anywhere in the civilized world: "To talk, in an age like ours, of not educating any particular class of human beings or of deliberately holding any fraction or race of men at a permanently lower level of industrial or political opportunity is to talk a language as stale—and as pathetic—as that of the complacent memo-

---

[56]*Ibid.*, p. 117.
[57]*Sewanee Review* 15 (1907):1–30.
[58]*Ibid.*, pp. 21–22, 25.
[59](New York: Longmans, Green and Co., 1909).

rial upon the coffin of an Egyptian mummy."[60] The South was to be democratic, then, while rigidly maintaining the color line.

Murphy again stressed the argument that white Southerners lived in constant danger of being corrupted by their contact with a subjugated people: "In any society human life in general tends to become as cheap as the life of its humblest representatives"; "no man, except the peculiarly strong and great, is at his best when habitually dealing with forms of manhood lower than his own."[61] But at this point Murphy retreated to his earlier admonitions: the superior whites, the "ascendant" ones, must guide the white South lest it stumble and fall as low as the Negroes.[62]

To give further force to his argument against "repression," Murphy listed its debilitating effects on the blacks: debased and demoralized, they lose all incentive, pride, and hope for the future; they become listless, dependent, careless of property rights and social order.[63] One sees again that his central concern is not the black but the white man. Thus it is understandable that he goes on to say that repression will destroy the black man's incentive to work and create a class with no stake in preserving the South, a seething cauldron of discontent. Years earlier John C. Calhoun ("the Marx of the Master Class," in Richard Hofstadter's felicitious phrase) had expressed similar alarm that the oppressed blacks would unite to overthrow their masters and urged stricter controls, along with a grand alliance with the Northern bourgeoisie. By Murphy's day that alliance had come to pass.

Actually, Murphy never specifically acknowledged a fear of black rebellion. His writing frequently has a murky quality, which makes it difficult to know precisely what he meant. But he did write in *The Basis of Ascendancy*: "Keep him forever in his bankruptcy and his destitution without a life to attract him or a treasure to conserve, and these millions will become a *despising and devouring menace* to the wholesale stability of our own life, and

[60] *Ibid.*, p. 94.
[61] *Ibid.*, pp. 125–27.
[62] *Ibid.*, pp. 198–200.
[63] *Ibid.*, pp. 57–111.

a noisome indictment of the perversity or the incapacity of our statesmanship" (italics added).[64]

Although he admitted the "perversity" and "incapacity" of his race in dealing with the black man, he insisted that it was "supremely necessary that this problem become in us no occasion of our industrial and political undoing."[65]

To Murphy's mind, one of the best ways to cooperate with the blacks was to ensure them minimal economic and educational opportunities. He did not mean by this equality of opportunity, but, like William Garrott Brown and most of the other intellectuals, he urged whites to allow the blacks a chance to work and to acquire the rudiments of an education: "the South has sometimes abridged the negro's right to vote, but the South has not abridged his right, in any direction of human interest or of honest effort, to earn his bread."[66]

It may seem ironic that such a fervent spokesman for school segregation and for maintenance of the public school movement in the hands of whites would have been widely respected, particularly among black leaders, as one of the more dependable friends of Negro education.[67] Murphy worked closely with Booker T. Washington on a number of occasions and championed Tuskegee Institute and its advocacy of practical education for blacks. Blacks as well as liberal whites appreciated his repeated assertion that the South had a duty to provide adequate support for the separate black schools. He resolutely opposed the recurring proposal to limit school appropriations to the amount of taxes paid by each

---

[64]*Ibid.*, p. 111.

[65]*Ibid.*, p. 245.

[66]*Ibid.*, p. 187.

[67]See Booker T. Washington, "The Present South," *Atlantic Monthly* 94 (1904):547–49; Kelly Miller, "Problems of the Present South," *Dial* 37 (1904):88–91; Booker T. Washington, "The Negro and the 'Solid South,'" *Independent* 67 (1909):1195–99. Robert Russa Moton, a black writer associated with Hampton Institute in Virginia, wrote to Murphy that *The Basis of Ascendancy* was the "fairest and most perfect statement from every viewpoint of the situation in general, and our American race problem in particular, that I have ever seen" (Moton to Murphy, September 22, 1909, Murphy Papers).

race.[68] He never insisted that financial appropriations be equal or that the radical disparity in the two systems be removed, but one must remember that at the time many whites opposed all Negro education of whatever kind.

In addition, Murphy went beyond mere homilies on the need for Negro education. A moralist at heart, he attempted to establish both moral principles and practical justifications for it, and in so doing he almost broke out of the racial lockstep. To the complaint that "education ruins a good field hand" he replied, "Education brings its dangers. But the risk of making fools is of smaller import than the larger chance of making men."[69] As proof he offered, as he had many times, what amounted to a gratuitous insult to blacks: no graduate of Tuskegee or Hampton Institute, he said, had ever been charged with assaulting a white woman.[70]

By 1909 he had come to understand, although dimly, racism's destructive effect on Negro identity, and thought that education for blacks might counteract their negative self-concept. Citing Mill, he contended that downtrodden and "ignorant" people lose a sense of dignity and faith in their ability to control their futures. Always first concerned for the welfare of the whites, he insisted that they could not afford to have the blacks regard themselves with contempt. Education might provide an opportunity for the race to develop "leaders" of the right type. Blacks needed leaders, he warned, "scholars, artists, prophets," to give them pride of accomplishment. Education brings the Negro into the "companionship of other educated Negroes. It appropriates him in behalf of a common standpoint. It introduces him into the collective intelligence of his people. He comes to share their racial interests. He is involved within the formative tendencies of class-consciousness and enters into the heritage of race ideals, policies, and antipathies."[71]

[68]Murphy, *Basis of Ascendancy*, pp. 94–99.
[69]*Ibid.*, p. 54.
[70]*Ibid.*, p. 55.
[71]*Ibid.*, p. 92.

Murphy uncritically accepted the common notions about African "savages" and, like most white writers, sincerely—if gratuitous-
ly—lauded their achievements since coming to America. What was
unusual was that he sensed a future relationship between the
American Negro and Africa. He predicted that, as the Western
powers had forced their way into Africa, Africa would one day
force its way into the consciousness of the colonial nations, particularly that of their non-white inhabitants. When that day comes,
the American Negro would not be unchanged. "I well know,"
Murphy acknowledged, "that among some of the intelligent
negroes of America the very subject of Africa is like the skeleton
in the closet. They would keep well within the background their
affinity with an older and weaker world, that their own origin may
be forgotten in the process."[72] But as the Negro "cannot escape
the Africa of his past, so he cannot escape, and will not desire to
escape, the Africa of his future."[73] "As the reemergence of Africa
becomes however, increasingly evident, and as the varied questions
presented by its own people appear and reappear within the consciousness of the modern world, I have no manner of doubt as to
the responses of the representatives of the race in the United
States." His prophecy was that they would develop "a new and
higher sense of their relation to the world. Through the grace of a
broader service of the now broader negro group, their own struggle
will become less a struggle for themselves alone, and still less a
struggle to lose themselves within the identity of another social
mass. The very stress and truths of their stewardship will make
forever impossible their self-obliteration or their self-despair."[74]

Murphy's dreams of racial "cooperation" and of a future African
identity for American blacks were not enough to emancipate him
from his heritage. In his moments of clearest vision, he could see
that true cooperation demanded complete equality, at least in the
laws and institutions of society, but he continued to yearn for

[72] *Ibid.*, p. 87.
[73] *Ibid.*, p. 82.
[74] *Ibid.*, pp. 88–90.

cooperation between unequals. He knew that inequality inevitably leads to exploitation of the weaker race, but he could not surrender his faith in the white South. Thus he demanded the impossible—that the white South, while it kept the Negro ignorant, politically powerless, and socially isolated, be tolerant and humane in its "dealing" with him. He could not see that he would perpetuate the very repression he claimed to oppose as long as he insisted upon White Supremacy as the permanent feature of Southern life.

9

WOODROW WILSON AND THE TRIUMPH OF WHITE SUPREMACY

IT IS A FACT OF CONSIDERABLE IMPORTANCE that Woodrow Wilson was born and raised in the South. He represented the best of the Southern mind and in many ways transcended not only the region but the age. His vision of international harmony and a peaceful world made safe for democracy attest to his hope for man. He brought integrity, intelligence, leadership, and democratic idealism to the presidency; he was partially responsible for a splendid array of social legislation. In addition, he was the first genuinely learned man to sit in the White House since Jefferson and Adams. Yet under his direction and with his full approval the federal government strengthened the color line and supported the forces of racism in America. Wilson "was characteristically a Southerner in his attitude toward the Negro," Arthur S. Link has said, and "like most Southerners of the upper class, his tolerance and kindliness to the Negro were motivated by a strong paternalistic feeling."[1] He was repelled, but not angered, by white racism.

[1] *Wilson: Road to the White House*, p. 3. Anyone familiar with Link's voluminous writings on Wilson will see that I have drawn heavily on his work. For the most part, I have no quarrel with Link's view of Wilson's racial thought, particularly that expressed in his earlier works. He has rather consistently sought to show the "Southernness" of Wilson's thinking about race. Recently, however, he has argued that Wilson must be understood as an American with emancipated ideas about nationalism, the relationship of government to the economy, and the Negro. Wilson was a "progressionist and paternalist," Link said in 1970, and was free from the assumptions and thoughts of the racist

Southern gentlemen of the sort he personified, though they might practice "tolerance and kindliness" toward Negroes, reserved their ultimate loyalties for the white South.

Wilson arrived at his views in a manner entirely normal for a white Southerner of his class and time. "After all," he observed once, "no man comes from the people in general. We are each of us derived from some small group of persons in particular; and unless we were too poor to have any family life at all, it is the life and associations of that family that have chiefly shaped us in our youth."[2] Through his own family Wilson received an early and convincing introduction to orthodox Southern attitudes about race. His father, the Reverend Joseph Ruggles Wilson, though born in Ohio, became a zealous advocate of the South. He was clerk of the newly created Southern Presbyterian Church—the Southern branch had officially established itself in his church. When war broke out in 1861 he converted his large church in Augusta, Georgia, into a Confederate hospital and, later, into a makeshift prison for captured Union soldiers. One Sunday, spurred on by a rumor of an impending battle, he dismissed his congregation and urged them to spend the Sabbath working in the local munitions arsenal.[3]

Throughout his life Woodrow Wilson remained inordinately proud of his father and of his Southern heritage. The South, he was fond of repeating, was "the only place in the country, the only place in the world, where nothing has to be explained to me."[4] As he said in 1896, addressing a group of professional his-

South ("Woodrow Wilson: The American as Southerner," *Journal of Southern History* 36 [1970]:3-17). I have tried in these pages to demonstrate that to be a "progressionist and paternalist" was to be deeply rooted in racism. Moreover, to argue, as Link has done, that Wilson was emancipated from racism because he held views which educated, intelligent white Southerners considered "very advanced" is hardly to make the case for an emancipated mind. This chapter, then, offers an interpretation of Wilson that differs rather radically from Link's recent summing up.

[2] Wilson, "Mr. Cleveland as President," *Atlantic Monthly* 79 (1897):289; Link, *Wilson: Road to the White House*, p. 2.

[3] Ray Stannard Baker, *Woodrow Wilson: Life and Letters*, 8 vols. (New York: Doubleday, Page and Co., 1927-39),1:50-51.

[4] This oft-quoted remark can be found in Link, *Wilson: Road to the White House*, p. 3.

torians, there was "nothing to apologize for in the past of the South—absolutely nothing to apologize for."[5] He was far less emancipated from the romantic myths of the virtuous South than such men as Trent, Walter Page, or even William Garrott Brown. When he wrote *Division and Reunion, 1829–1889* in 1893, he gingerly sidestepped the slave issue, denying the Abolitionist charge of moral guilt while admitting that since slaves had "to be driven" to their work there were occasional instances of cruel punishment for "petty" infractions.[6] In any case, he reasoned, the Abolitionist attack had caused Southern attitudes to harden into an unyielding defense of slavery; moreover, "the slaves were too numerous and too ignorant to be set free." However, in 1890, when speaking candidly to a history seminar at Johns Hopkins, he claimed that slavery "had done more for the negro in two hundred and fifty years than African freedom had done since the building of pyramids."[7] In addition to betraying his ignorance of Africa (which was common among white writers at the time) the two comments contain an inherent contradiction, which Wilson failed to see: if the Negroes were "too ignorant" for freedom in 1860, what had slavery "done" for them?

When writing as a professional historian, Wilson made the customary attacks on Reconstruction for allowing unfit blacks to vote, even though, again in a manner common at the time, he glorified Jacksonian democracy for allowing the "common [white] man" to vote and to become an active participant in American politics. Secession, however, was another question altogether for Wilson. He could not denounce it, as Trent had, because of his love of the South and his father's secessionist loyalties, nor could he justify it entirely. He resolved the dilemma by concluding

---

[5] *Annual Report of the American Historical Association, 1896*, 2 vols. (Washington, D.C.: U.S. Government Printing Office, 1897), 1:295. In characteristic fashion, Wilson linked the statement to a larger view of history—he assured his audience that "no past should ever be regretted"—and announced that "the Southerner is proud of the past of his region, and he is cordially ready to accept the present and to help forward the tasks of the future."

[6] *Division and Reunion, 1829–1889* (New York: Collier Books, 1961), pp. 115–16.

[7] Quoted in Henry Louis Bragdon, *Woodrow Wilson: The Academic Years* (Cambridge: Harvard University Press, 1967), p. 237.

that Dixie was constitutionally right but historically wrong. The South, he wrote in *Division and Reunion*, "had stood still while the rest of the country had undergone profound changes; and standing still, she retained the old principles which had once been universal. But she and her principles, it turned out, had been caught in the great national drift, and were to be overwhelmed."[8] Wilson continued this line of thinking and later said that he "rejoiced" that the Confederacy had failed, though he was not really departing from the view he had expressed years before: "I recognize and pay loving tribute to the virtues of the leaders of secession, to the purity of their purpose, to the righteousness of the cause which they thought they were promoting—and to the immortal courage of the soldiers of the Confederacy."[9] He felt a bond of "intellectual consanguinity" with men of his own "race and breeding," he said, that allowed him to "speak [his] mind frankly upon any theme."[10]

In the next fifteen years Wilson appears to have given little, if any, thought to the race question. An ambitious man, after a brief and unsuccessful attempt at practicing law in Atlanta, he left the South for good in 1883. He received a doctorate at Johns Hopkins in 1886, working under Adams, published his dissertation, *Congressional Government*, and settled down, first at Bryn Mawr, then

[8]Pp. 178–79.

[9]"I yield to no one precedence in love for the South," Wilson said in 1880, "but *because* I love the South, I rejoice in the failure of the Confederacy. Suppose that secession had been accomplished? Conceive of this Union divided into two separate and independent sovereignties!" (Ray Stannard Baker and William E. Dodd, eds., *The Public Papers of Woodrow Wilson*, 6 vols. [New York: Harper and Brothers, 1925–27], 1:56). Wilson was young, only twenty-four, when he spoke these words. In later years, during the writing of his multivolume history of the United States, he spoke more objectively about secession and Reconstruction, but his basic views had not changed (see his *A History of the American People*, 10 vols. [New York: Harper and Brothers, 1901], 8:121–40, 9:46–53; Wilson, "The Reconstruction of the Southern States," *Atlantic Monthly* 83 [1901]:1–15). In Reconstruction, he wrote, one found "a vast 'laboring, landless, homeless class,' once slaves, now free; unpracticed in liberty, unschooled in self-control; never sobered by the discipline of self-support, never established in any habit of prudence; excited by freedom they did not understand, exalted by false hopes; bewildered and without leaders, and yet insolent and aggressive; sick of work, covetous of pleasure,—a host of dusky children untimely put out of school" (p. 6).

[10]"Leaderless Government," address before the Virginia Bar Association, August 4, 1897, reprinted in Baker and Dodd, *Public Papers of Woodrow Wilson*, 1:336–37.

at Wesleyan University, then, in 1890, at Princeton. In 1902 he
became president of Princeton and immediately went to work to
revitalize and transform that old Presbyterian school into a
national university. His goal was to put Princeton "in the nation's
service," to be achieved by updating the faculty and the curriculum and by attracting better students.[11] Part of his plan included a
bold attempt to abolish the privileged upper-class eating clubs and
to replace them with quadrangles where students and resident
faculty advisers would live, eat, and learn together in a democratic
manner.[12] Something of the old egalitarianism of the yeoman
South may have prompted him to take up this unpopular and
unsuccessful cause, but it always stopped short at the color line: at
the very time when he was attempting to democratize the student
body, he also introduced a policy of discouraging Negroes from
applying to Princeton. He justified his actions on the basis that
blacks would not be happy at Princeton, though there had been
black students there for years, and that their presence would com-
plicate life for the large number of Southern whites who traditionally attended the school.[13]

Wilson had been telling his students for years that only a homo-
geneous people can have a stable constitutional government.[14] As
a public spokesman for "responsible government," he approved
the disfranchisement of the "ignorant and hostile" black voters,
though he did not quite approve of the methods employed to
achieve it. Like most Americans, he also supported American
imperialism in the Philippines. As he put it in the *Atlantic
Monthly*, the white Anglo-Saxon Christians might "moralize" and

[11]These years are described in copious detail in Bragdon, *Wilson: The Academic
Years.*

[12]*Ibid.,* pp. 316–26.

[13]Arthur S. Link, "The Negro as a Factor in the Campaign of 1912," *Journal of
Negro History* 32 (1947):87. Writing about this incident, Link says: "Although he never
shared the anti-Negro sentiment of many of his contemporaries, there is no doubt that
Wilson remained largely a Southerner on the race issue." Actually, he continues, "Mrs.
Wilson felt much more strongly about the necessity of drawing the color line than did
her husband, but both were opposed to social relations between the races" (*Wilson:
Road to the White House,* p. 502).

[14]Bragdon, *Wilson: The Academic Years,* p. 260.

"uplift" the Filipino and the Southern Negro: "it is the aid of our character they need, and not the premature aid of our institutions."[15] But on the whole he had little to say about the race issue, and when he emerged as a major aspirant for the presidency few Americans knew much about his racial attitudes.[16]

During the campaign of 1912 he would have liked to ignore the issue, but black and white liberals and reformers badgered him into taking a stand. To his mind this was politically inexpedient because few Southern blacks voted and Northern Negroes traditionally voted for the party of Lincoln.[17] Besides, raising the question of Negro rights would only arouse animosity in the white South, as demonstrated by its outrage over Theodore Roosevelt's "dinner" with Booker T. Washington. Wilson did consent to meet quietly with militant blacks, including W. E. B. Du Bois and William Monroe Trotter, and with white liberals like Oswald Garrison Villard, the influential editor of the New York *Evening Post*. However, he kept them at bay with vague statements of the sort he had made to other black leaders when asked what he would do for the Negro. In August, 1912, he specifically promised Villard, whose paper was now supporting him, that he would make federal appointments without regard to color and would create a National Race Commission to study racism in America. He also promised to speak out against lynchings—"every honest man must do so," he told Villard.[18] His words seemed sincere, and he had also been widely reported as saying to one moderate black leader, "should I become President of the United States [Negroes] may count on

[15]"Democracy and Efficiency," *Atlantic Monthly* 87 (1901):298.

[16]In the South Wilson's harshest critic was Tom Watson, who attempted to erode his support by portraying him as an advocate of social equality between the races—one of Watson's most scurrilous pamphlets was "The Nigger and the Governor of New Jersey." Yet attempts to interject the race issue into the campaign failed (Link, "The Negro as a Factor in the Campaign of 1912," pp. 83-84).

[17]Nevertheless, Wilson's campaign managers approved such organizations as the National Negro Wilson League in Virginia, and Wilson himself sanctioned the formation of the National Independent Political League of Washington, D.C. (*ibid.*, p. 85).

[18]Quoted in *ibid.*, p. 89. See also Link, *Wilson: Road to the White House*, pp. 503-4; Henry J. Blumenthal, "Woodrow Wilson and the Race Question," *Journal of Negro History* 47 (1963):9.

me for absolute fair dealing and for everything by which I could assist in advancing the interests of the race in the United States."[19] Villard, Du Bois, and the others were reassured, to the point of discounting Wilson's choice of Josephus Daniels as his campaign manager. Du Bois resigned from the Socialist Party, campaigned for Wilson, and in the N.A.A.C.P. magazine, the *Crisis*, urged that America should "elect Woodrow Wilson President . . . and prove once and for all if the Democratic party dares to be Democratic when it comes to the black man."[20]

Du Bois had deceived himself, as he would soon learn. Upon taking office, Wilson not only bestowed high offices on white Southerners but reneged on his promises to blacks and followed a clear anti-Negro policy. He remained silent on lynchings; he refused to create a National Race Commission. When Villard came to Washington to protest, Wilson refused to see him. In fact, after the first few years in office Wilson saw very few blacks or representatives of groups sympathetic to blacks. The hardest blow came when Wilson's Southern Cabinet members, William McAdoo, Secretary of the Treasury, and Postmaster General Albert S. Burleson, introduced the color line in their departments. Blacks now began to be herded into separate offices, separate lunch rooms, rest rooms; separate drinking fountains appeared.[21] Some segregated facilities had been introduced during the Roosevelt and Taft administrations, particularly in the Bureau of Engraving,[22]

[19] Quoted in Oswald Garrison Villard, "The President and Segregation at Washington," *North American Review* 198 (1913):800. Villard could not forget, as he prepared to vote in 1912, that Wilson, a white Southerner, introduced the color line at Princeton and during the campaign surrounded himself with white Southerners, not the least of whom was Josephus Daniels.

[20] Quoted in Link, *Wilson: Road to the White House*, p. 505. The large Negro community of Washington, D.C., hoped that the New Freedom might also include them in specific ways (Constance McLaughlin Green, *Washington: Capital City, 1789-1950*, 2 vols. [Princeton: Princeton University Press, 1963], 2:222).

[21] Villard, "The President and Segregation at Washington," pp. 800-804; Blumenthal, "Woodrow Wilson and the Race Question," p. 10; Kathleen Long Wolgemuth, "Woodrow Wilson and Federal Segregation," *Journal of Negro History* 44 (1959):158-73; and "Woodrow Wilson's Appointment Policy and the Negro," *Journal of Southern History* 24 (1958):461-63.

[22] August Meier and Elliott M. Rudwick, "The Rise of Segregation in the Federal Bureaucracy, 1900-1930," *Phylon* 28 (1967):178-84.

but with Wilson the progress of segregation was accelerated and spread dramatically from the Treasury and the Office of the Postmaster General to the Department of State, War, and the Navy. When Wilson announced that he was appointing a black man to be registrar of the Treasury, a post traditionally held by a Negro, a Southern Congressional contingent, led by racist-progressives James K. Vardaman, Ben Tillman, and Hoke Smith, objected. Thomas Dixon, author of the widely acclaimed racist Broadway play and movie *Birth of a Nation*, wrote Wilson, "I am heartsick over the pronouncement that you have appointed a Negro to boss white girls. . . . Please let me as one of your best friends utter my passionate protest. Unless you withdraw his name the South can never forgive you."[23] Thus confronted, Wilson withdrew the nomination and assured everyone, including his friend Dixon, that he had a "plan of concentration" for blacks in the civil service.[24]

Wilson's refusal to stand against the Southern opposition was symptomatic of the racial policies the new administration would follow.[25] Since 1865 presidents from both parties had used the appointment of Negroes to a few federal offices as a small but symbolically important way of rewarding and reassuring blacks. As a result, certain posts were considered "black" jobs. Occasionally there had been opposition from Southerners, which Taft experienced when he appointed a Negro to the position of registrar of the Treasury, but he remained adamant; Wilson gave in. Du Bois, Trotter, and Villard were shocked, and their chagrin mounted when Wilson appointed whites to such traditionally black jobs as

[23]Dixon to Wilson, June 27, 1913, quoted in Wolgemuth, "Woodrow Wilson's Appointment Policy," p. 463.

[24]*Ibid.*, p. 463. Villard reported that one of McAdoo's colleagues in the Cabinet had been heard to say that "the South is in the saddle and negroes should only hold laborer's positions under the government" (Villard, "The President and Segregation at Washington," p. 806). Wilson's "plan," if he really had one, immediately ran into opposition from the National Association for the Advancement of Colored People and from scattered white liberals like Villard. Together, his opponents were able to slow down the progress of segregation in federal agencies, but integration has not yet been restored (Wolgemuth, "Woodrow Wilson and Federal Segregation," p. 171; Meier and Rudwick, "The Rise of Segregation in the Federal Bureaucracy," pp. 180–84).

[25]The following account of Wilson's appointment policies rests on the articles cited in n. 24.

the recordership of deeds, which had been held by a Negro since 1881, and removed blacks from office and replaced them with whites: he turned out a black assistant attorney general (one of Taft's appointments) and a black auditor of the navy and replaced both men with whites.

Compared to Taft or even Grover Cleveland, a Democrat who owed no political or historical debts to Negroes, Woodrow Wilson emerges as a reactionary. At every turn, his policies marked a step backward. Taft appointed seventeen Negroes to federal jobs. Wilson appointed one, and though he named a black man to be minister to Liberia, another traditionally "black" job, he hesitated two years before doing so. Taft retained fourteen Negroes in federal office; Wilson retained six. Wilson thus reduced the number of positions that had been secured for Negroes from thirty-one to seven.[26]

"Politics" alone will not explain Wilson's reactionary practices. His reform proposals did need Southern congressional support, and he did sincerely believe that the "race issue" should not be further aggravated by publicity, but it is hard to see how the appointment of a few Negroes to governmental offices would have caused even the Vardamans and Tillmans to block legislation of the New Freedom.[27] Moreover, he did fight to retain a black municipal court judge in Washington, D.C., and suffered no repris-

---

[26]Wolgemuth, "Woodrow Wilson's Appointment Policy," pp. 458-70.

[27]The key issues in the New Freedom as defined by Wilson between 1912 and 1916 were economic, specifically, a downward revision of the tariff, reassertion of government control over banking and the currency, and regulation of trusts. The majority of Southern congressmen favored these and exerted pressure on Wilson to broaden his program to include such measures as the Rural Credits Act of 1916 and the Lever Warehouse Act of 1914. Yet even so, Link has concluded, Wilson "practically sacrificed the Negroes on the altar of political expediency, by allowing segregation in the governmental departments, dismissal and downgrading of Negro civil servants in the South, and the like, in order to win Southern support for his program" (Arthur S. Link, "The South and the New Freedom: An Interpretation," *American Scholar* 20 [1951]:324). For a rejoinder to this view, see Richard Abrams' argument that Southern Congressmen hardly needed placating to vote for the Underwood tariff and the other fiscal reforms brought about by the New Freedom. Southerners, Abrams has written, tended to divide along traditional lines of "conservative" and "liberal" responses to economic issues (Richard Abrams, "Woodrow Wilson and the Southern Congressmen, 1913-1916," *Journal of Southern History* 22 [1956]:417-37).

als on that occasion.[28] He had embraced the basic assumptions of White Supremacy, as indicated by his actions and thoughts in late 1913, when he and William Jennings Bryan, Secretary of State, agreed that they had better send a white man to Haiti, rather than a Negro diplomat because Haiti was in turmoil. Better send a white man, who could handle the trouble. Then, when the trouble subsided, a black man could be sent.[29]

This decision epitomizes the limited, constricted vision of the Southern intellectual. Wilson knew that black people were inferior, but his acceptance of this doctrine does not explain the nature of his racism. He was a benign, decent man like Murphy and Brown; he did not hate or despise black people; he harbored no conscious desire to add to their yoke. His racism sprang not so much from his feelings about blacks as from his assumptions about whites: he believed that they were rational and good, or would be if led by men of vision and high ideals, like himself. Wilson said little about blacks, gave them little thought, preferred to ignore them, but he had boundless confidence in the redemption of white men, in the face of overwhelming evidence to the contrary—from riots to finger chopping.

The problem, then, lay in the special way the Southern intellectuals regarded themselves—as rational and good, and hence emancipated from racism. That unconscious self-image prevented them from seriously examining their own minds and was the source of their many complacent identifications of themselves with the Real South and their praise for Southerners (meaning themselves) who had learned to think clearly. It lay behind their division of the South into the two polar camps of the rational and the irrational, the reasonable and the sentimental. Projecting this image onto the white South, they then redeemed it by elevating it to the status of the "Real South." Thus they could say, with Wilson and the most "liberal" of his generation, that Negroes would be granted the suffrage when they "qualified." The whites, of course—under the direction of the Real South—would be the judges.

[28] Blumenthal, "Woodrow Wilson and the Race Question," pp. 7-8.
[29] Wolgemuth, "Woodrow Wilson's Appointment Policy," p. 464.

The inability of Wilson and Southern intellectuals in general to understand blacks was in reality their inability to understand themselves. They never grasped the fact that they too, like the blacks and the white masses, were under the sway of a set of controlling assumptions and mythologies. Wilson, in one of his infrequent speeches to blacks, indicated this identification of himself with rationality and goodness. "I was born and raised in the South," he reassured a skeptical audience of Northern Negroes in 1912: "there is no place where it is easier to cement friendships between the races than there. You may feel assured of *my entire comprehension of the ambitions of the negro race* and my willingness and desire to deal with that race fairly and justly" (my italics).[30] One might be tempted to write his words off as campaign talk, but anyone who had been listening to his "race and class" all along would have heard those words a thousand times from the Southern white intellectuals.

Who might have helped Wilson and the Southern intellectuals to see that their racial thought expressed what Reinhold Niebuhr has called the "covert prejudice" inherent in assuming that one's own mind is the mind of man, "the final bar of judgment before which all nations and peoples must be brought"? Not Northern white intellectuals, certainly; with few exceptions, they had long ago given way to the same racist assumptions as those of the Southern whites. In reality, only the black intellectuals of the Du Bois persuasion could have brought the point home, but Wilson and the intellectuals preferred to listen to Booker T. Washington, in whom they found a mirror of their own values.

One might argue that the Southerners were protecting themselves by ignoring Du Bois and the world he portrayed in *The Souls of Black Folk*. His message was a brutal one: the white South, indeed all of white America, was destroying the souls of black folk, daily and without mercy. That message was simply too much for the white intellectuals to believe. Not even John Spencer Bassett could bring himself to think that the white South was corrupt beyond redemption. Asking Southerners to denounce the white

[30] Quoted in Link, *Wilson: Road to the White House*, p. 502.

South was tantamount to asking them to disown their fathers, their families, their teachers, their schools, their friends, their memories—in short, themselves, since they were, as Wilbur J. Cash said of the Confederate soldier, "the South in little." Wilson and his contemporaries could not leap over the barriers of time and place. They could not, when it came to the black man, transcend their age. Their only recourse was in faith and optimism.

BIBLIOGRAPHICAL ESSAY

A full-dress bibliography of the writings of and about the generation of intellectuals treated in this book would be an Olympian task, if not an impossibility. Their writings lie scattered throughout scores of magazines, newspapers, college bulletins and alumni publications, and obscure religious journals. Morever, several of them regularly wrote unsigned editorials and book reviews and gave hastily prepared speeches which have not always survived in accessible places. Then, too, a number wrote miscellaneous articles and speeches which give little or no insight into their intellectual development or social thought. The following essay is intended to supplement the footnotes by offering a brief comment on the more significant published and unpublished sources available.

The Walter Hines Page Papers in the Houghton Library, Harvard University, offer the richest collection of manuscripts to the student of Page and his generation. His correspondence was extensive, and the collection includes countless letters to him from many prominent Americans as well as hundreds of letters from his own hand. Happily, many other Page letters are reprinted in Burton J. Hendrick, *The Life and Letters of Walter H. Page* (3 vols.; Garden City, N.Y.: Doubleday, Page and Co., 1922-25), and in Hendrick, *The Training of an American: The Earlier Life and Letters of Walter H. Page, 1855-1913* (Boston: Houghton Mifflin Co., 1928). For my study, the latter volume was the most important.

The collection of William Garrott Brown Papers in the Duke University Library is another rich vein for understanding Southern thought. Like Page, Brown lingered over his correspondence, which was written with patrician grace and style. When he died in 1914 John Spencer Bassett, his friend, thought of preparing a biography based on Brown's papers which he had received from the family. He never did so, but he did deposit the letters in the Trinity College Library. Thanks to Bassett, the collection has a full set of clippings from Brown's writings, including the twenty travel pieces he did for the Boston *Evening Transcript* in 1904. Bassett also bound the pieces into a small, makeshift book, which he entitled *The South at Work* and placed in the college library. Also in the Duke University Library is a large holding of the Thomas Nelson Page Papers which shed some light on Page's literary career, particularly in terms of how he was regarded by his many admirers, North and South.

Of special importance to the historian are several other manuscript collections in the Duke University Library of the men who graced Trinity College at the turn of the century. Unfortunately, the John Spencer Bassett Papers are skimpy, made up mostly of photocopies and odds and ends from his published writings. Several of his letters, however, may be found in the Trinity College Papers, a voluminous collection which includes letters, copies of speeches, clippings, memoranda by and about President John C. Kilgo, Professor Edwin Mims, President William P. Few, and sundry others. Duke also houses individual collections of the personal papers of Kilgo and Few. The Kilgo Papers, particularly the well-preserved manuscripts of his sermons, reveal a body of thought which historians would do well to consider. One should supplement these sermons with D. W. Newsom, ed., *The Chapel Talks of John Carlisle Kilgo* (Nashville: Publishing House of the Methodist Episcopal Church, South, 1922). Those wishing to study William P. Few's thinking in depth ought to consult Robert H. Woody, ed., *The Papers and Addresses of William Preston Few* (Durham: Duke University Press, 1951).

The Edgar Gardner Murphy Papers in the University of North Carolina Library may be consulted with some profit, though clippings make up the bulk of this small collection. Deeper reservoirs of cultural and intellectual history are to be found in the Edwin A. Alderman Papers in the Alderman Library, University of Virginia; the Edwin Mims Papers in the Joint Universities Library, Nashville, Tennessee; and the William E. Dodd Papers at the Library of Congress. Woodrow Wilson's public and private papers reveal little about the intellectual community in the South, but the following published papers are indispensable for understanding Wilson: Ray Stannard Baker, *Woodrow Wilson: Life and Letters* (8 vols.; Garden City: Doubleday, Page and Company, 1927-39); Ray Stannard Baker and William E. Dodd, eds., *The Public Papers of Woodrow Wilson* (6 vols.; New York: Harper and Brothers, 1925-27); and Arthur S. Link *et al.*, eds., *The Papers of Woodrow Wilson* (11 vols. to date; Princeton: Princeton University Press, 1966-). This comprehensive edition supersedes the other two publications. The following manuscript holdings also contain letters to and from the men studied in this book: the Herbert Baxter Adams Papers in the Johns Hopkins University Library; the Frederick Bancroft Papers and the Brander Matthews Papers in the Columbia University Library; the Yates Snowden Papers in the University of South Carolina Library; and the Benjamin Newton Duke Papers in the Duke University Library.

In addition to the above, biographical information is readily available for most of the men treated in this book. Walter Page has never received full biographical treatment, partly, one suspects, because of the sheer size of the several laudatory volumes written and edited by Burton J. Hendrick. He has, however, been analyzed, sometimes harshly, in shorter pieces: Robert D. W. Conner, "Walter Hines Page: A Southern Nationalist" (in Howard W. Odum, ed., *Southern Pioneers in Social Interpretation* [Chapel Hill: University of North Carolina Press, 1925]), reflects the sympathetic attitude found in Hendrick; so, too, does Edwin Mims's remembrance in *The Advancing South* (New York: Doubleday, Page, and Co., 1926); Charles G. Sellers, Jr., in "Walter Hines Page and the Spirit of the New South" (*North Carolina Historical Review* 29 [1952]:481-99), has written the most informative summary. For insight into the long-standing antagonism to

Page and his ideas, see Edd W. Parks, *Segments of Southern Thought* (Athens: University of Georgia Press, 1938). William Garrott Brown, whose short and rather uneventful life hardly merits a full biography, has been sympathetically remembered by John Spencer Bassett in "My Recollections of William Garrott Brown" (*South Atlantic Quarterly* 16 [1917]:97-107), and by William P. Few in "William Garrott Brown" (*South Atlantic Quarterly* 13 [1914]:67-74). Brown's work as a historian and man of letters has been surveyed in Wendell Holmes Stephenson's *Southern History in the Making* (Baton Rouge: Louisiana State University Press, 1964). In this book and in *The South Lives in History* (Baton Rouge: Louisiana State University Press, 1955) Stephenson has gathered together his historiographic essays on Brown, Bassett, Trent, Dodd, and several other Southern historians of the day. Brown's racial and political thoughts have been analyzed in Bruce Clayton, "The Racial Thought of a Southern Intellectual at the Beginning of the Century: William Garrott Brown" (*South Atlantic Quarterly* 63 [1964]:93-103); "An Intellectual on Politics: William Garrott Brown and the Ideal of a Two-Party South" (*North Carolina Historical Review* 42 [1965]:319-34). The life and writings of Thomas Nelson Page have been critically studied in Harriet Holman, "The Literary Career of Thomas Nelson Page, 1884-1910" (Ph.D. dissertation, Duke University, 1947). Theodore L. Gross's *Thomas Nelson Page* (New York: Twayne Publishers, 1967) is briefer and less satisfactory. For a nostalgic look at Page, see Rosewell Page, *Thomas Nelson Page: A Memoir of a Virginia Gentleman by His Brother* (New York: Charles Scribner's Sons, 1923).

William P. Trent's life and writings—including his years at Columbia University after he left the South—are clearly outlined in Franklin T. Walker's "William P. Trent—A Critical Biography" (Ph.D. dissertation, George Peabody College for Teachers, 1943). John Spencer Bassett's scholarly and rather uneventful life presents little allure to the biographer, but Wendell Holmes Stephenson's two essays in *Southern History in the Making* should be supplemented with Earl W. Porter, *Trinity and Duke, 1892-1924: The Foundations of Duke University* (Durham: Duke University Press, 1964), which has the best account to date of the Bassett affair. William E. Dodd's life has been fully treated in Robert Dallek, *Democrat and Diplomat: The Life of William E. Dodd* (New York: Oxford University Press, 1968). Edwin Mims's early years are adequately surveyed in Leah Parks, "Edwin Mims and *The Advancing South*: A Study of a Southern Liberal" (Master's thesis, Vanderbilt University, 1964). Henry Y. Warnock's "Andrew Sledd, Southern Methodists, and the Negro: A Case Study" (*Journal of Southern History* 31 [1965]:251-71) is a model study.

Three of the more prominent college presidents—Kilgo, Alderman, and Kirkland—have received competent, if uncritical, biographical study in Paul Neff Garber, *John C. Kilgo* (Durham: Duke University Press, 1937); Dumas Malone, *Edwin A. Alderman: A Biography* (New York: Doubleday, Doran and Co., 1940); and Edwin Mims, *Chancellor Kirkland of Vanderbilt* (Nashville: Vanderbilt University Press, 1940).

The two child labor reformers, A. J. McKelway and Edgar Gardner Murphy, have been treated in Hugh C. Bailey, *Liberalism in the New South* (Coral Gables, Fla.: University of Miami Press, 1969). Bailey's biography, *Edgar Gardner Murphy: Gentle Progressive* (Coral Gables, Florida: University of Miami Press, 1968), outlines his career but misses the subtleties of Murphy's mind. Herbert J. Doherty, Jr.,'s "Alexander J. McKelway: Preacher to Progressive" (*Journal of Southern History* 24 [1958]:177-90) is a brief but informative study of McKelway as a child labor reformer. Doherty also centers on McKelway and Murphy in an important article, "Voices of Protest from the New South, 1875-1910" (*Mississippi Valley Historical Review* 42 [1955-56]:45-66).

For understanding Woodrow Wilson I have relied heavily on Arthur S. Link's many studies and biographical volumes. In *Wilson: The Road to the White House* (Princeton: Princeton University Press, 1947) and in *Wilson: The New Freedom* (Princeton: Princeton University Press, 1956) he presents a strong case for Wilson's "Southernness" on the race issue. In "The Negro as a Factor in the Campaign of 1912" (*Journal of Negro History* 32 [1947]:81-99) he asserts that Wilson "remained largely a Southerner on the race issue." Of late, however, in "Woodrow Wilson: The American as Southerner" (*Journal of Southern History* 36

[1970]:3-17) Link has reversed himself and says that Wilson, though a Southerner, held progressive views on the race issue and was "very advanced" in his thinking about the Negro. Within the last fifteen years, however, a number of scholars have exposed the extent of racist attitudes and practices in the Wilson administration. The following articles detail Wilson's racism and the racism of the era: Kathleen Long Wolgemuth, "Woodrow Wilson's Appointment Policy and the Negro" (*Journal of Southern History* 24 [1958]:457-71); "Woodrow Wilson and Federal Segregation" (*Journal of Negro History* 44 [1959]:158-73);Henry J. Blumenthal, "Woodrow Wilson and the Race Question" (*Journal of Negro History* 47 [1963]:1-21); and Nancy J. Weiss, "The Negro and the New Freedom: Fighting Wilsonian Segregation" (*Political Science Quarterly* 84 [1969]:61-79). However, August Meier and Elliott M. Rudwick, in "The Rise of Segregation in the Federal Bureaucracy, 1900-1930" (*Phylon* 28 [1967]:178-84), have argued that racial segregation did not start with Wilson, though his administration introduced a dramatic increase in its extent. For the response of the black community of Washington, D.C., to Wilson's actions, see Constance McLaughlin Green, *Washington: Capital City, 1879-1950* (2 vols.; Princeton: Princeton University Press, 1963).

The question of the relationship between the South—i.e., Southern votes in Congress—and Wilson's New Freedom is debated in Arthur S. Link, "The South and the New Freedom: An Interpretation" (*American Scholar* 20 [1951]:314-24); Dewey Grantham, Jr., "Southern Congressional Leaders and the New Freedom" (*Journal of Southern History* 13 [1947]:439-59); and in Richard Abrams, "Woodrow Wilson and the Southern Congressmen, 1913-1916" (*Journal of Southern History* 22 [1956]:417-37). Link and Grantham contend that Southern support was crucial for the New Freedom, while Abrams argues that Southerners hardly needed persuading to vote for its modest aims.

* * *

Among general historical interpretations of the South Wilbur J. Cash, *The Mind of the South* (New York: Alfred A. Knopf, 1941), must rank near the top of any student's list of required reading. Cash and his book will be better understood by reading the late Joseph L. Morrison's masterful biography, *W. J. Cash: Southern Prophet, A Biography and Reader* (New York: Alfred A. Knopf, 1967). Cash should be set over against the exhaustive researches of C. Vann Woodward, whose books include *Origins of the New South, 1877–1913* (Baton Rouge: Louisiana State University Press, 1951), *The Burden of Southern History* (Baton Rouge: Louisiana State University Press, 1960), and *The Strange Career of Jim Crow* (2d rev. ed.; New York: Oxford University Press, 1966). Also indebted to Cash and Woodward is Paul Gaston, *The New South Creed* (New York: Alfred A. Knopf, 1970), which subjects the emerging myths of the New South to critical examination. An older and much more sanguine interpretation of the public school movement is Charles W. Dabney's *Universal Education in the South* (2 vols.; Chapel Hill: University of North Carolina Press, 1936). Dabney fondly and carefully researched what he could not remember of those halcyon days, but he could not put the movement into historical perspective because he shared the assumptions of the men he praised. The same should be said of Edgar Gardner Murphy, *Problems of the Present South: A Discussion of Certain of the Educational, Industrial and Political Issues in the Southern States* (New York: The Macmillan Co., 1904), which has several informative chapters on the mood of the era, and Edwin Mims, *The Advancing South* (New York: Doubleday, Page, and Company, 1926), which fondly remembers the educational crusade. More recent and more critical studies are Louis R. Harlan, *Separate and Unequal: Public School Campaigns and Racism in the Southern Seaboard States, 1901–1915* (Chapel Hill: University of North Carolina Press, 1958), and Harold W. Mann, *Atticus Greene Haygood: Methodist Bishop, Editor, and Educator* (Athens: University of Georgia Press, 1965).

The relationship between racism and politics is fully explored in William A. Mabry, "The Disfranchisement of the Negro in the South" (Ph.D. dissertation, Duke University, 1933). For the Northern response see Rayford W. Logan, *The Negro in American Life and Thought: The Nadir, 1877–1901* (New York: The Dial

Press, 1954), and Paul Herman Buck, *The Road to Reunion, 1865–1900* (Boston: Little, Brown and Co., 1937). Both books deal with conditions in the South as well. There are several good studies of racial conditions in the individual states. Among the better ones are Albert D. Kirwan, *Revolt of the Rednecks: Mississippi Politics, 1876–1925* (Lexington: University of Kentucky Press, 1951); Vernon Lane Wharton, *The Negro in Mississippi, 1865–1890* (Chapel Hill: University of North Carolina Press, 1947); George Brown Tindall, *South Carolina Negroes, 1877–1900* (Columbia: University of South Carolina Press, 1952); Frenise A. Logan, *The Negro in North Carolina, 1876–1894* (Chapel Hill: University of North Carolina Press, 1964); and Helen G. Edmonds, *The Negro and Fusion Politics in North Carolina* (Chapel Hill: University of North Carolina Press, 1951). On this subject, as on all others, Woodward's writings ought to be consulted, specifically his incisive biography of the Georgia Populist who soured on the Negro and became a belligerent racist, *Tom Watson: Agrarian Rebel* (New York: The Macmillan Co., 1938). The careers of other racist politicians are carefully traced in Francis Butler Simkins, *Pitchfork Ben Tillman, South Carolinian* (Baton Rouge: Louisiana State University Press, 1944); Dewey W. Grantham, Jr., *Hoke Smith and the Politics of the New South* (Baton Rouge: Louisiana State University Press, 1958); and Oliver H. Orr, Jr., *Charles Brantley Aycock* (Chapel Hill: University of North Carolina Press, 1961). Josephus Daniels speaks candidly of his role in North Carolina's racist campaigns to disfranchise and segregate the Negro: see his autobiographical volumes, *Tar Heel Editor* (Chapel Hill: University of North Carolina Press, 1939) and *Editor in Politics* (Chapel Hill: University of North Carolina Press, 1941). Daniels' memoirs should be supplemented with Joseph L. Morrison, *Josephus Daniels, the Small-d Democrat* (Chapel Hill: University of North Carolina Press, 1966) and *Josephus Daniels Says... An Editor's Political Odyssey from Bryan to Wilson to F. D. R.* (Chapel Hill: University of North Carolina Press, 1962).

The industrial evolution in the South has yet to be analyzed as cogently as such issues as race, education, and politics. Philip Alexander Bruce's *The Rise of the New South* (Philadelphia: George

Barrie & Sons, 1905) presents useful information within a limited perspective; Holland Thompson's slender analysis, *The New South* (New Haven: Yale University Press, 1919), does little more than reflect the euphoria of the era. Broadus Mitchell's *The Rise of the Cotton Mills in the South* (Baltimore: Johns Hopkins Press, 1921) remains a standard work on the textile industry, but readers should consult chap. 11 of Woodward's *Origins of the New South, 1877-1913*. Recent studies, such as William H. Nicholls' *Southern Tradition and Regional Progress* (Chapel Hill: University of North Carolina Press, 1960), tend to stress social ideas about economic development, rather than economic data. Robert L. Brandfon's *Cotton Kingdom of the New South: A History of the Yazoo Mississippi Delta from Reconstruction to the Twentieth Century* (Cambridge, Mass.: Harvard University Press, 1967) is a step in the right direction.

The South's social history, as Woodward lamented over twenty years ago, has not received adequate attention from historians. The Fugitive-Agrarian writers who issued *I'll Take My Stand: The South and the Agrarian Tradition* (New York: Harper & Brothers, 1930) rightfully called attention to neglected phases of the region's cultural background, particularly religion. Most of their own writings about the South, however, centered on their beloved Old South or on their contemporary "enemies." Donald Davidson's collections of essays, *Still Rebels, Still Yankees* (Baton Rouge: Louisiana State University Press, 1957) and *Attack on Leviathan* (Chapel Hill: University of North Carolina Press, 1938), reflect the anger and mood of the conservative intellectuals of the 1920s and 1930s who thought that Southern culture was being destroyed by machines, factories, and modern ideas. See also the writings of Allen Tate, *Reactionary Essays on Poetry and Ideas* (New York: Charles Scribner's Sons, 1936), particularly the essay, "The Profession of Letters in the South"; Frank L. Owsley, "A Key to Southern Liberalism" (*Southern Review* 3 [1937]:28-38); and John Donald Wade, "What the South Figured, 1865-1914" (*Southern Review* 3 [1937]:360-67). For a sketchy overview of religion, see Kenneth L. Bailey, *Southern White Protestantism in the Twentieth Century* (New York: Harper and Row, 1964).

INDEX

Abbott, Lyman, 113, 120

Adams, Herbert Baxter: historical seminar at Johns Hopkins, 9, 33, 34, 40; and scientific history, 35, 36, 37; and Trent, 64, 75; and Bassett, 84, 85, 86; and Wilson, 208

Advancing South, The (Mims), 10, 27, 61, 72

Alabama: child labor in, 143, 144, 145, 151; disfranchisement in, 196

Alabama Child Labor Committee, 144, 145, 148. *See also* Murphy, Edgar Gardner

Alderman, Edwin A., 7, 56, 128; biographical sketch, 11; on industrialism, 21; as college president, 21, 56–57; "The Growing South," 27; education of, 32; on education, 51, 101, 107, 111, 126; and Walter Page, 56–57; and education crusade, 113, 116, 117, 120; on disfranchisement, 159, 187; and Woodrow Wilson, 172, 174

Arnold, Matthew, 9, 32, 66, 70, 154

Ashby, Irene, 143, 144, 146

Atlanta, Ga.: reaction to Sledd affair, 77–84 *passim*; race riot in, 187, 191

Atlantic Monthly, 7, 22–23, 49

Aycock, Charles B.: and racism, 113, 140, 153; and education crusade, 113–15; and child labor reform, 150

Baldwin, William H., 113, 115, 120

Bancroft, Frederick, 97, 98, 99

Basis of Ascendancy, The (Murphy), 199–204

Baskerville, William, 12, 37

Bassett, John Spencer, 7, 11, 25, 72, 77, 124, 134; biographical sketch, 9–10; on industrialism, 22; education of, 33, 34; criticizes racism, 58, 84–103, 182, 183; on Southern writing, 109; criticizes Solid South, 158, 159

Beveridge, Albert J., 151; Beveridge bill, 147, 148

Birmingham, Ala.: and industrialism, 20–21, 139; as New South city, 133; and child labor reform, 146–47

Blacks. *See* Negroes

Boyd, William K., 101, 103

Brown, William Garrott, 7, 46, 56, 150, 197, 201, 207, 213; biographical sketch, 8; *The Lower South in American History*, 8, 165; on industrialism, 20, 23–24; family background, 25; "The South at Work," 27, 139–41; and education, 29–30; education of, 34, 37; on Southern identity, 38; and "Bassett affair," 91, 97; on "Real South," 111; as critic of politics, 114, 154, 155, 160, 165–72, 175–77; economic views of, 133, 136–41; and child labor, 139, 141; and Woodrow Wilson, 172–77; racial thought of, 191–95

Bruce, Philip A., 24, 191; racism of, 188–90; *The Plantation Negro as a Freedman*, 189

227

THE JOHNS HOPKINS UNIVERSITY PRESS

This book was composed in Baskerville text and display
by Jones Composition Company. It was printed by
Universal Lithographers, Inc. on 55-lb. Sebago Regular
and bound by L. H. Jenkins, Inc. in Interlaken Matte
cloth.